BATMAN

THE DARK PRINCE CHARMING

STORY AND ART BY
MARINI

BATMAN CREATED BY BOB KANE WITH BILL FINGER

JIM CHADWICK EDITOR – ORIGINAL SERIES
LIZ ERICKSON ASSISTANT EDITOR – ORIGINAL SERIES
JEB WOODARD GROUP EDITOR – COLLECTED EDITIONS
SCOTT NYBAKKEN EDITOR – COLLECTED EDITION
STEVE COOK DESIGN DIRECTOR – BOOKS
LOUIS PRANDI PUBLICATION DESIGN
CHRISTY SAWYER PUBLICATION PRODUCTION

MARIE JAVINS EDITOR-IN-CHIEF, DC COMICS

DANIEL CHERRY III SENIOR VP – GENERAL MANAGER
JIM LEE PUBLISHER & CHIEF CREATIVE OFFICER
JOEN CHOE VP – GLOBAL BRAND & CREATIVE SERVICES
DON FALLETTI VP – MANUFACTURING OPERATIONS & WORKFLOW MANAGEMENT
LAWRENCE GANEM VP – TALENT SERVICES
ALISON GILL SENIOR VP – MANUFACTURING & OPERATIONS
NICK J. NAPOLITANO VP – MANUFACTURING ADMINISTRATION & DESIGN
NANCY SPEARS VP – REVENUE

FRANÇOIS PERNOT – CEO OF DARGAUD-LOMBARD
YVES SCHLIRF – EDITOR-IN-CHIEF OF DARGAUD BENELUX
PHILIPPE RAVON – GRAPHIC DESIGNER AND ART DIRECTOR
LAURENT DUVAULT – DIRECTOR OF DEVELOPMENT
CLAUDE PEDRONO – PUBLISHING DIRECTOR
HÉLÈNE WERLÉ – PRESS COORDINATOR
VALÉRIE BENIEST – EDITORIAL ASSISTANT
FLORENCE QUADT – TECHNICAL PUBLISHER

BATMAN: THE DARK PRINCE CHARMING
Published by DC Comics. Compilation and all new material Copyright © 2021
DC Comics. All Rights Reserved. Originally published in single magazine form in
Batman: The Dark Prince Charming 1-2. Copyright © 2017, 2018 DC Comics. All Rights
Reserved. All characters, their distinctive likenesses, and related elements featured in
this publication are trademarks of DC Comics. The stories, characters, and incidents
featured in this publication are entirely fictional. DC Comics does not read
or accept unsolicited submissions of ideas, stories, or artwork.

DC Comics, 2900 West Alameda Ave., Burbank, CA 91505
Printed by Transcontinental Interglobe, Beauceville, QC, Canada. 6/11/21. First Printing.
ISBN: 978-1-77951-021-1

Library of Congress Cataloging-in-Publication Data is available.

I was working on my *Eagles of Rome* comic book when Batman knocked at my door. Actually, he crashed through my window, like he usually does when he's in a hurry. He looked down at me and said, "Enrico, I want you to write and draw a story about me."

I admit, I was a little surprised, thinking, "Who's gonna pay for my window?"
"Let me think about that offer for five minutes," I replied.
After two seconds I said, "Okay."

But then I had some additional questions.
"Can I tell the story I want and draw it in my own style? Can I design a new Bat-costume and a new Batmobile? Can I include Catwoman (for selfish reasons), Harley Quinn and the Joker?"
Batman agreed. But with one condition.
"What is it?" I asked.
"No white socks," he replied.
"What?"
"You don't draw me in white socks, ever," Batman answered. "I wear black."
"Sure, no problem," I replied (thinking, "Whatever.").

I still had one more question, though. "Who's gonna pay for my window?"
But he had already vanished. He does that.

I swear that's what truly happened.

You don't say no to Batman, especially when he's standing right in front of you. And since I had already planned to do a noir crime story next, I was already in the mood. This Batman story you are about to read is—what else?—a crime story. Let's say it's a noir with some green and purple stains.

A childhood dream came true.

So thank you, DC, for giving me the opportunity to spend some time in Gotham City and hang out with your fantastic characters.

Some big thanks go to the legendary artist and publisher Jim Lee and to executive director Sandy Resnick, to Dargaud-Lombard's CEO, François Pernot, to Laurent Duvault and to my friend and Dargaud's editor-in-chief Yves Schlirf, for making it all happen.

I'd like to thank my DC editor, Jim Chadwick. It's great to work with you.

Thank you very much, Philippe Ravon. You're an excellent graphic designer. It's always a pleasure to team up with you.

I love Bruce Timm and Paul Dini's Harley Quinn. Thanks to them for having created such a wonderful character.

A big hug goes to my buddy and Batman expert Juan Ortega. Your advice and moral support were most welcome.

I especially want to thank my family for coming along with me on this wild Batman trip.

In conclusion, I want to thank all the Batman friends out there. I hope you enjoy what follows.

Enrico Marini
August 25, 2017

"I'm not here to play."

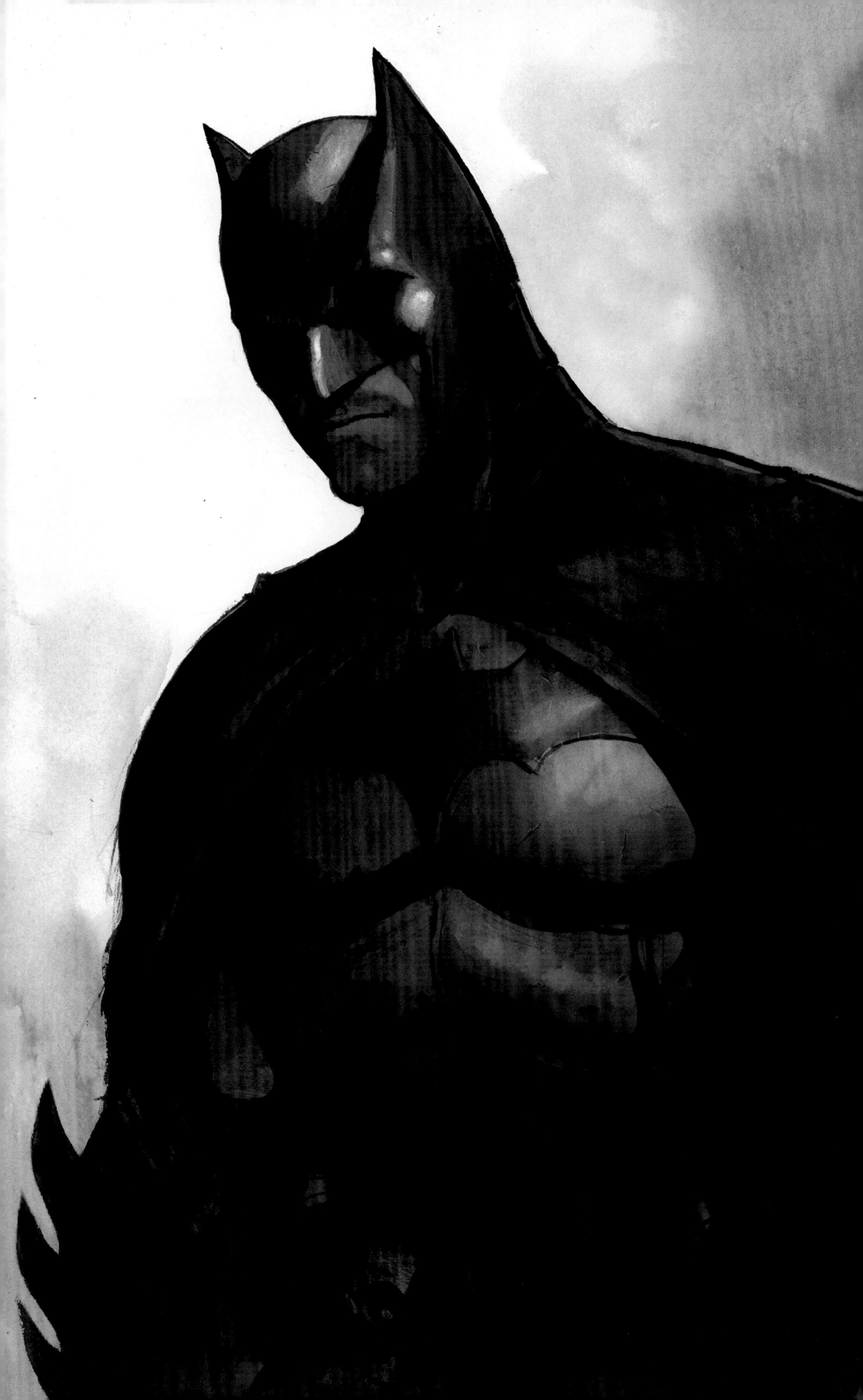

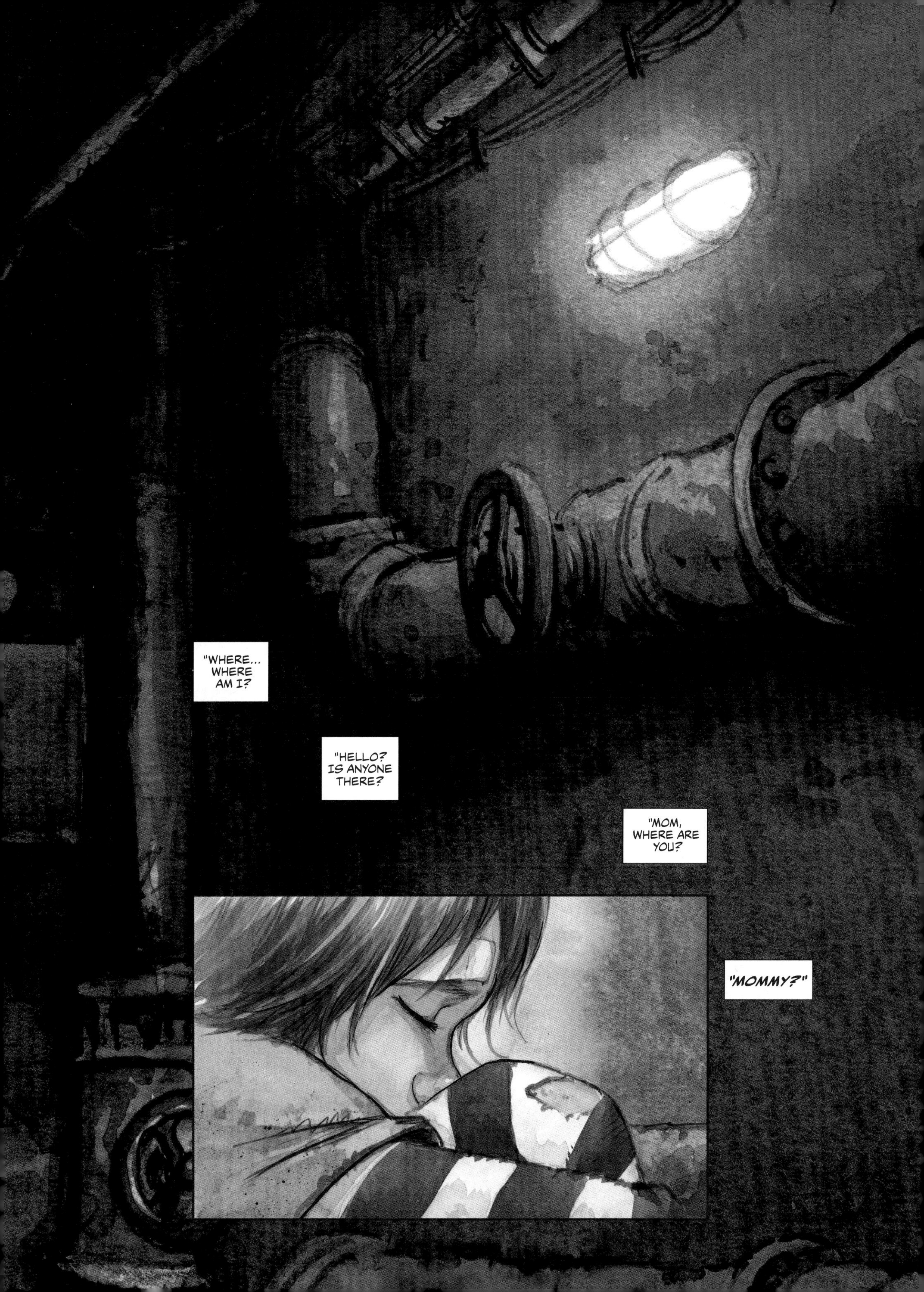
"WHERE... WHERE AM I?
"HELLO? IS ANYONE THERE?
"MOM, WHERE ARE YOU?
"MOMMY?"

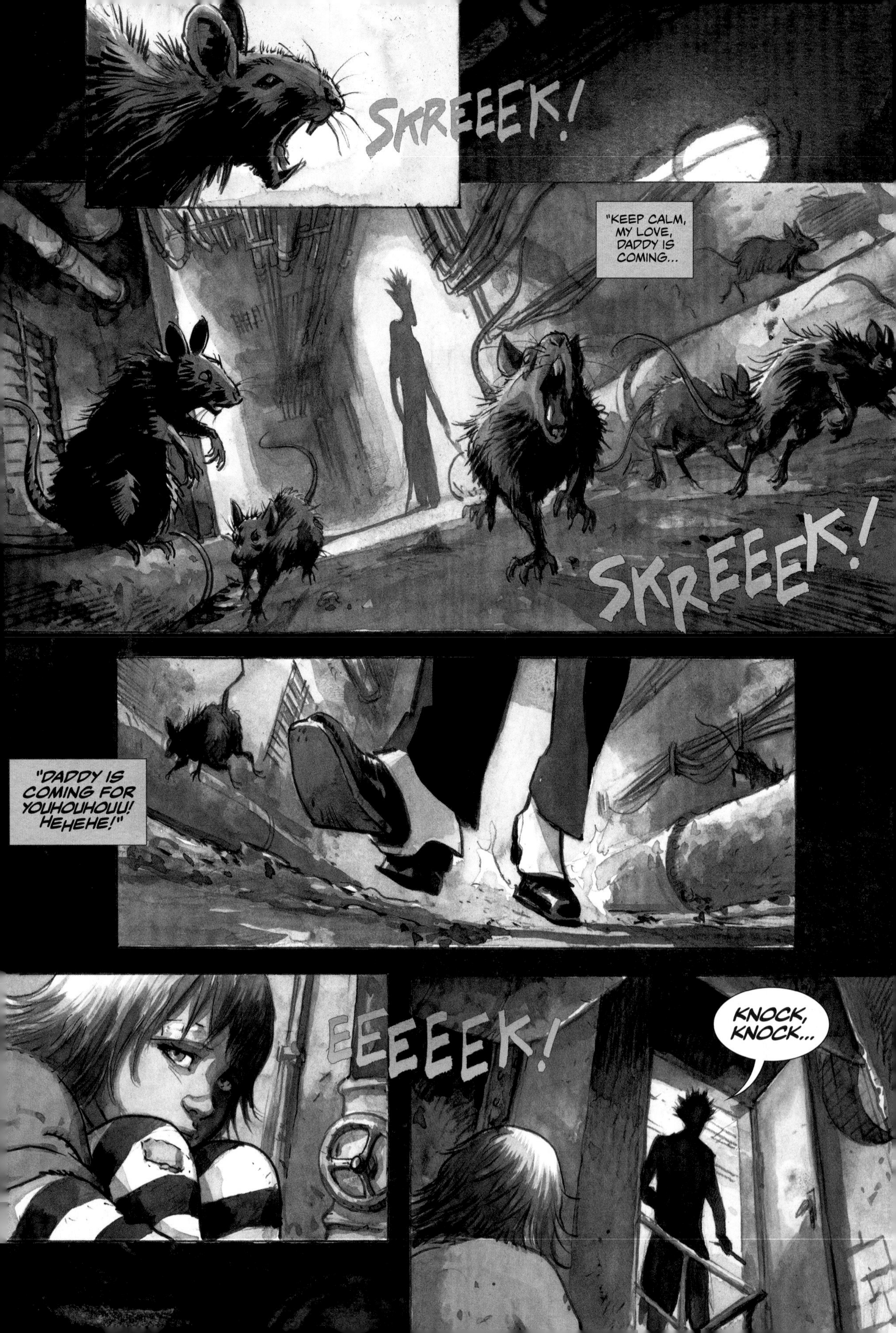
SKREEEK!
"KEEP CALM, MY LOVE, DADDY IS COMING...
SKREEEK!
"DADDY IS COMING FOR YOUHOUHOUU! HEHEHE!"
EEEEEK!
KNOCK, KNOCK...

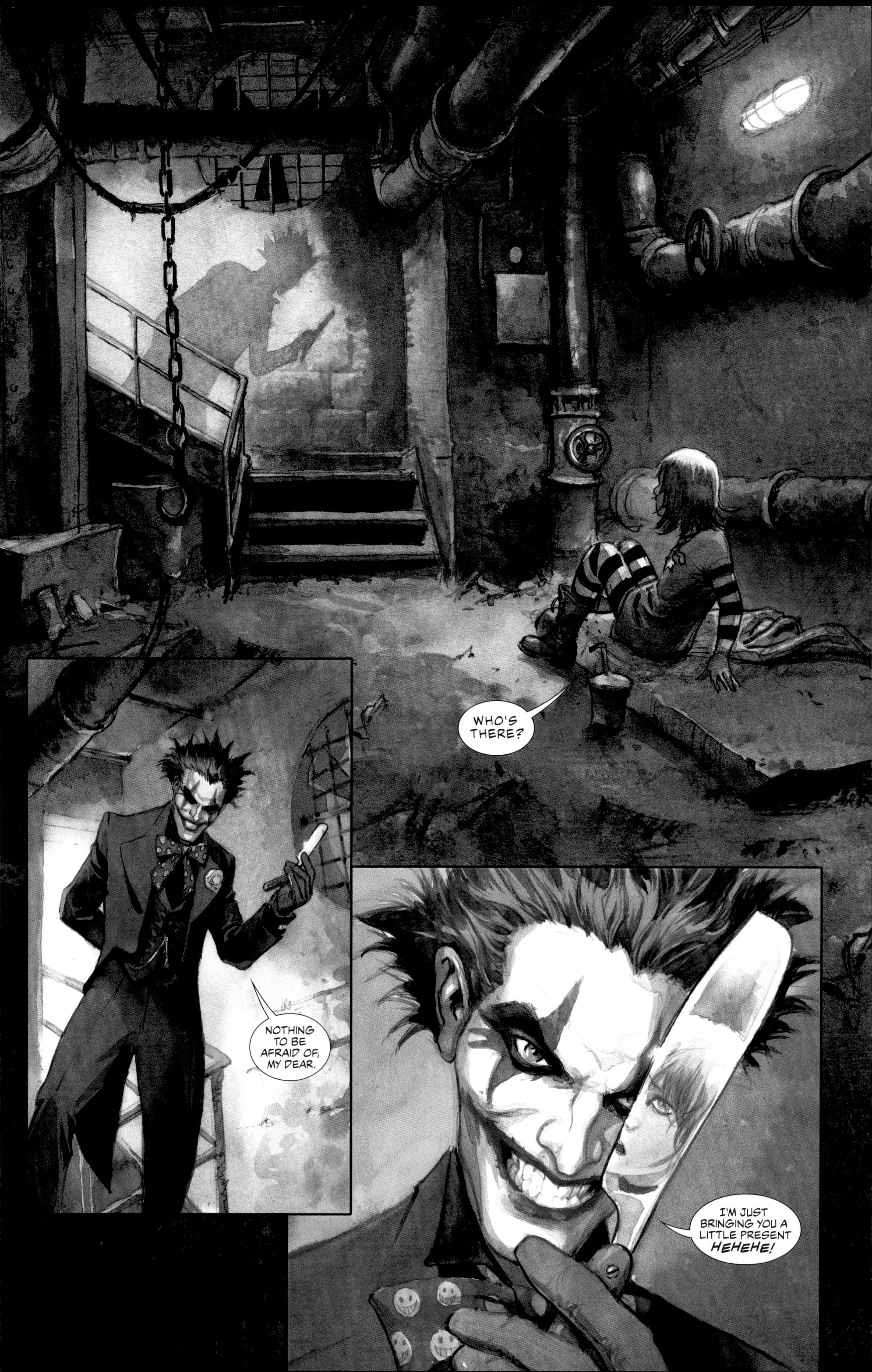
WHO'S THERE?
NOTHING TO BE AFRAID OF, MY DEAR.
I'M JUST BRINGING YOU A LITTLE PRESENT HEHEHE!

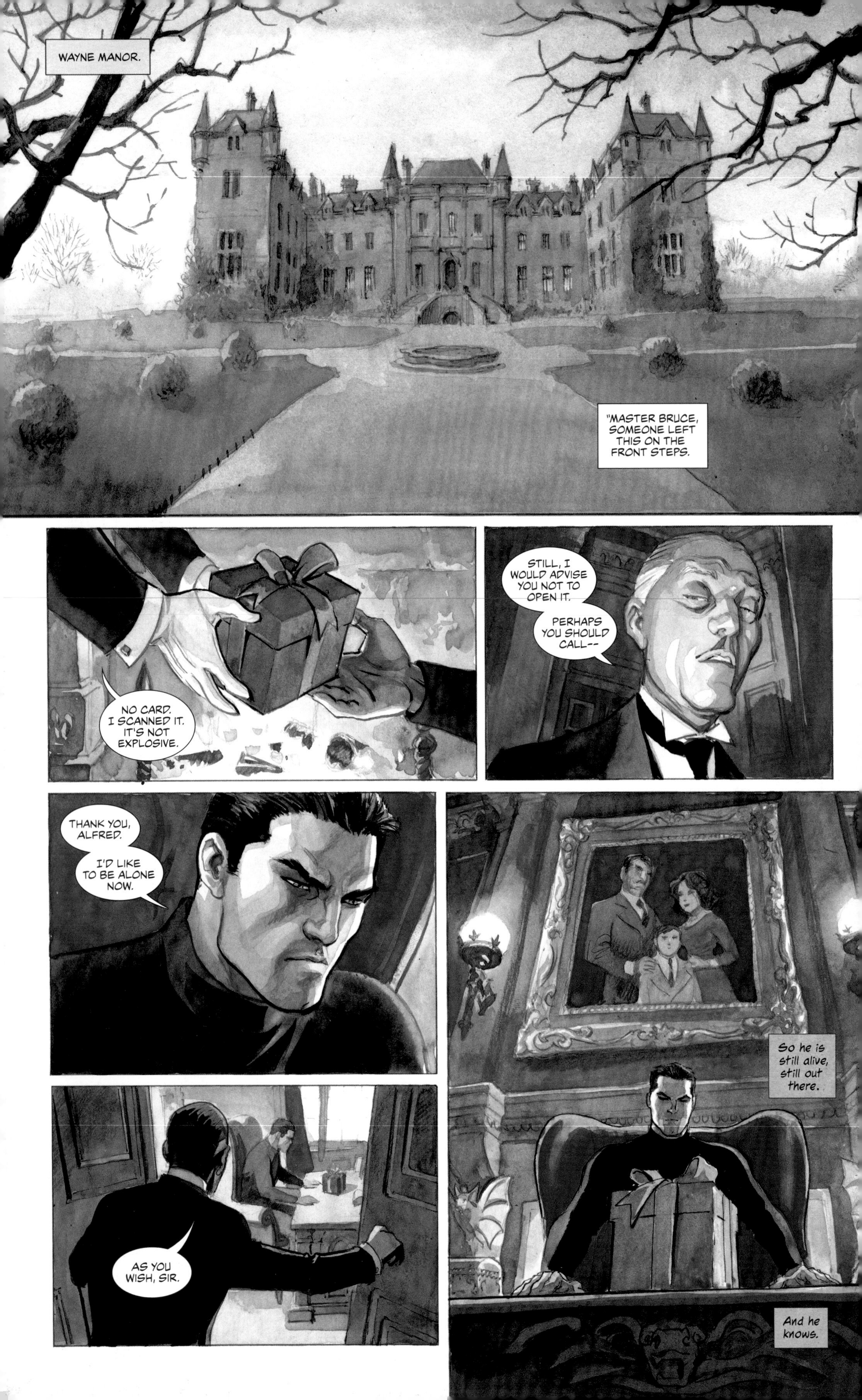
WAYNE MANOR.
"MASTER BRUCE, SOMEONE LEFT THIS ON THE FRONT STEPS.
NO CARD. I SCANNED IT. IT'S NOT EXPLOSIVE.
STILL, I WOULD ADVISE YOU NOT TO OPEN IT.
PERHAPS YOU SHOULD CALL--
THANK YOU, ALFRED.
I'D LIKE TO BE ALONE NOW.
AS YOU WISH, SIR.
So he is still alive, still out there.
And he knows.

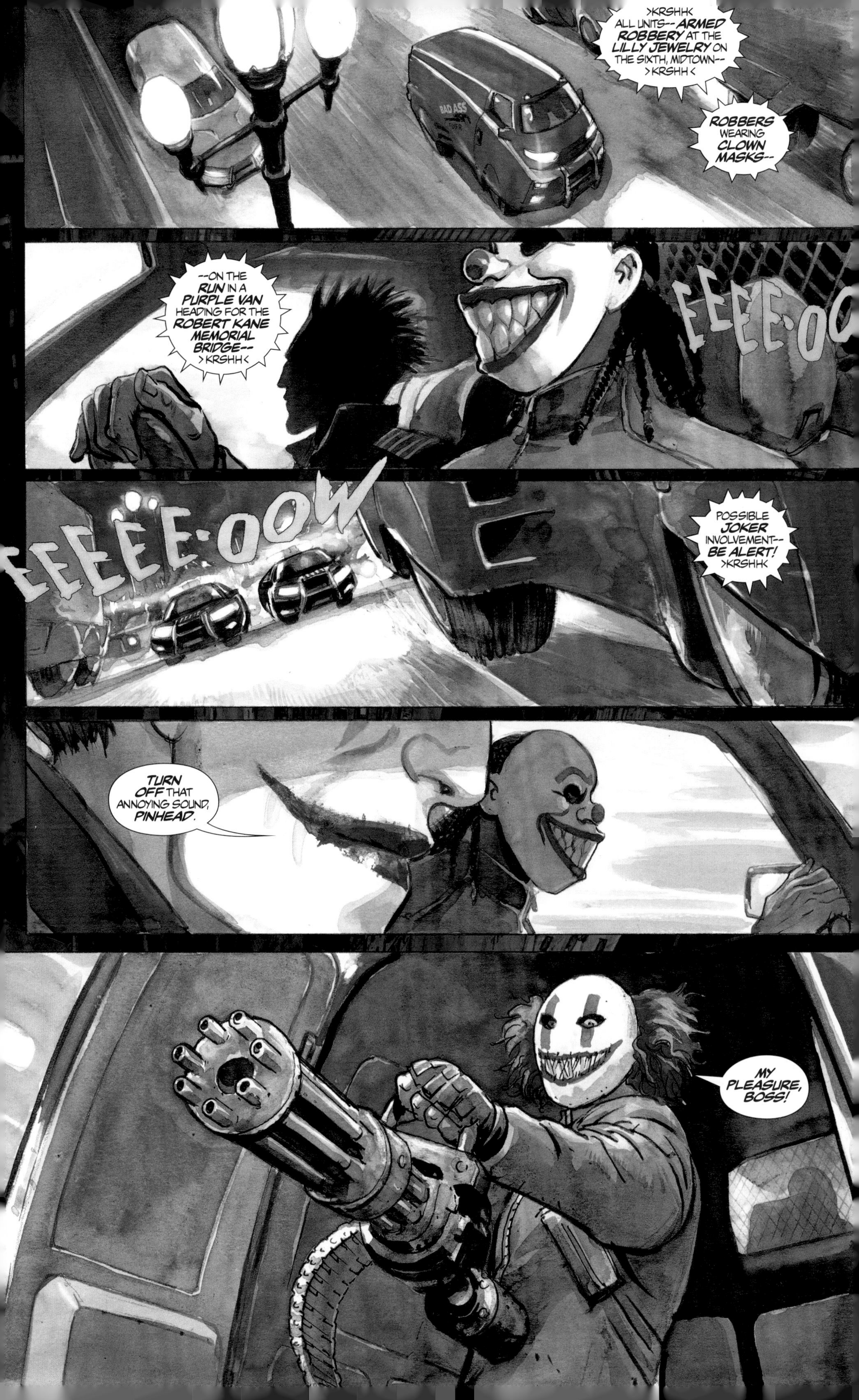
>KRSHH< ALL UNITS-- ARMED ROBBERY AT THE LILLY JEWELRY ON THE SIXTH, MIDTOWN-- >KRSHH<
ROBBERS WEARING CLOWN MASKS--
--ON THE RUN IN A PURPLE VAN HEADING FOR THE ROBERT KANE MEMORIAL BRIDGE-- >KRSHH<
EEEE-OO
EEEEE-OOW
POSSIBLE JOKER INVOLVEMENT-- BE ALERT! >KRSHH<
TURN OFF THAT ANNOYING SOUND, PINHEAD.
MY PLEASURE, BOSS!

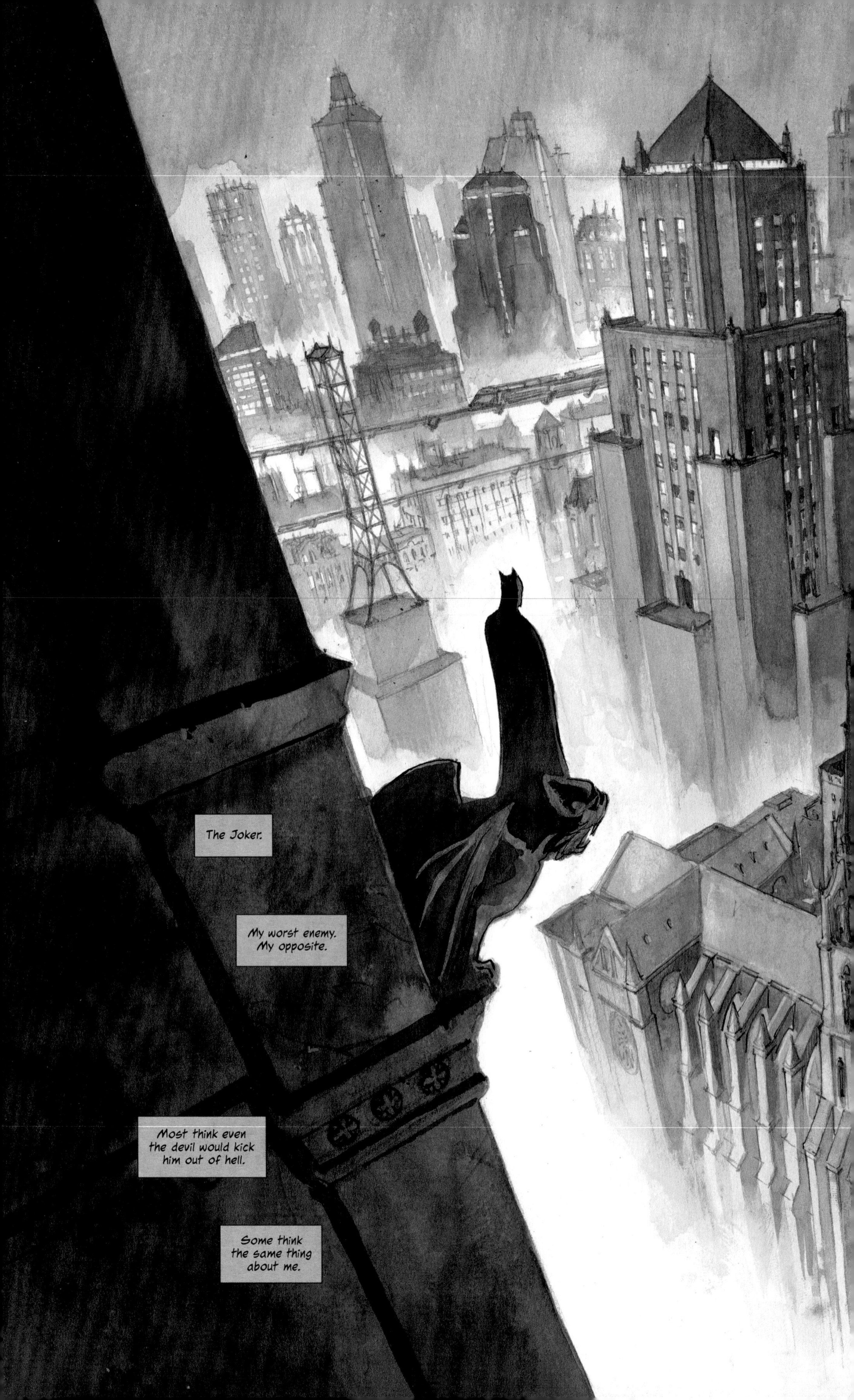
The Joker.
My worst enemy. My opposite.
Most think even the devil would kick him out of hell.
Some think the same thing about me.

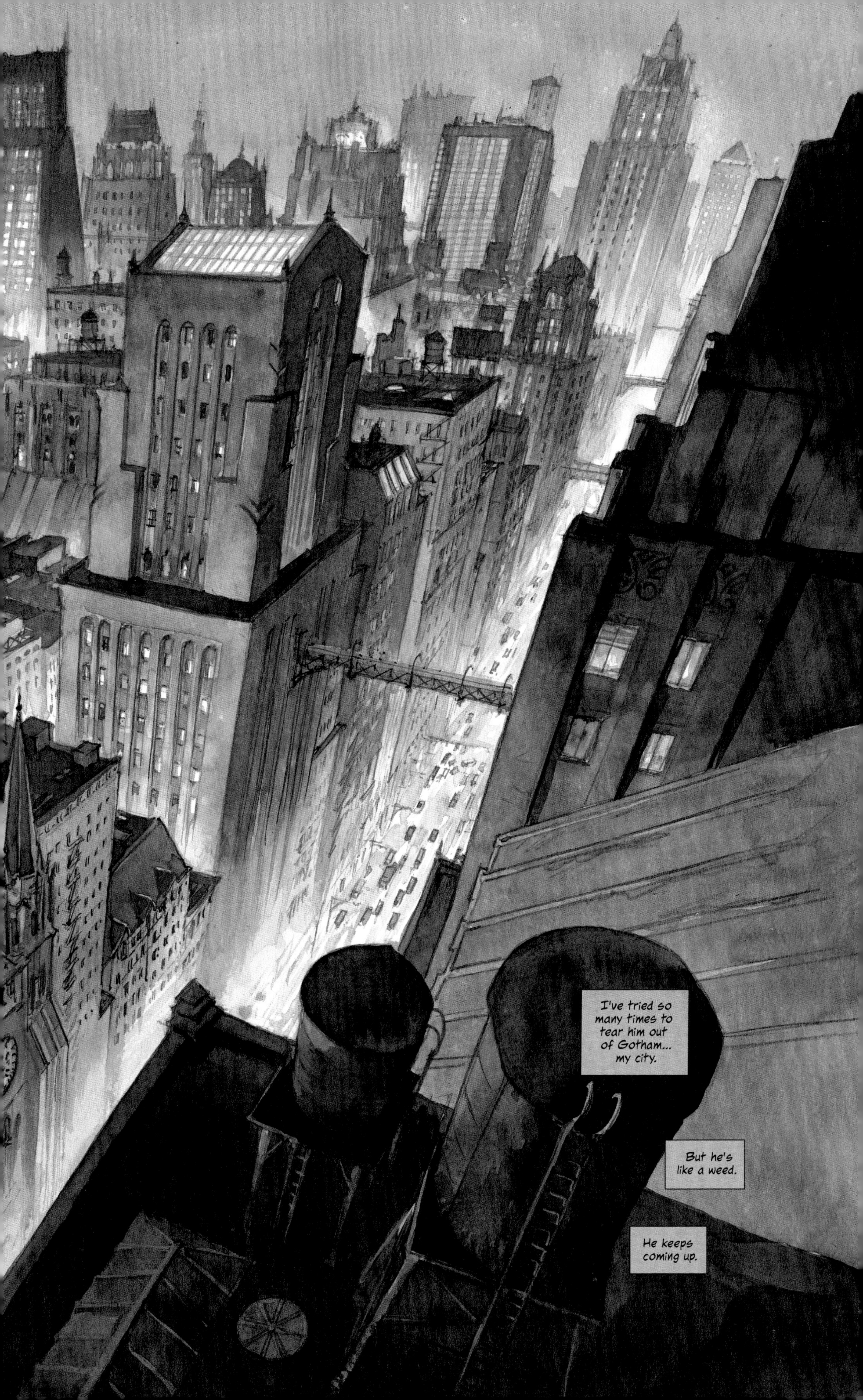
I've tried so many times to tear him out of Gotham... my city.
But he's like a weed.
He keeps coming up.

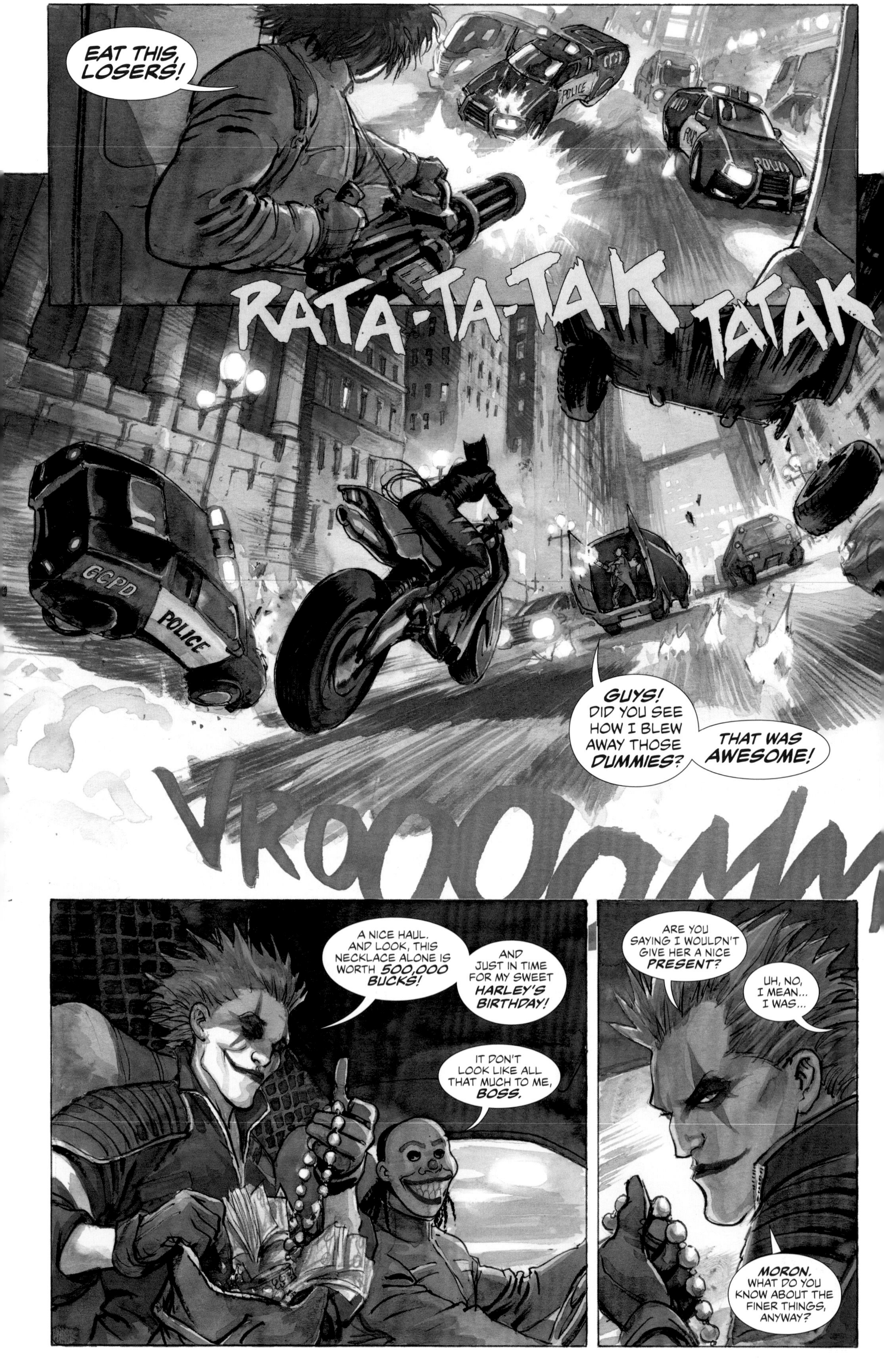
EAT THIS, LOSERS!
POLICE
RATA-TA-TAK TATAK
GCPD
POLICE
GUYS! DID YOU SEE HOW I BLEW AWAY THOSE DUMMIES?
THAT WAS AWESOME!
VROOOOMM
A NICE HAUL. AND LOOK, THIS NECKLACE ALONE IS WORTH 500,000 BUCKS!
AND JUST IN TIME FOR MY SWEET HARLEY'S BIRTHDAY!
IT DON'T LOOK LIKE ALL THAT MUCH TO ME, BOSS.
ARE YOU SAYING I WOULDN'T GIVE HER A NICE PRESENT?
UH, NO, I MEAN... I WAS...
MORON. WHAT DO YOU KNOW ABOUT THE FINER THINGS, ANYWAY?

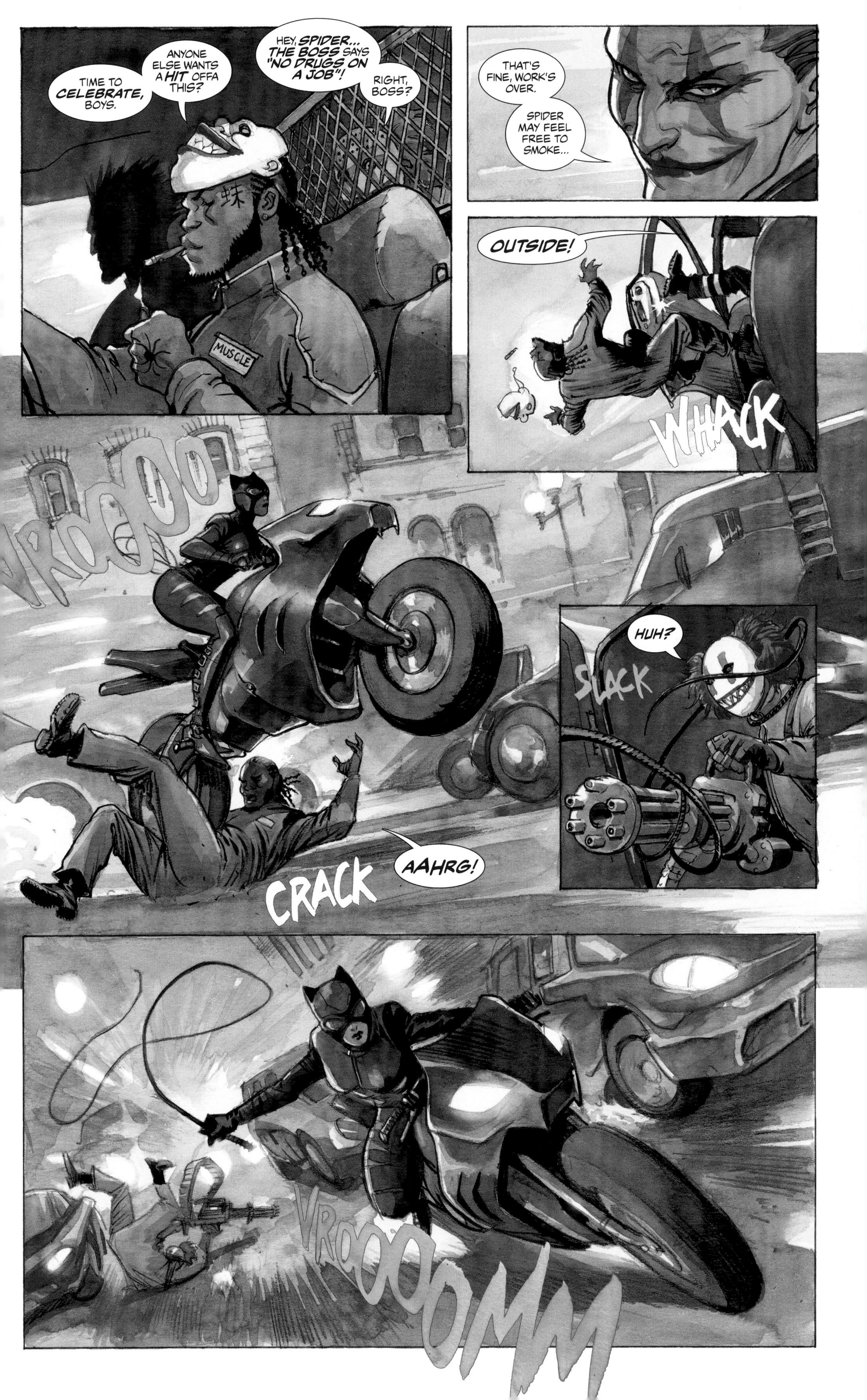
TIME TO CELEBRATE, BOYS.
ANYONE ELSE WANTS A HIT OFFA THIS?
HEY, SPIDER... THE BOSS SAYS "NO DRUGS ON A JOB"!
RIGHT, BOSS?
MUSCLE
THAT'S FINE, WORK'S OVER.
SPIDER MAY FEEL FREE TO SMOKE...
OUTSIDE!
WHACK
VROOOO
HUH?
SLACK
AAHRG!
CRACK
VROOOOMM

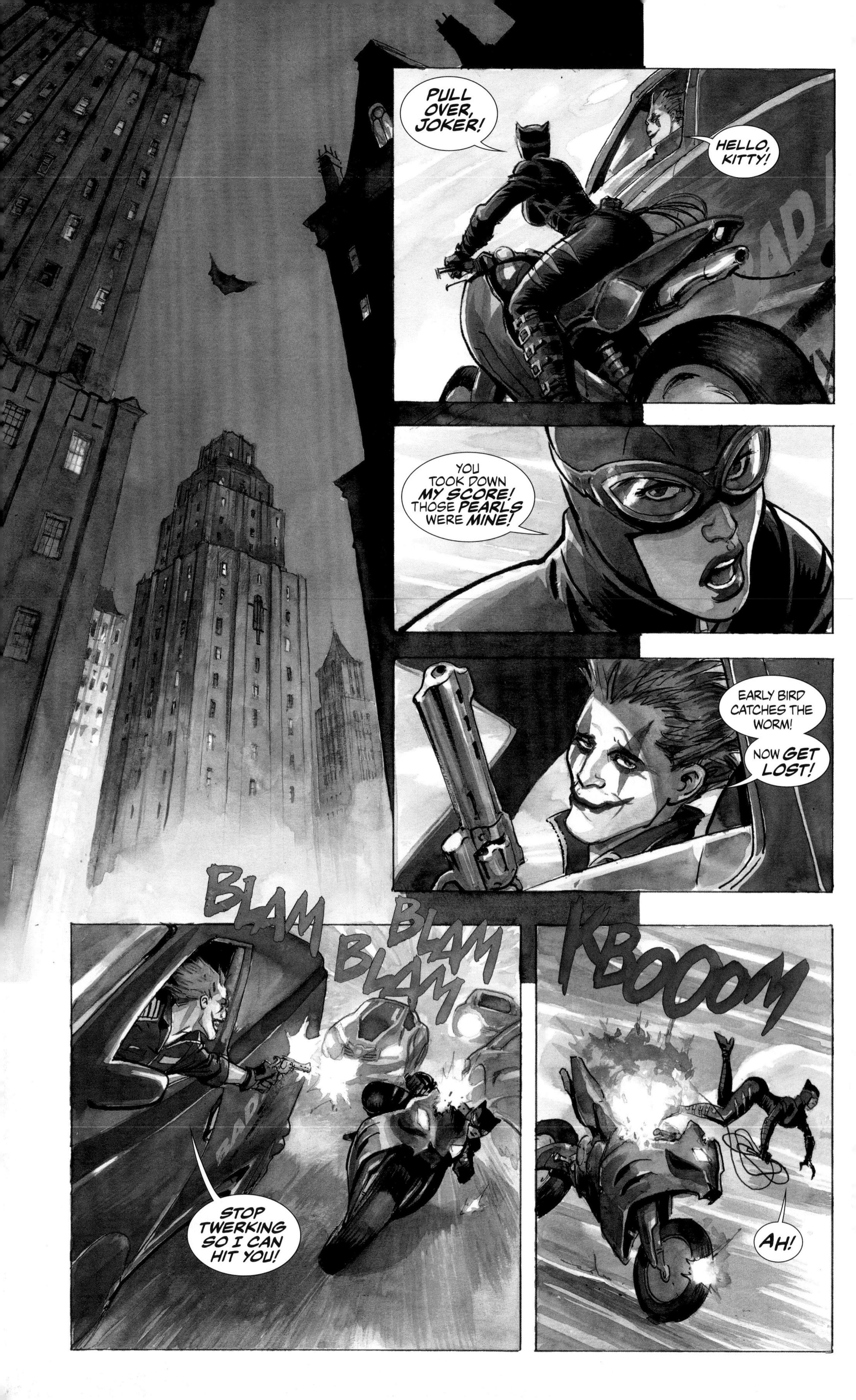
PULL OVER, JOKER!
HELLO, KITTY!
YOU TOOK DOWN MY SCORE! THOSE PEARLS WERE MINE!
EARLY BIRD CATCHES THE WORM!
NOW GET LOST!
BLAM BLAM BLAM
STOP TWERKING SO I CAN HIT YOU!
KBOOOOM
AH!

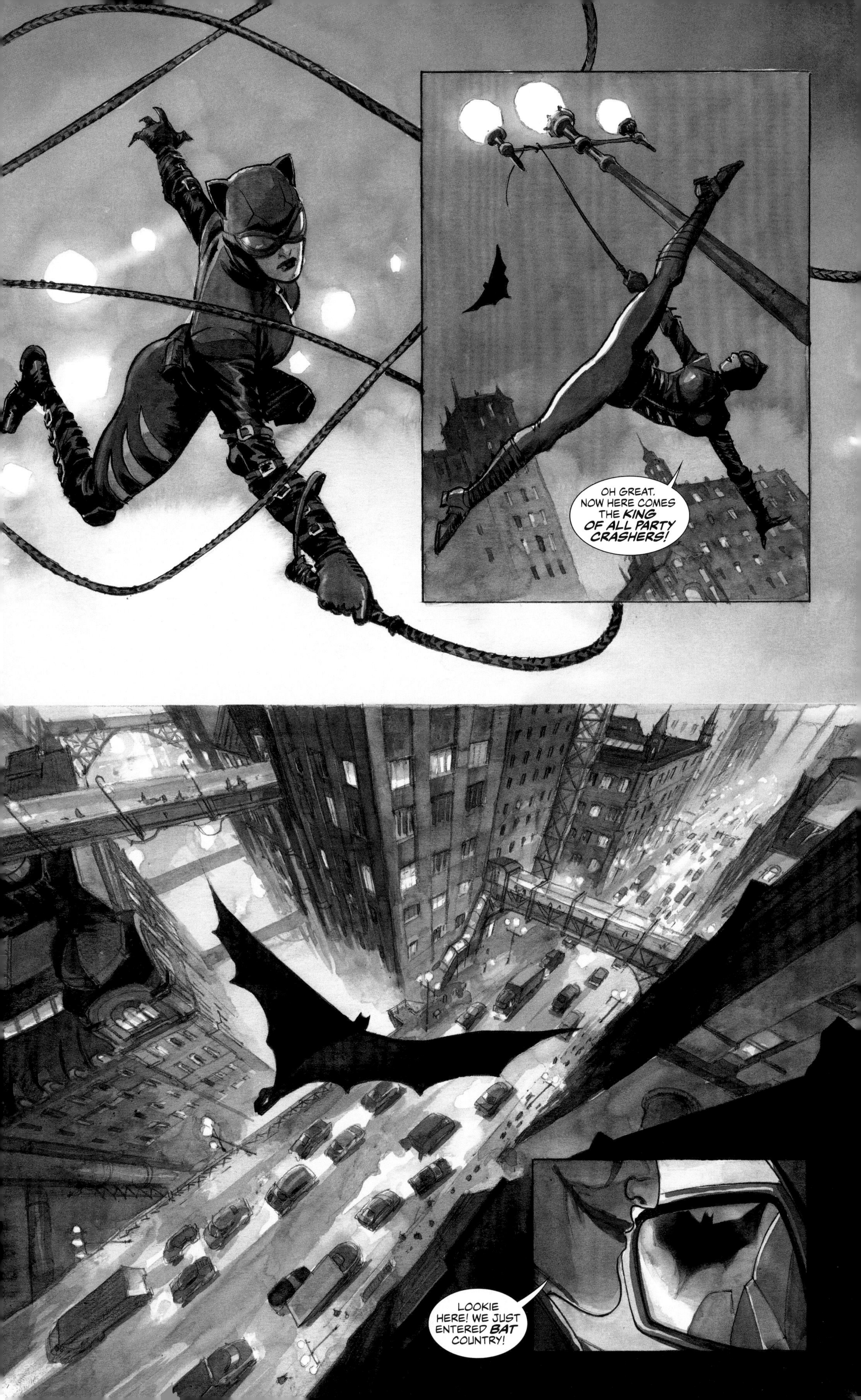
OH GREAT. NOW HERE COMES THE KING OF ALL PARTY CRASHERS!
LOOKIE HERE! WE JUST ENTERED BAT COUNTRY!

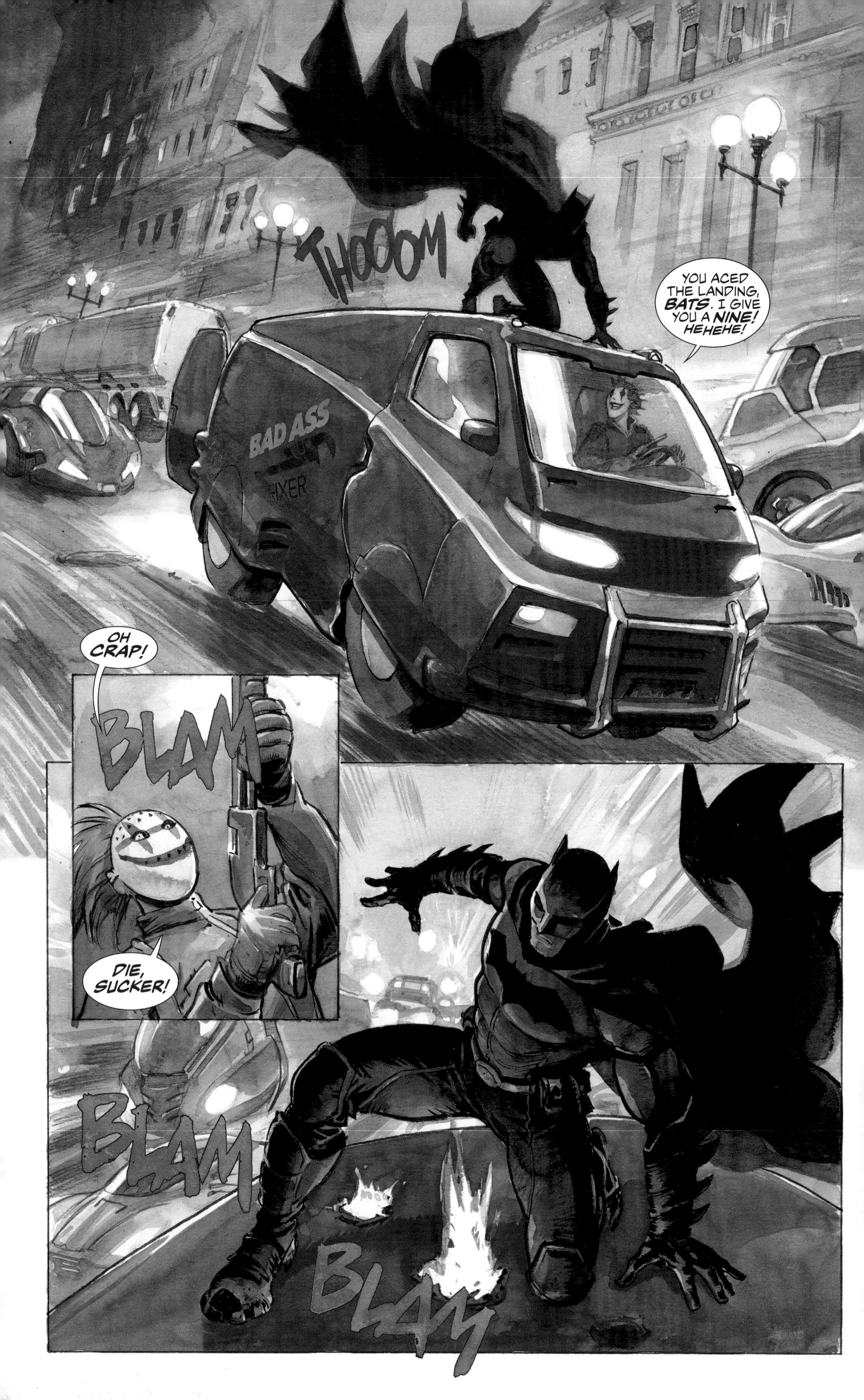
THOOOM
YOU ACED THE LANDING, BATS. I GIVE YOU A NINE! HEHEHE!
BAD ASS
OH CRAP!
BLAM
DIE, SUCKER!
BLAM
BLAM

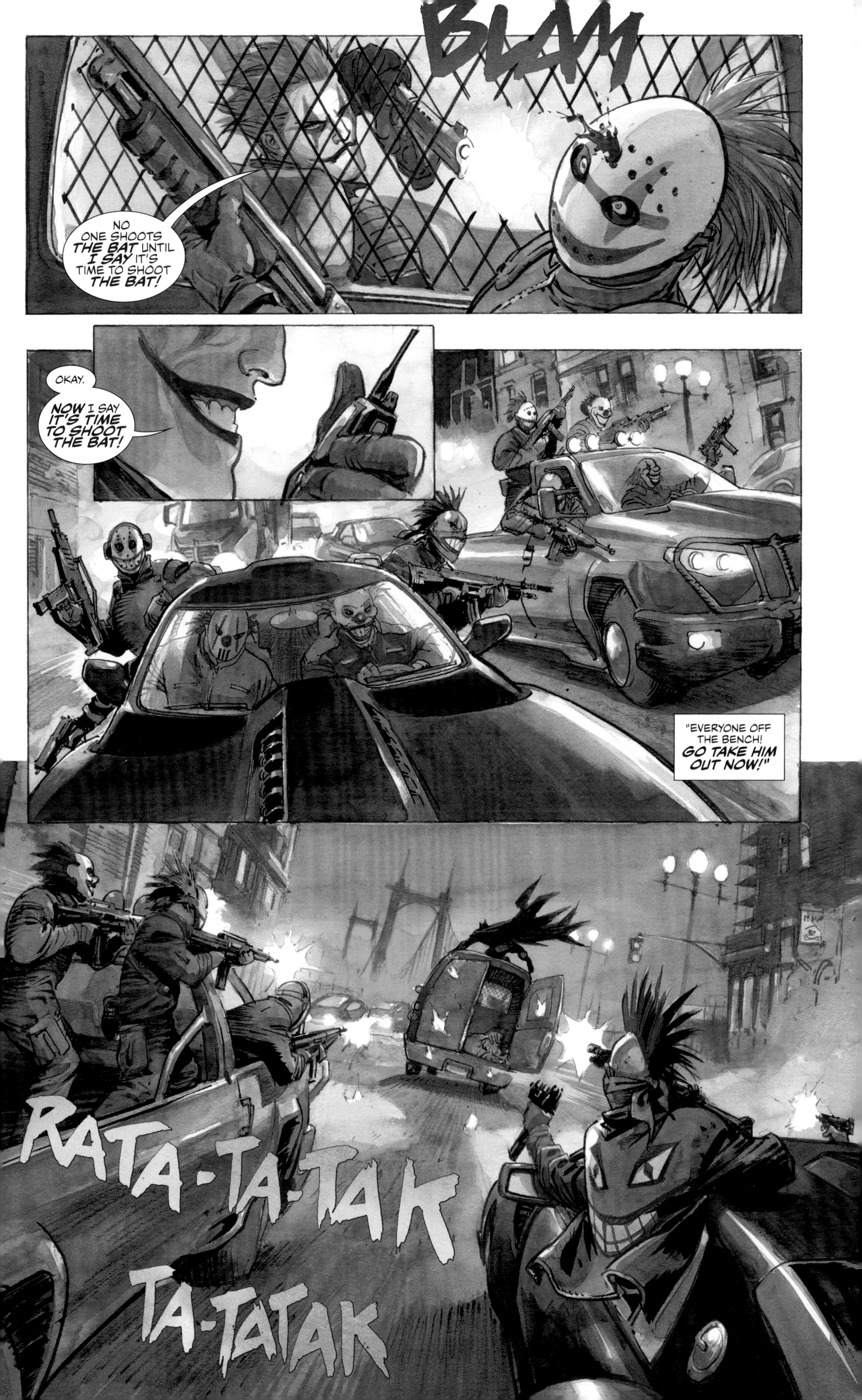
BLAM
NO ONE SHOOTS THE BAT UNTIL I SAY IT'S TIME TO SHOOT THE BAT!
OKAY.
NOW I SAY IT'S TIME TO SHOOT THE BAT!
"EVERYONE OFF THE BENCH! GO TAKE HIM OUT NOW!"
RATA-TA-TAK
TA-TATAK

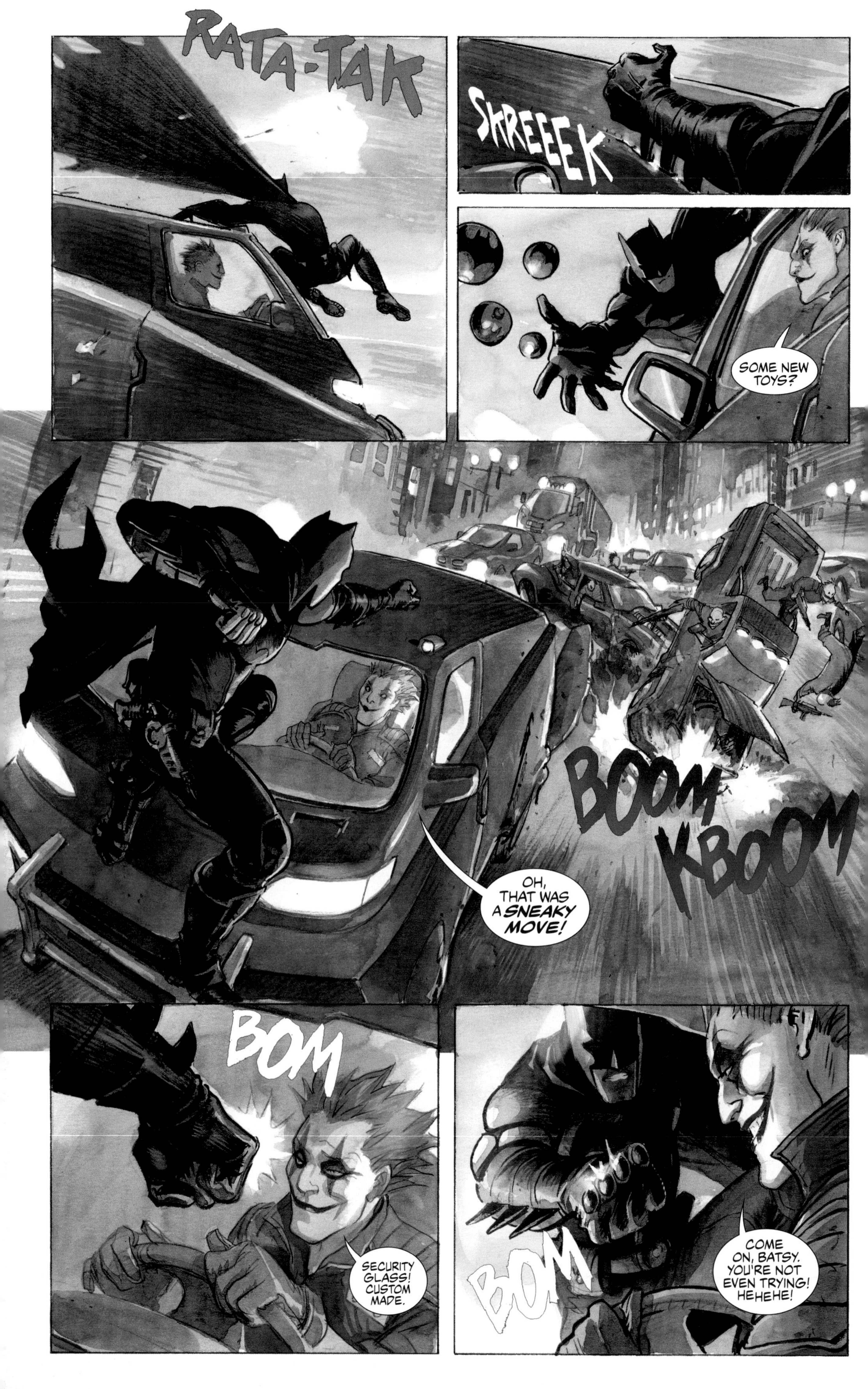
RATA-TAK
SKREEEEK
SOME NEW TOYS?
OH, THAT WAS A SNEAKY MOVE!
BOOM
KBOOM
BOM
SECURITY GLASS! CUSTOM MADE.
BOM
COME ON, BATSY. YOU'RE NOT EVEN TRYING! HEHEHE!

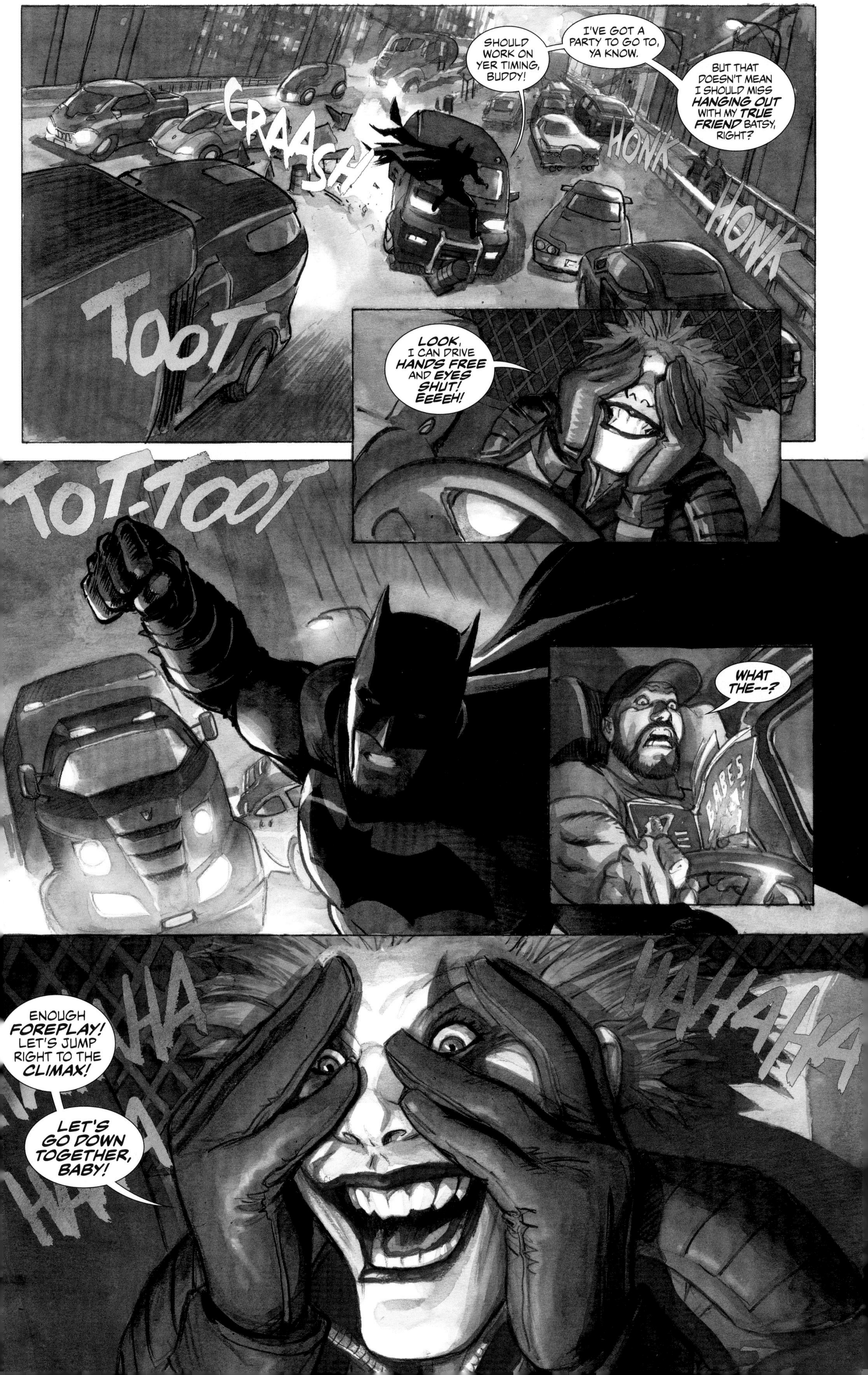
CRAAASH
SHOULD WORK ON YER TIMING, BUDDY!
I'VE GOT A PARTY TO GO TO, YA KNOW.
BUT THAT DOESN'T MEAN I SHOULD MISS HANGING OUT WITH MY TRUE FRIEND BATSY, RIGHT?
HONK
HONK
TOOT
LOOK, I CAN DRIVE HANDS FREE AND EYES SHUT! EEEEH!
TOT-TOOT
WHAT THE--?
BABES
HA HA
HAHAHA
ENOUGH FOREPLAY! LET'S JUMP RIGHT TO THE CLIMAX!
LET'S GO DOWN TOGETHER, BABY!

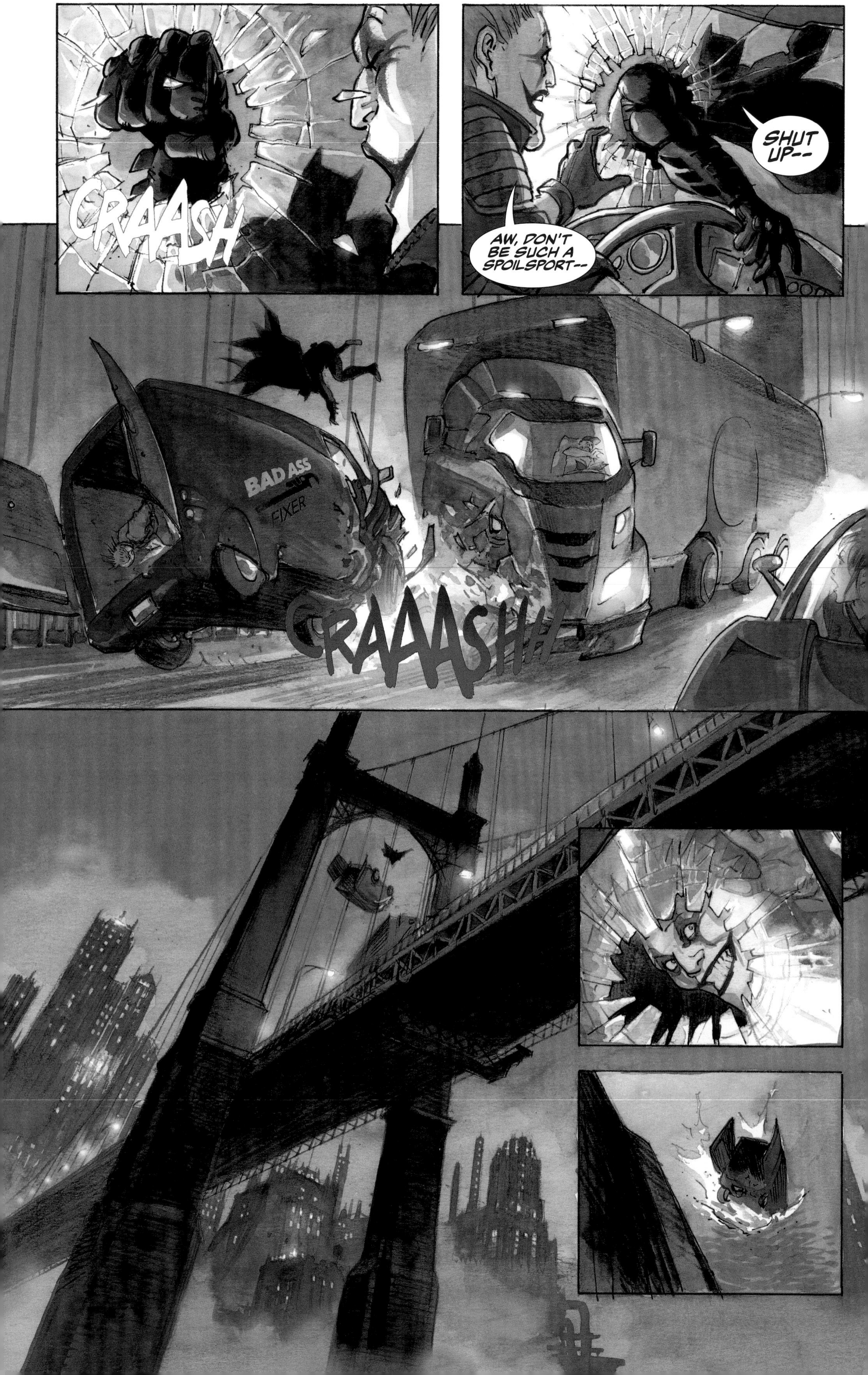
CRAAASH
AW, DON'T BE SUCH A SPOILSPORT--
SHUT UP--
BAD ASS
FIXER
CRAAASHH

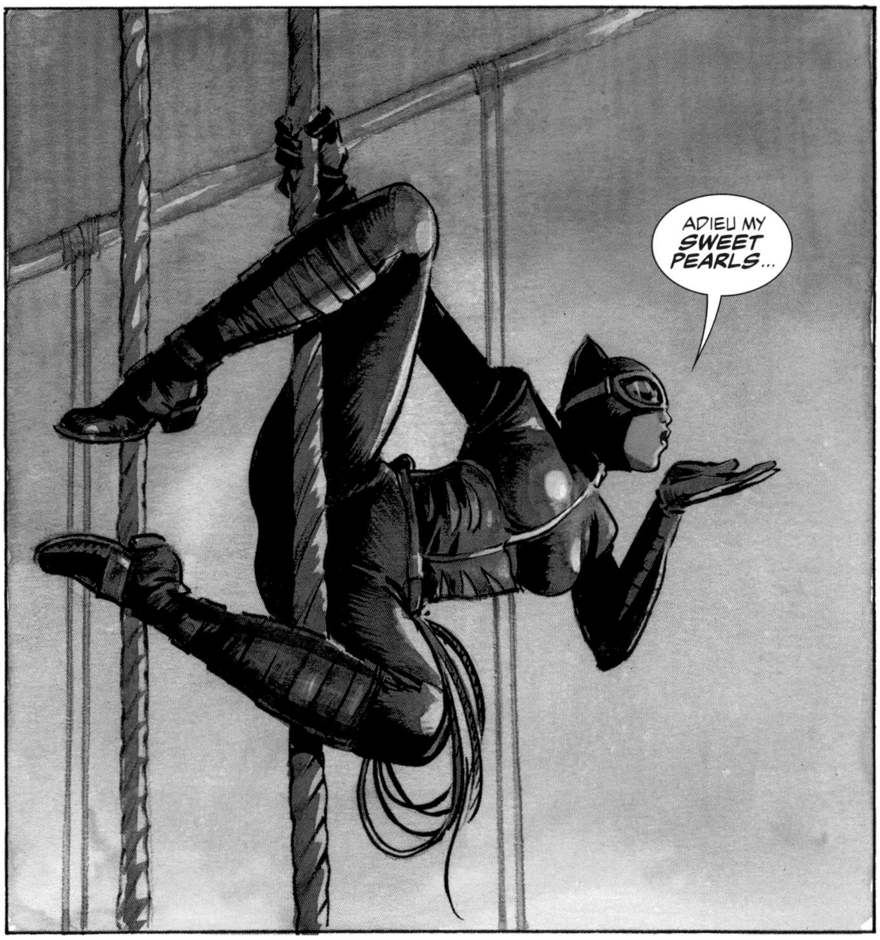
ADIEU MY SWEET PEARLS...

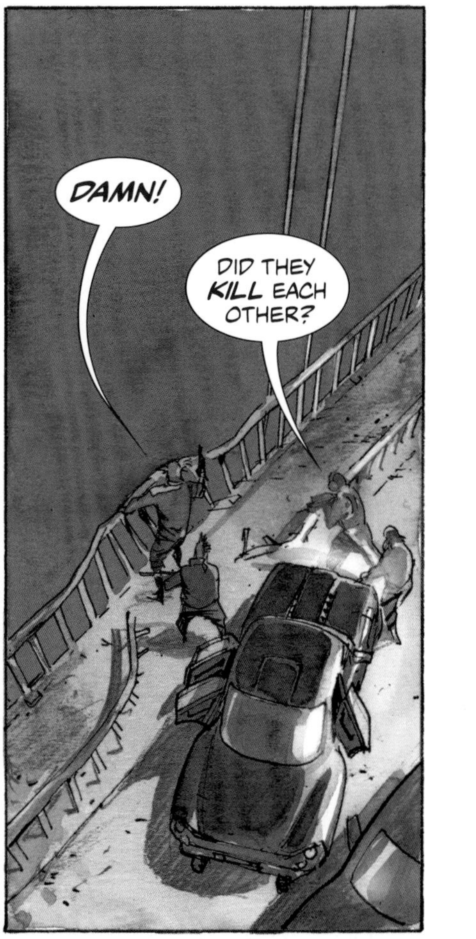
DAMN!
DID THEY KILL EACH OTHER?

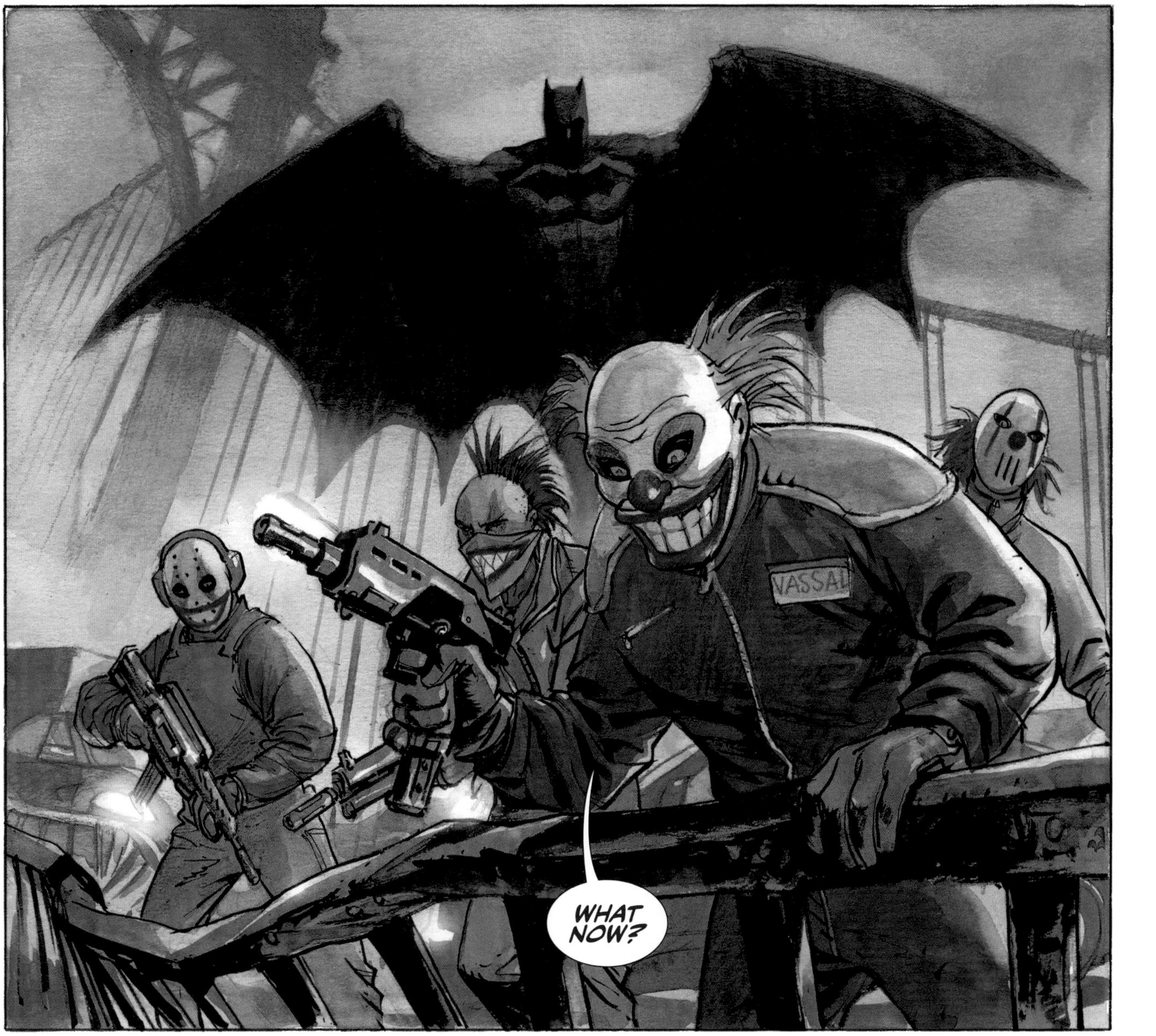
VASSAL
WHAT NOW?

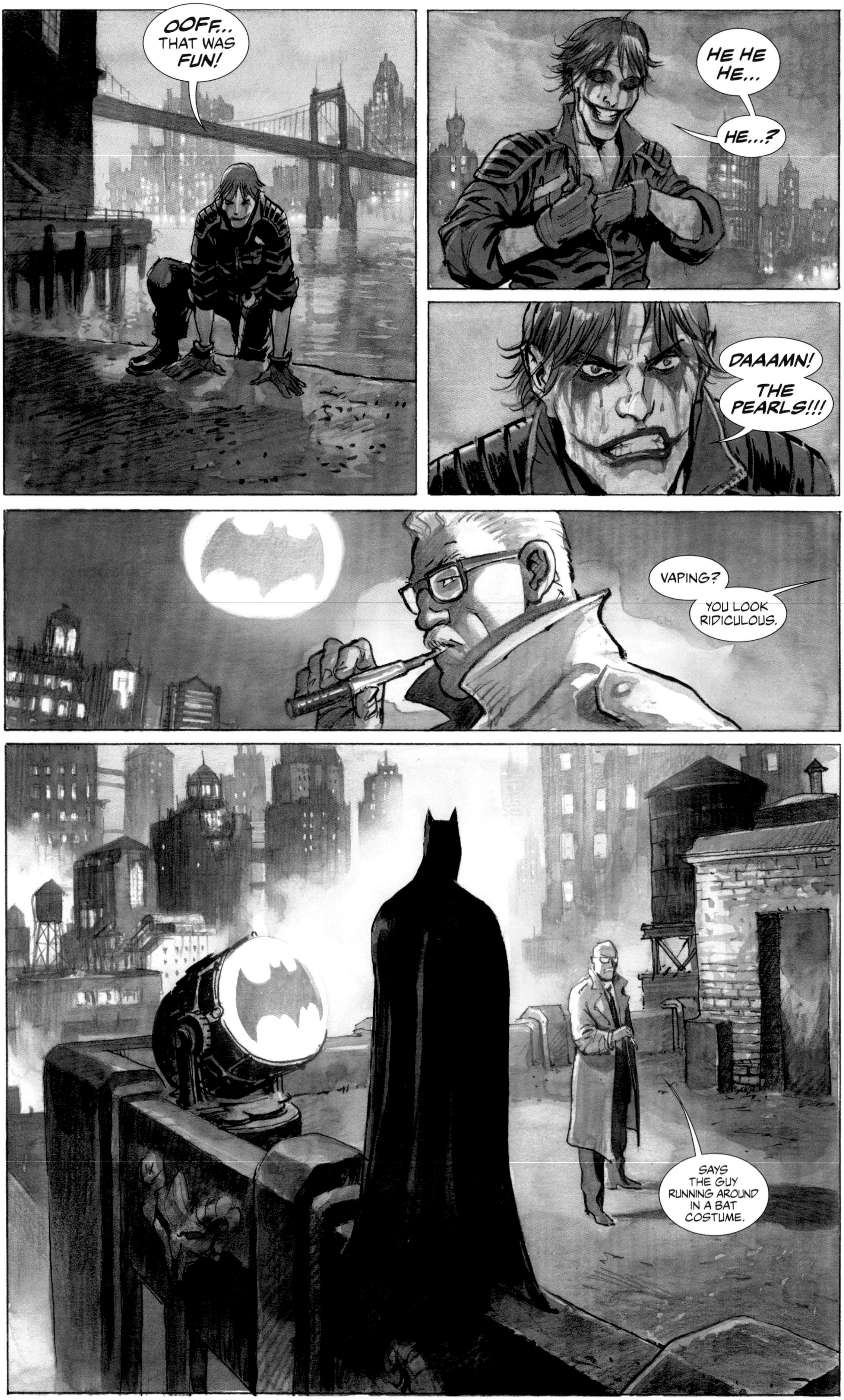
OOFF... THAT WAS FUN!
HE HE HE...
HE...?
DAAAMN!
THE PEARLS!!!
VAPING?
YOU LOOK RIDICULOUS.
SAYS THE GUY RUNNING AROUND IN A BAT COSTUME.

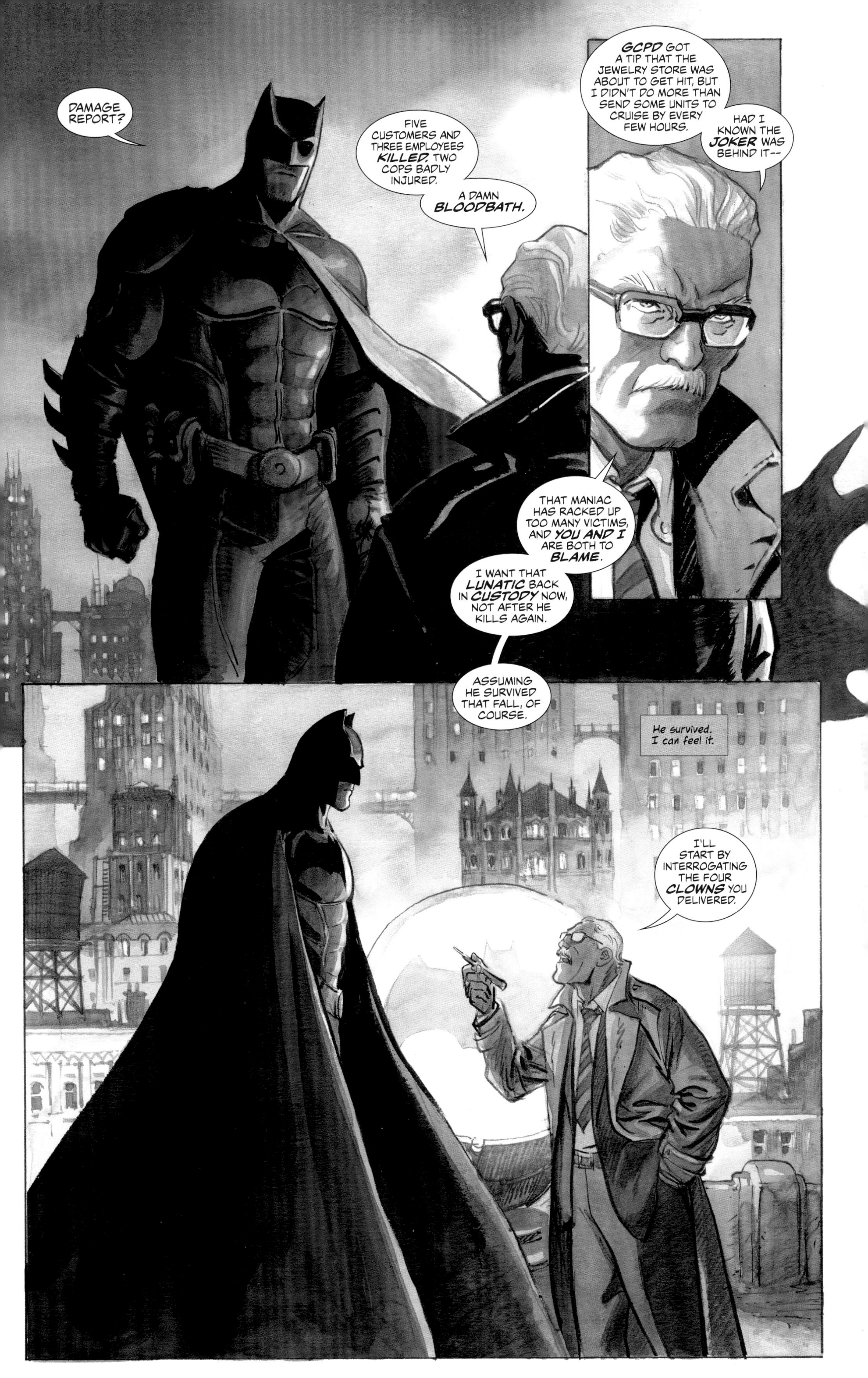
DAMAGE REPORT?
FIVE CUSTOMERS AND THREE EMPLOYEES KILLED. TWO COPS BADLY INJURED.
A DAMN BLOODBATH.
GCPD GOT A TIP THAT THE JEWELRY STORE WAS ABOUT TO GET HIT, BUT I DIDN'T DO MORE THAN SEND SOME UNITS TO CRUISE BY EVERY FEW HOURS.
HAD I KNOWN THE JOKER WAS BEHIND IT--
THAT MANIAC HAS RACKED UP TOO MANY VICTIMS, AND YOU AND I ARE BOTH TO BLAME.
I WANT THAT LUNATIC BACK IN CUSTODY NOW, NOT AFTER HE KILLS AGAIN.
ASSUMING HE SURVIVED THAT FALL, OF COURSE.
He survived. I can feel it.
I'LL START BY INTERROGATING THE FOUR CLOWNS YOU DELIVERED.

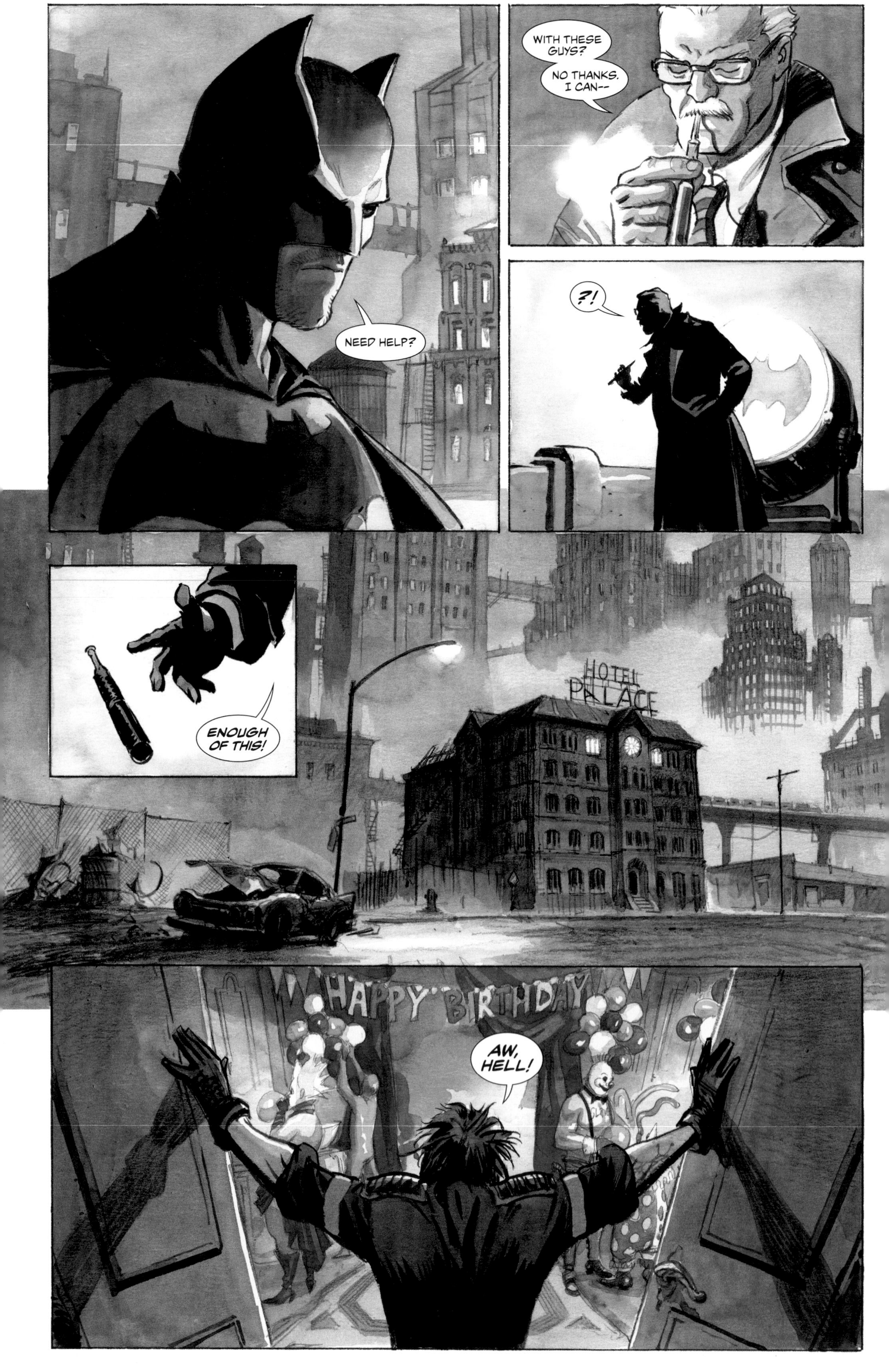
NEED HELP?
WITH THESE GUYS?
NO THANKS. I CAN--
?!
ENOUGH OF THIS!
HOTEL PALACE
HAPPY BIRTHDAY
AW, HELL!

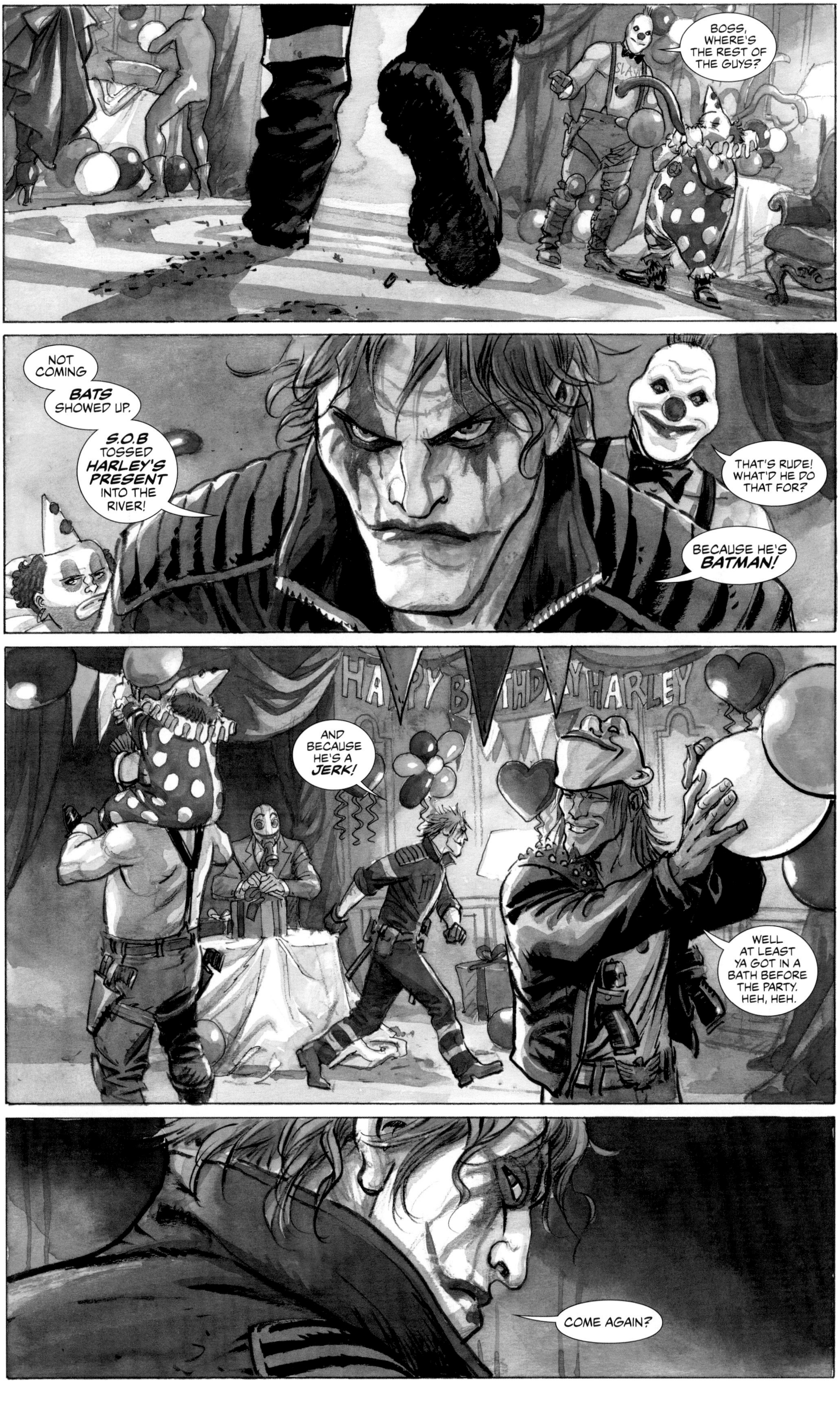
BOSS, WHERE'S THE REST OF THE GUYS?
NOT COMING
BATS SHOWED UP.
S.O.B TOSSED HARLEY'S PRESENT INTO THE RIVER!
THAT'S RUDE! WHAT'D HE DO THAT FOR?
BECAUSE HE'S BATMAN!
HAPPY BIRTHDAY HARLEY
AND BECAUSE HE'S A JERK!
WELL AT LEAST YA GOT IN A BATH BEFORE THE PARTY. HEH, HEH.
COME AGAIN?

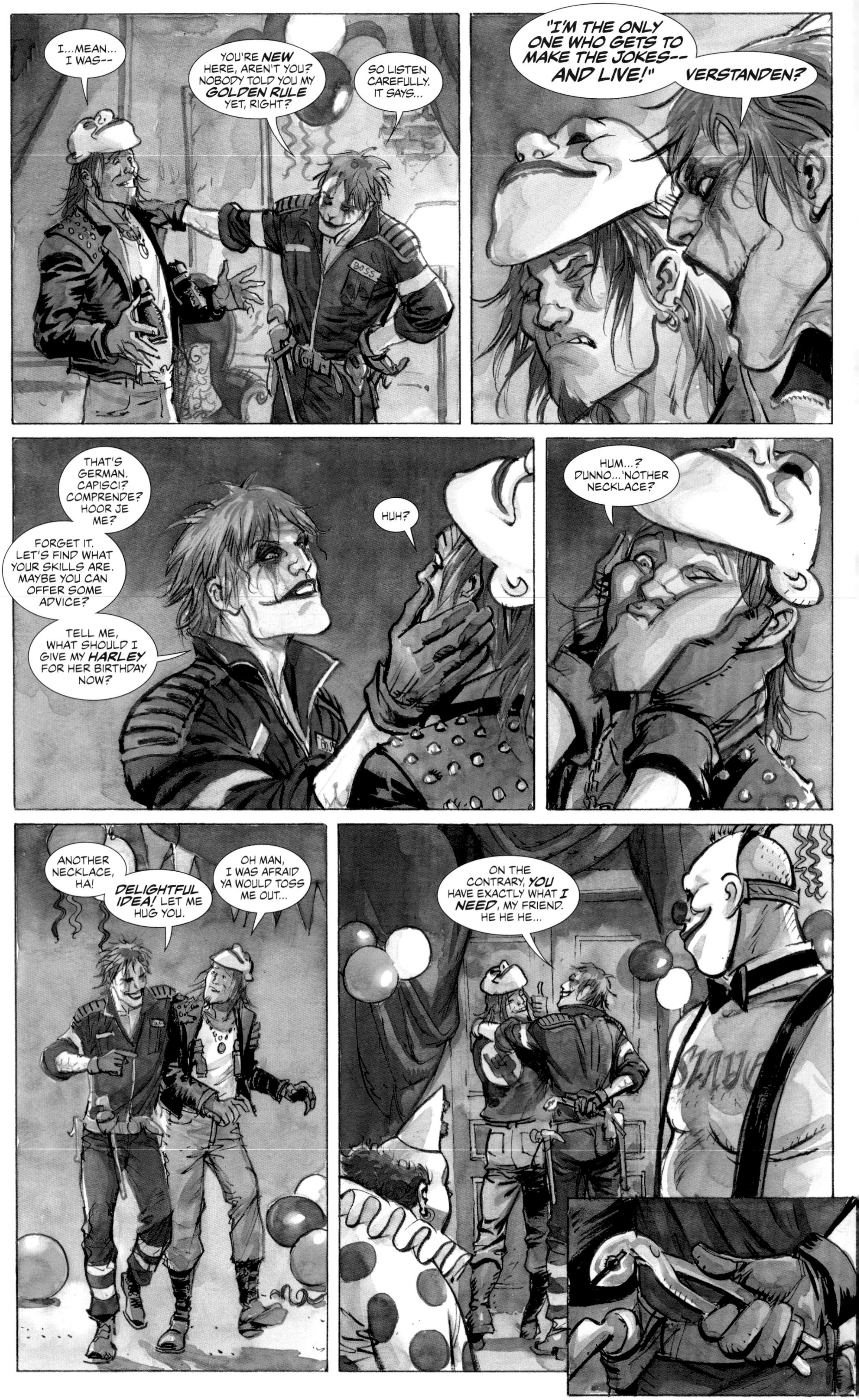
I...MEAN... I WAS--
YOU'RE NEW HERE, AREN'T YOU? NOBODY TOLD YOU MY GOLDEN RULE YET, RIGHT?
SO LISTEN CAREFULLY. IT SAYS...
"I'M THE ONLY ONE WHO GETS TO MAKE THE JOKES-- AND LIVE!"
VERSTANDEN?
BOSS
THAT'S GERMAN. CAPISCI? COMPRENDE? HOOR JE ME?
FORGET IT. LET'S FIND WHAT YOUR SKILLS ARE. MAYBE YOU CAN OFFER SOME ADVICE?
TELL ME, WHAT SHOULD I GIVE MY HARLEY FOR HER BIRTHDAY NOW?
HUH?
HUM...? DUNNO...'NOTHER NECKLACE?
ANOTHER NECKLACE, HA!
DELIGHTFUL IDEA! LET ME HUG YOU.
OH MAN, I WAS AFRAID YA WOULD TOSS ME OUT...
ON THE CONTRARY, YOU HAVE EXACTLY WHAT I NEED, MY FRIEND. HE HE HE...

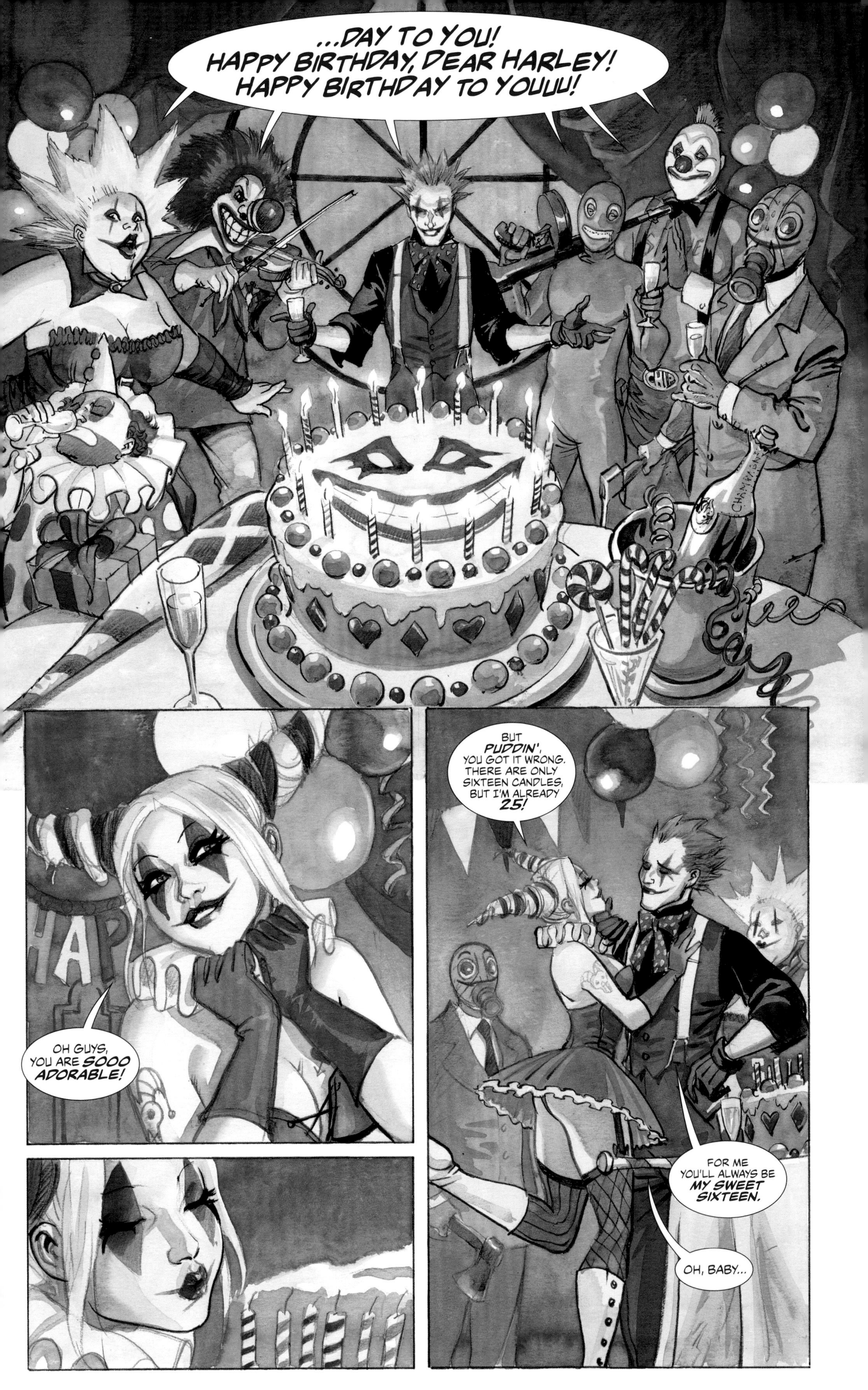
...DAY TO YOU!
HAPPY BIRTHDAY, DEAR HARLEY!
HAPPY BIRTHDAY TO YOUUU!
OH GUYS, YOU ARE SOOO ADORABLE!
BUT PUDDIN', YOU GOT IT WRONG. THERE ARE ONLY SIXTEEN CANDLES, BUT I'M ALREADY 25!
FOR ME YOU'LL ALWAYS BE MY SWEET SIXTEEN.
OH, BABY...

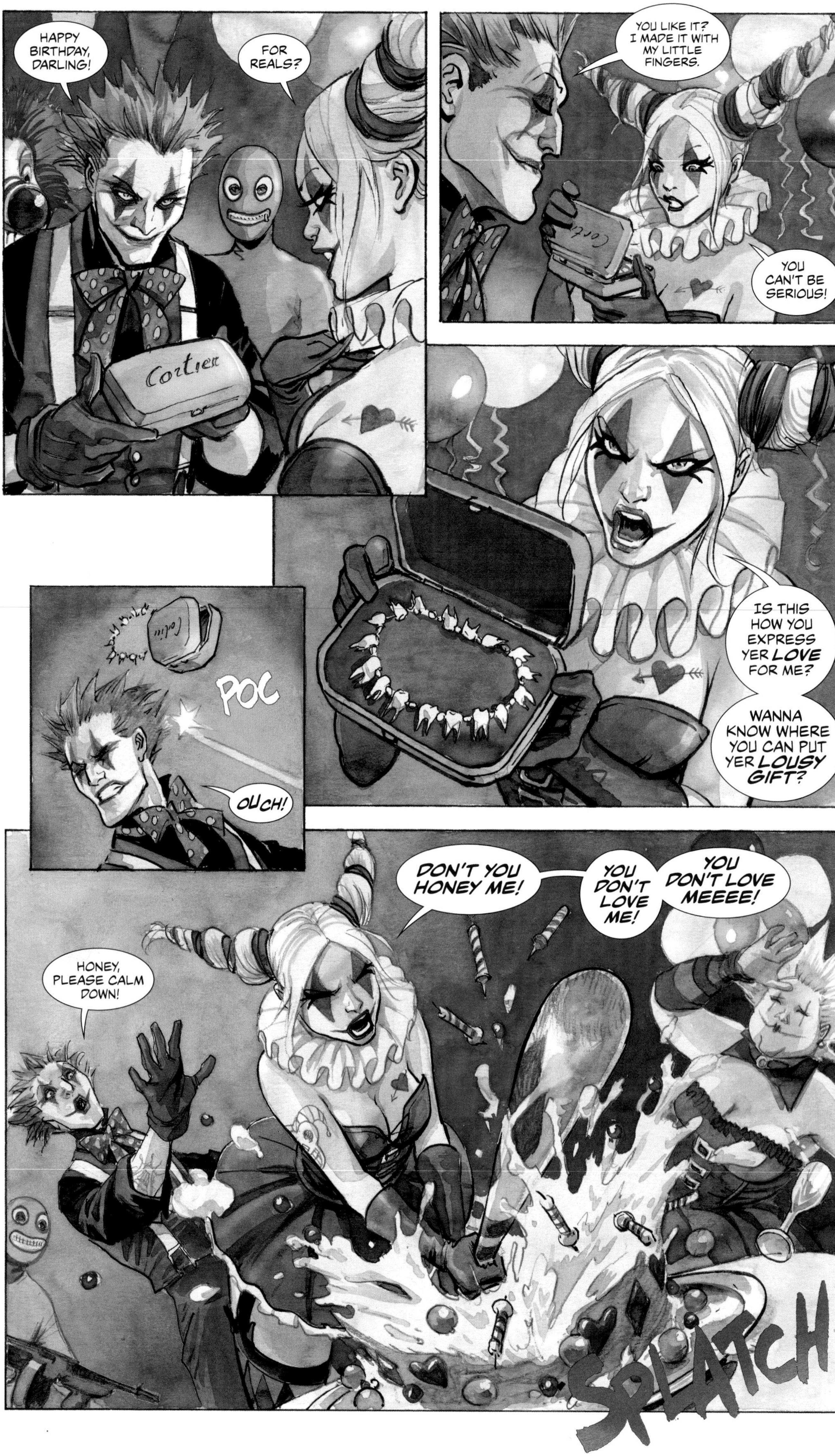
HAPPY BIRTHDAY, DARLING!
FOR REALS?
Cortier
YOU LIKE IT? I MADE IT WITH MY LITTLE FINGERS.
YOU CAN'T BE SERIOUS!
IS THIS HOW YOU EXPRESS YER LOVE FOR ME?
WANNA KNOW WHERE YOU CAN PUT YER LOUSY GIFT?
POC
OUCH!
HONEY, PLEASE CALM DOWN!
DON'T YOU HONEY ME!
YOU DON'T LOVE ME!
YOU DON'T LOVE MEEEE!
SPLATCH

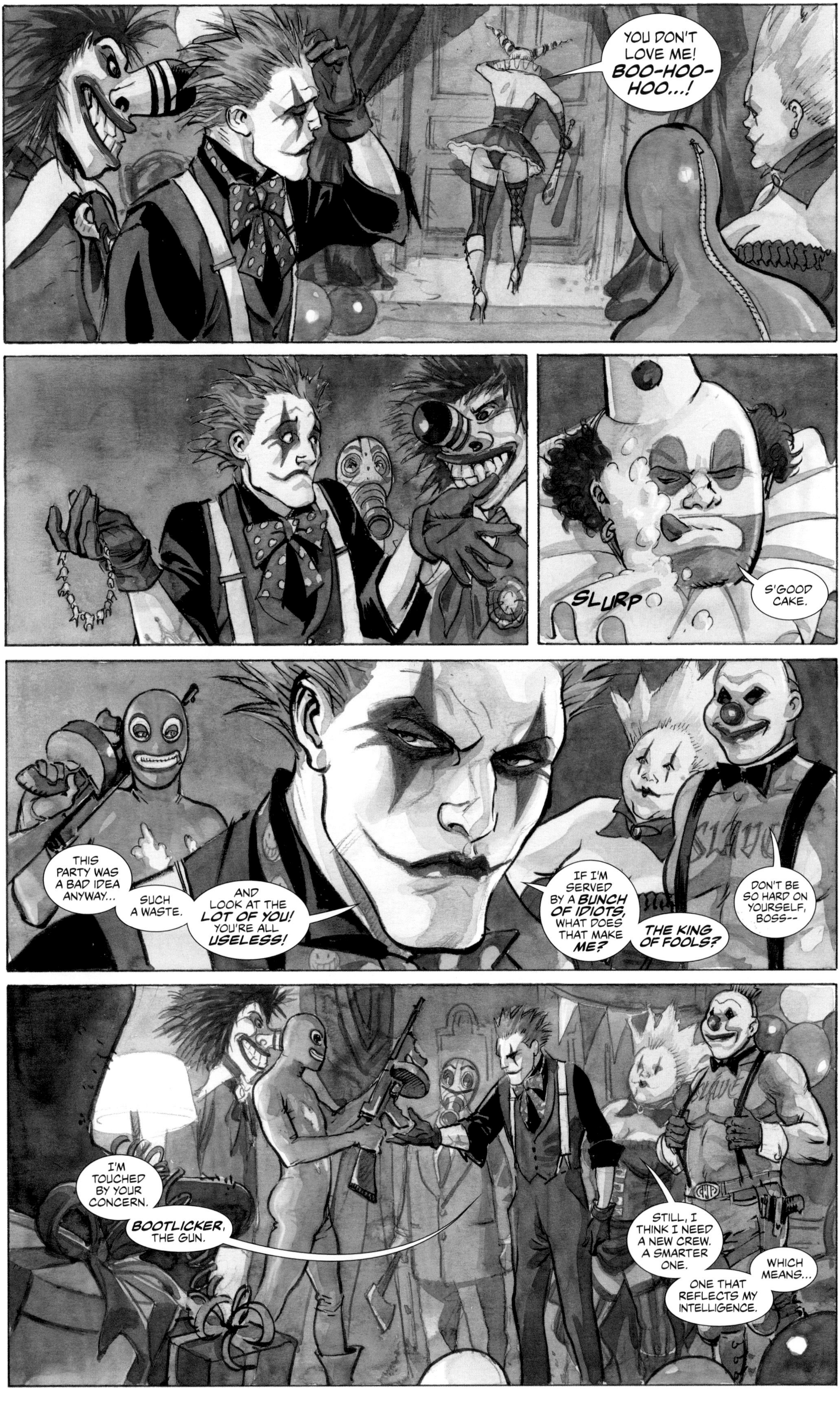
YOU DON'T LOVE ME! BOO-HOO-HOO...!
SLURP
S'GOOD CAKE.
THIS PARTY WAS A BAD IDEA ANYWAY...
SUCH A WASTE.
AND LOOK AT THE LOT OF YOU! YOU'RE ALL USELESS!
IF I'M SERVED BY A BUNCH OF IDIOTS, WHAT DOES THAT MAKE ME?
THE KING OF FOOLS?
DON'T BE SO HARD ON YOURSELF, BOSS--
I'M TOUCHED BY YOUR CONCERN.
BOOTLICKER, THE GUN.
STILL, I THINK I NEED A NEW CREW. A SMARTER ONE.
WHICH MEANS...
ONE THAT REFLECTS MY INTELLIGENCE.

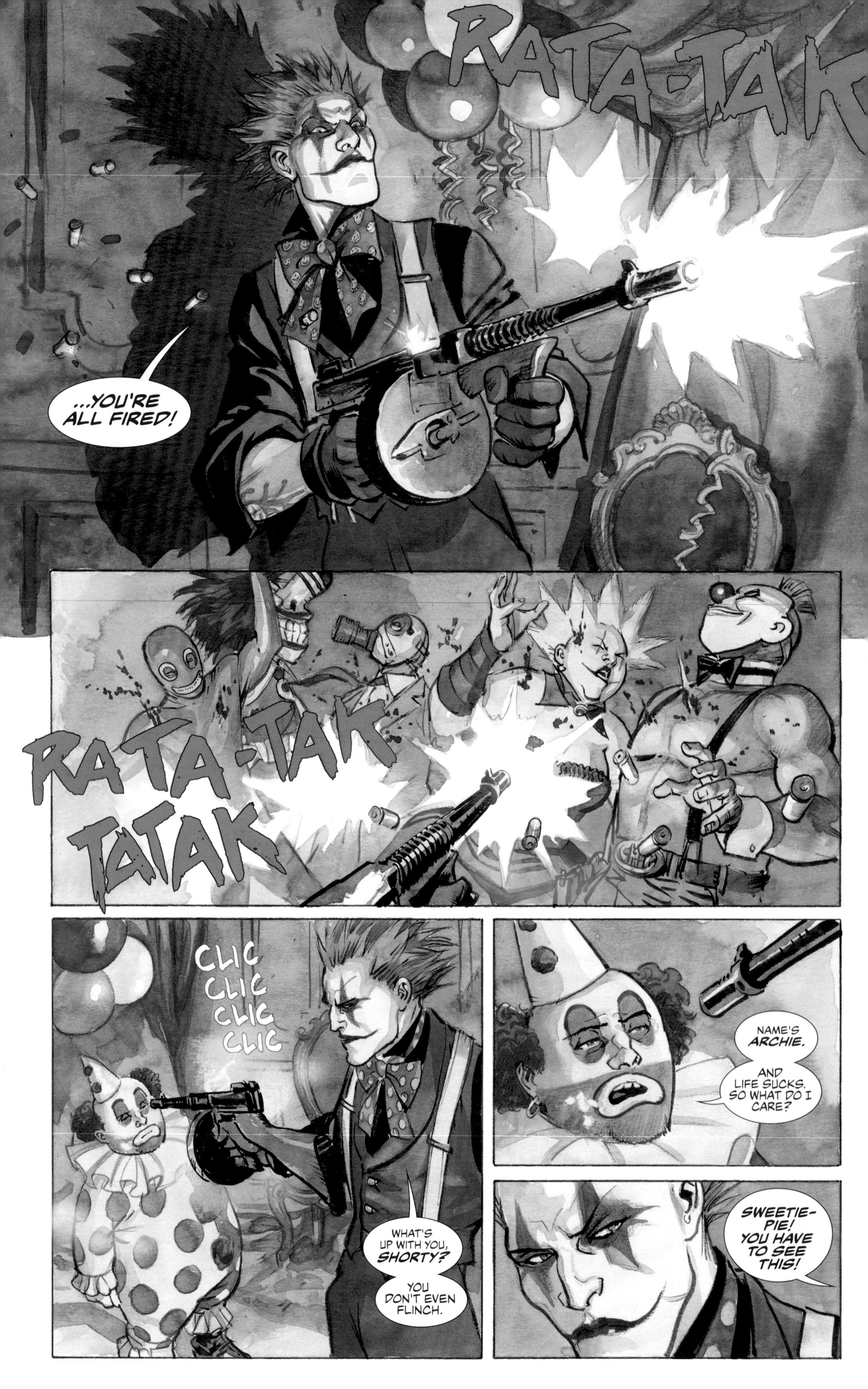
RATA-TAK
...YOU'RE ALL FIRED!
RATA-TAK TATAK
CLIC CLIC CLIC CLIC
WHAT'S UP WITH YOU, SHORTY?
YOU DON'T EVEN FLINCH.
NAME'S ARCHIE.
AND LIFE SUCKS. SO WHAT DO I CARE?
SWEETIE-PIE! YOU HAVE TO SEE THIS!

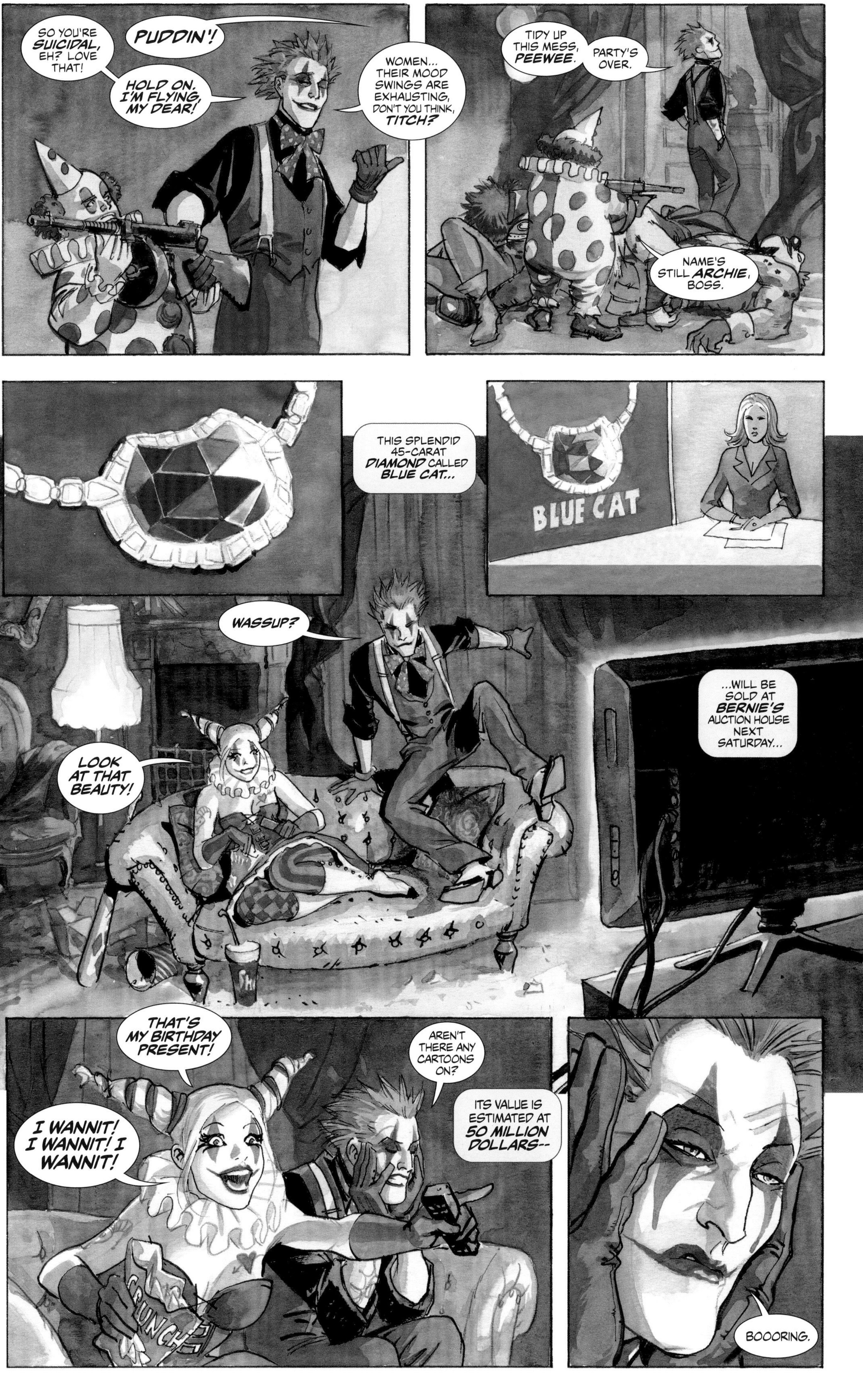

SO YOU'RE SUICIDAL, EH? LOVE THAT!
PUDDIN'!
HOLD ON. I'M FLYING, MY DEAR!
WOMEN... THEIR MOOD SWINGS ARE EXHAUSTING, DON'T YOU THINK, TITCH?
TIDY UP THIS MESS, PEEWEE.
PARTY'S OVER.
NAME'S STILL ARCHIE, BOSS.
THIS SPLENDID 45-CARAT DIAMOND CALLED BLUE CAT...
BLUE CAT
WASSUP?
...WILL BE SOLD AT BERNIE'S AUCTION HOUSE NEXT SATURDAY...
LOOK AT THAT BEAUTY!
THAT'S MY BIRTHDAY PRESENT!
AREN'T THERE ANY CARTOONS ON?
ITS VALUE IS ESTIMATED AT 50 MILLION DOLLARS--
I WANNIT! I WANNIT! I WANNIT!
BOOORING.

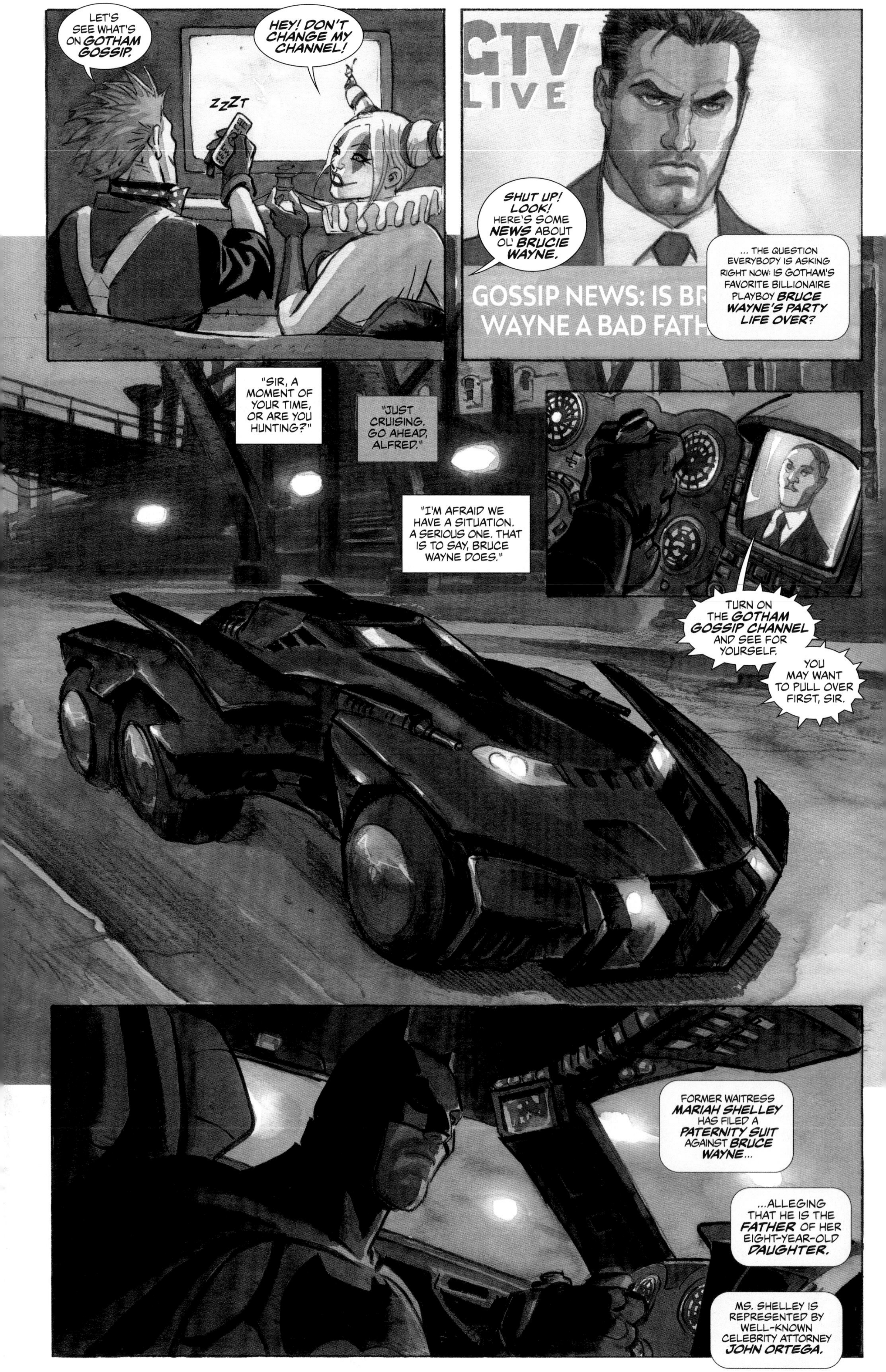
LET'S SEE WHAT'S ON GOTHAM GOSSIP.
HEY! DON'T CHANGE MY CHANNEL!
ZZZT
GTV LIVE
SHUT UP! LOOK! HERE'S SOME NEWS ABOUT OL' BRUCIE WAYNE.
GOSSIP NEWS: IS BR WAYNE A BAD FATH
... THE QUESTION EVERYBODY IS ASKING RIGHT NOW: IS GOTHAM'S FAVORITE BILLIONAIRE PLAYBOY BRUCE WAYNE'S PARTY LIFE OVER?
"SIR, A MOMENT OF YOUR TIME, OR ARE YOU HUNTING?"
"JUST CRUISING. GO AHEAD, ALFRED."
"I'M AFRAID WE HAVE A SITUATION. A SERIOUS ONE. THAT IS TO SAY, BRUCE WAYNE DOES."
TURN ON THE GOTHAM GOSSIP CHANNEL AND SEE FOR YOURSELF.
YOU MAY WANT TO PULL OVER FIRST, SIR.
FORMER WAITRESS MARIAH SHELLEY HAS FILED A PATERNITY SUIT AGAINST BRUCE WAYNE...
...ALLEGING THAT HE IS THE FATHER OF HER EIGHT-YEAR-OLD DAUGHTER.
MS. SHELLEY IS REPRESENTED BY WELL-KNOWN CELEBRITY ATTORNEY JOHN ORTEGA.

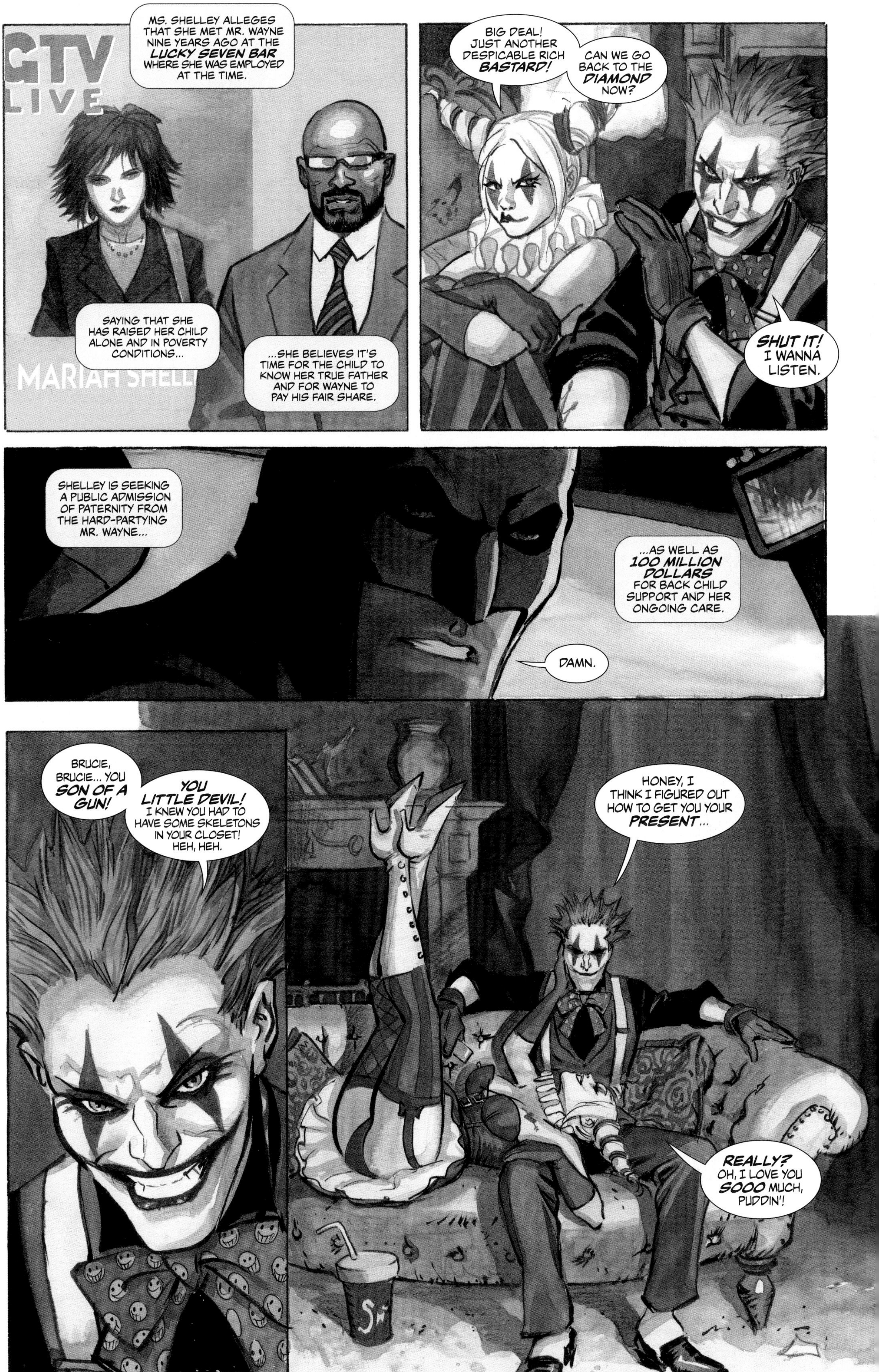
GTV LIVE
MS. SHELLEY ALLEGES THAT SHE MET MR. WAYNE NINE YEARS AGO AT THE LUCKY SEVEN BAR WHERE SHE WAS EMPLOYED AT THE TIME.
SAYING THAT SHE HAS RAISED HER CHILD ALONE AND IN POVERTY CONDITIONS...
...SHE BELIEVES IT'S TIME FOR THE CHILD TO KNOW HER TRUE FATHER AND FOR WAYNE TO PAY HIS FAIR SHARE.
BIG DEAL! JUST ANOTHER DESPICABLE RICH BASTARD!
CAN WE GO BACK TO THE DIAMOND NOW?
SHUT IT! I WANNA LISTEN.
SHELLEY IS SEEKING A PUBLIC ADMISSION OF PATERNITY FROM THE HARD-PARTYING MR. WAYNE...
...AS WELL AS 100 MILLION DOLLARS FOR BACK CHILD SUPPORT AND HER ONGOING CARE.
DAMN.
BRUCIE, BRUCIE... YOU SON OF A GUN!
YOU LITTLE DEVIL! I KNEW YOU HAD TO HAVE SOME SKELETONS IN YOUR CLOSET! HEH, HEH.
HONEY, I THINK I FIGURED OUT HOW TO GET YOU YOUR PRESENT...
REALLY? OH, I LOVE YOU SOOO MUCH, PUDDIN'!

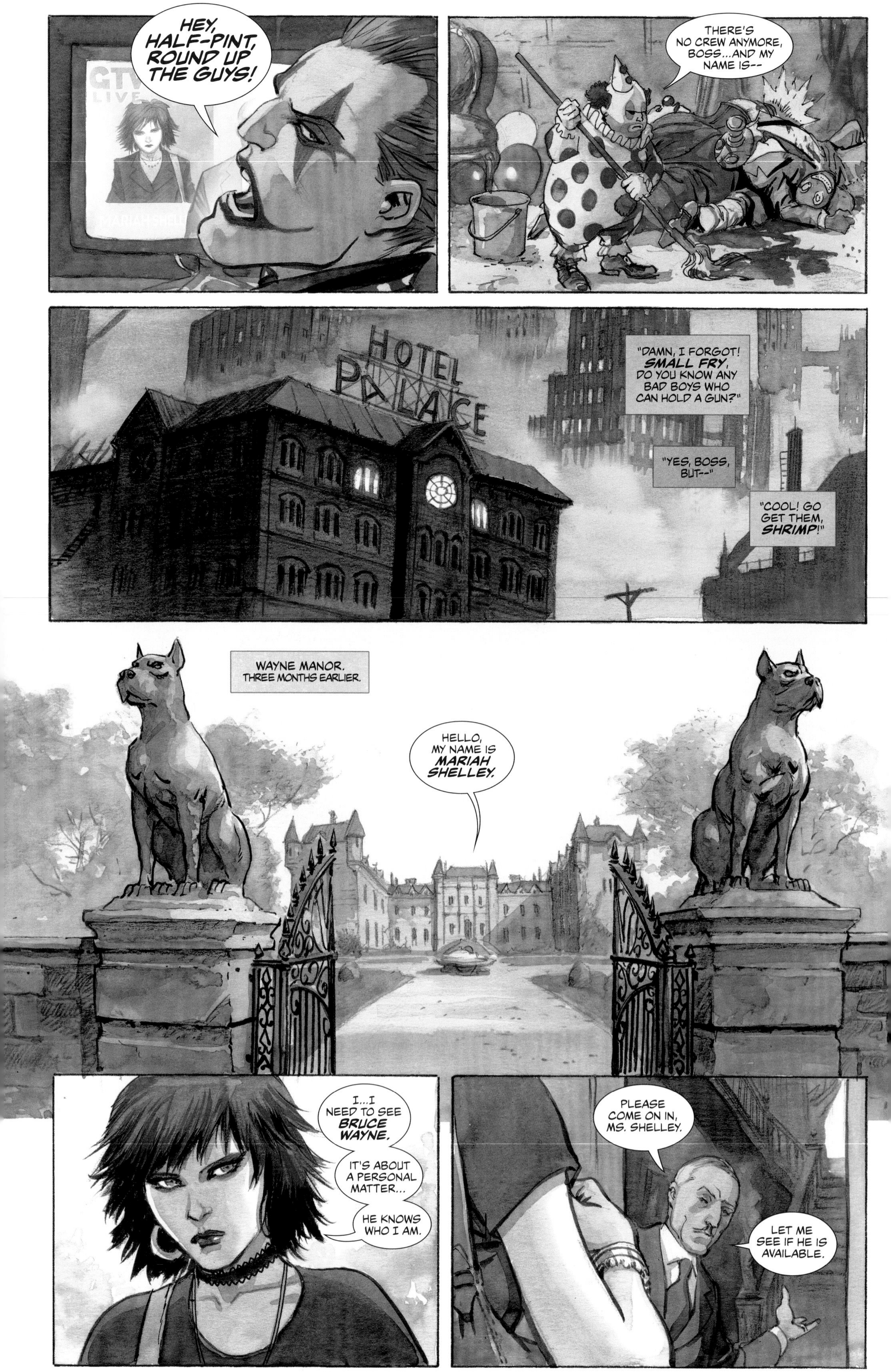
HEY, HALF-PINT, ROUND UP THE GUYS!
THERE'S NO CREW ANYMORE, BOSS...AND MY NAME IS--
HOTEL PALACE
"DAMN, I FORGOT! SMALL FRY, DO YOU KNOW ANY BAD BOYS WHO CAN HOLD A GUN?"
"YES, BOSS, BUT--"
"COOL! GO GET THEM, SHRIMP!"
WAYNE MANOR. THREE MONTHS EARLIER.
HELLO, MY NAME IS MARIAH SHELLEY.
I...I NEED TO SEE BRUCE WAYNE.
IT'S ABOUT A PERSONAL MATTER...
HE KNOWS WHO I AM.
PLEASE COME ON IN, MS. SHELLEY.
LET ME SEE IF HE IS AVAILABLE.

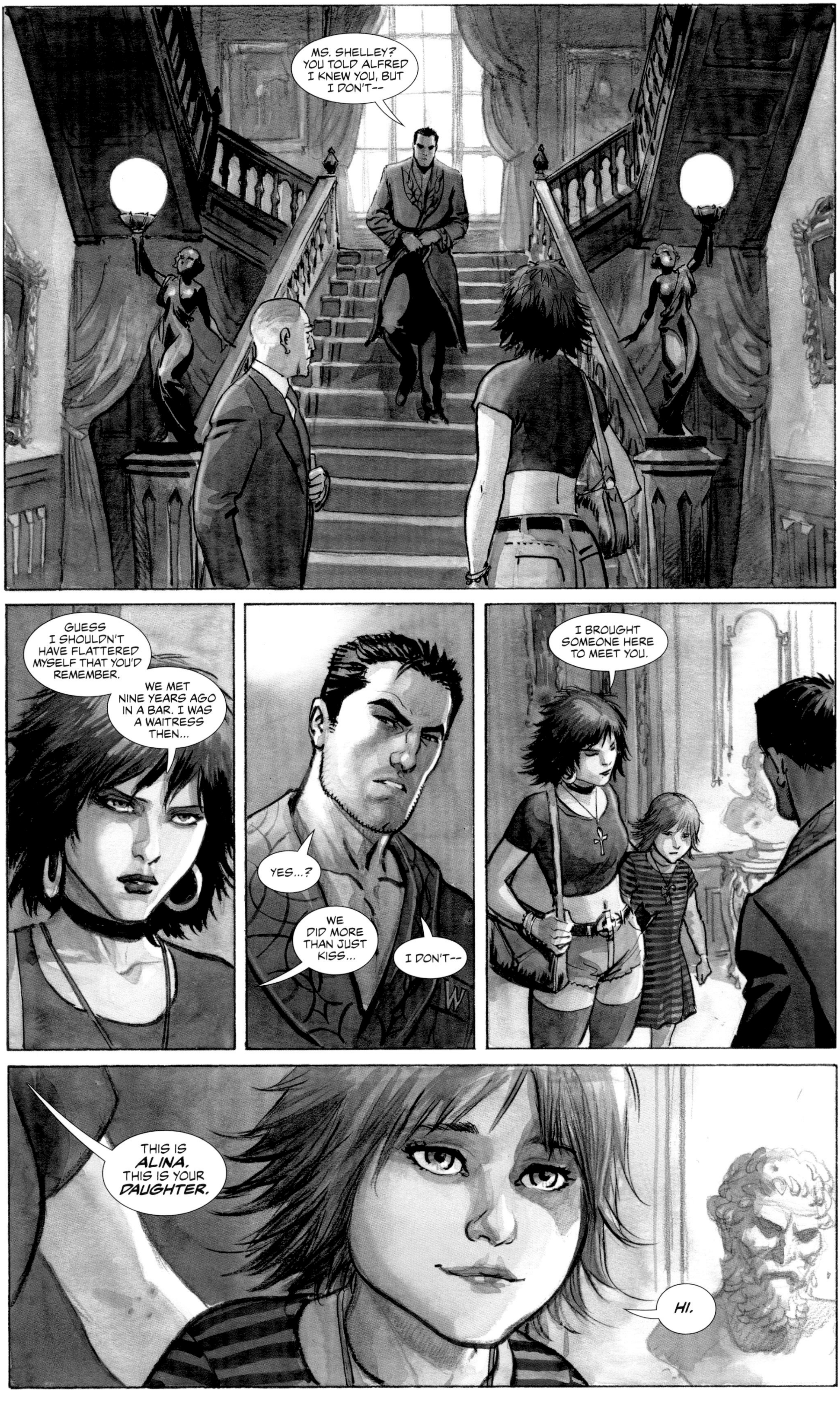
MS. SHELLEY? YOU TOLD ALFRED I KNEW YOU, BUT I DON'T--
GUESS I SHOULDN'T HAVE FLATTERED MYSELF THAT YOU'D REMEMBER.
WE MET NINE YEARS AGO IN A BAR. I WAS A WAITRESS THEN...
YES...?
WE DID MORE THAN JUST KISS...
I DON'T--
I BROUGHT SOMEONE HERE TO MEET YOU.
THIS IS ALINA. THIS IS YOUR DAUGHTER.
HI.

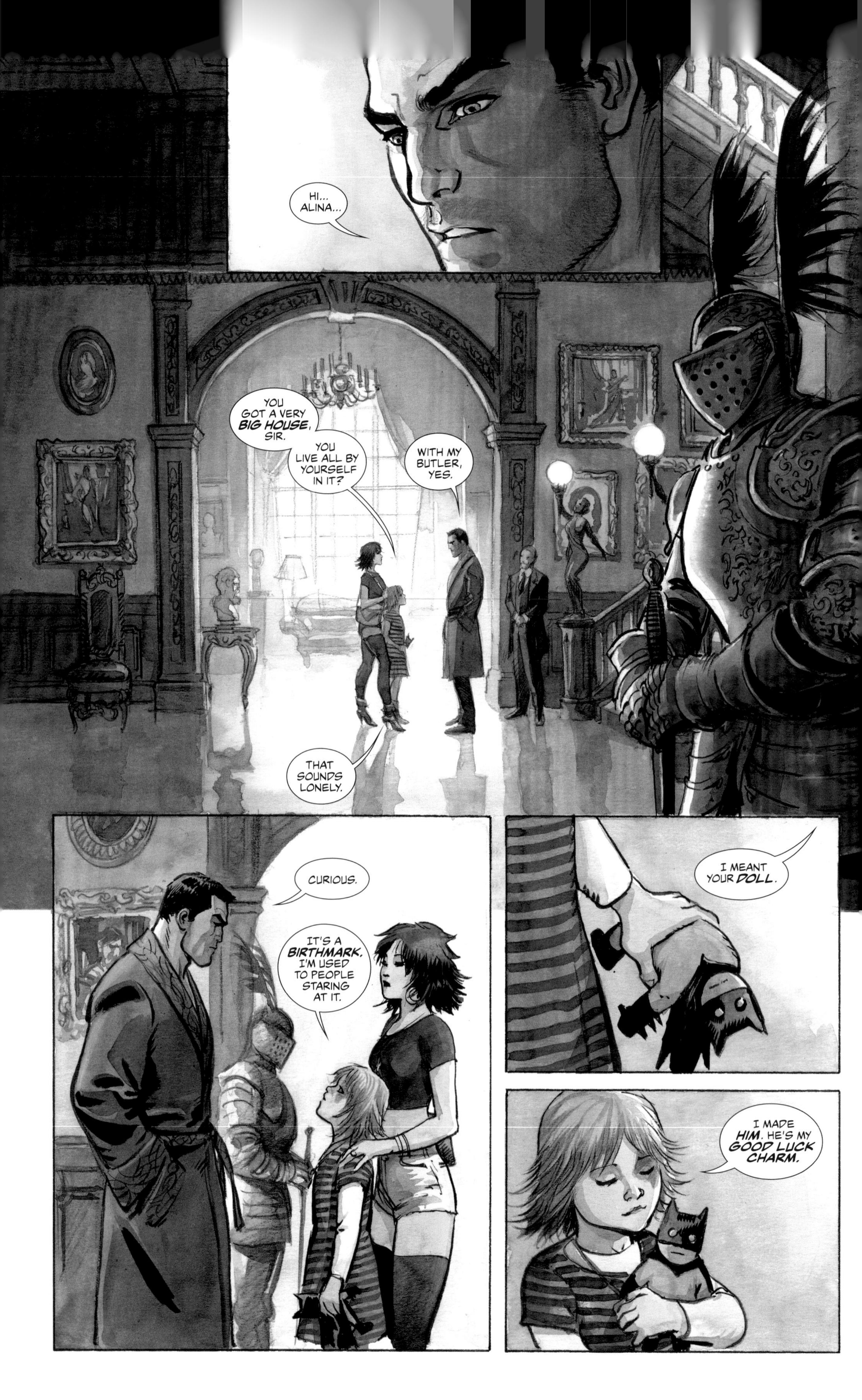
HI... ALINA...
YOU GOT A VERY BIG HOUSE, SIR.
YOU LIVE ALL BY YOURSELF IN IT?
WITH MY BUTLER, YES.
THAT SOUNDS LONELY.
CURIOUS.
IT'S A BIRTHMARK. I'M USED TO PEOPLE STARING AT IT.
I MEANT YOUR DOLL.
I MADE HIM. HE'S MY GOOD LUCK CHARM.

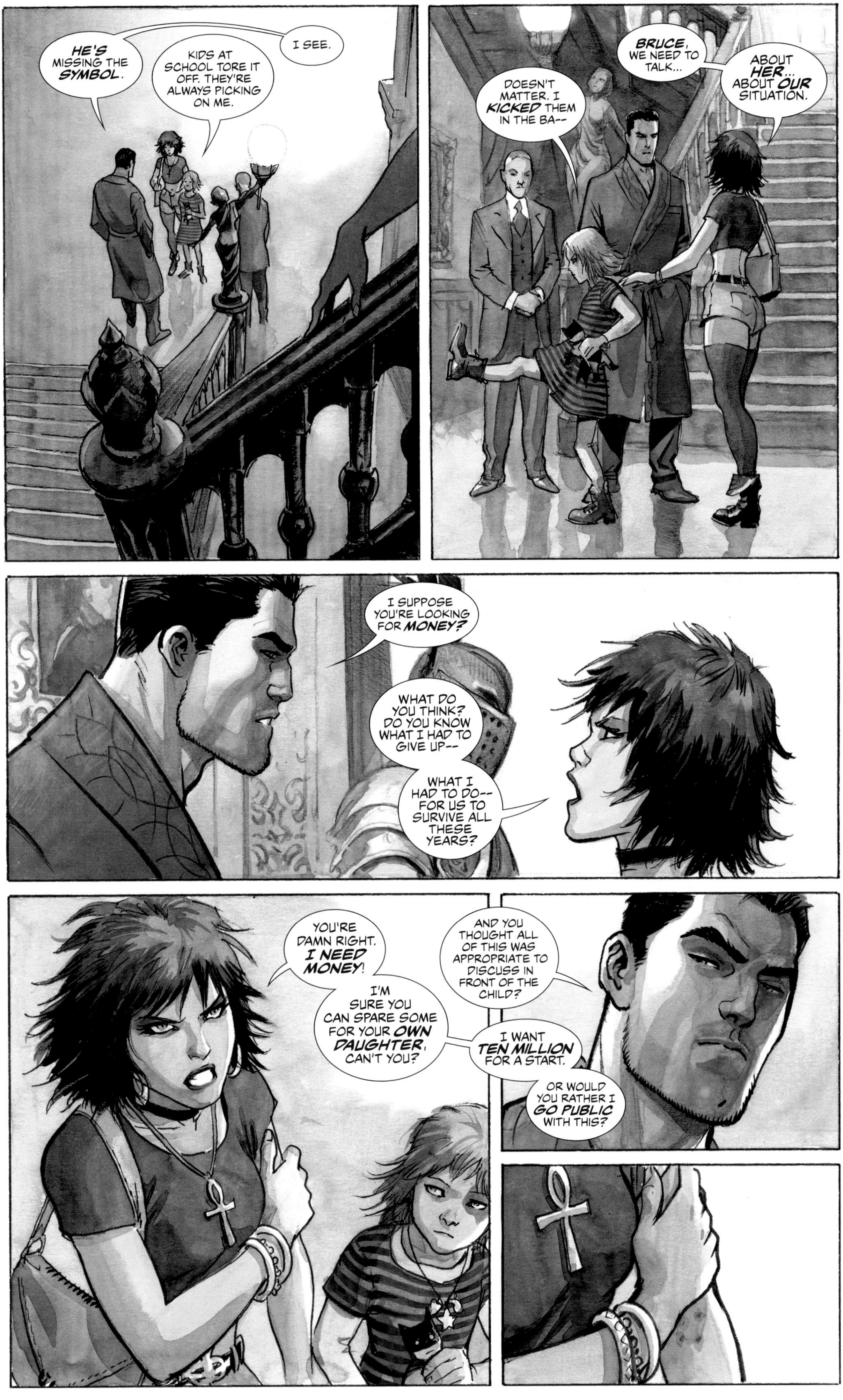
HE'S MISSING THE SYMBOL.
KIDS AT SCHOOL TORE IT OFF. THEY'RE ALWAYS PICKING ON ME.
I SEE.
DOESN'T MATTER. I KICKED THEM IN THE BA--
BRUCE, WE NEED TO TALK...
ABOUT HER... ABOUT OUR SITUATION.
I SUPPOSE YOU'RE LOOKING FOR MONEY?
WHAT DO YOU THINK? DO YOU KNOW WHAT I HAD TO GIVE UP--
WHAT I HAD TO DO-- FOR US TO SURVIVE ALL THESE YEARS?
YOU'RE DAMN RIGHT. I NEED MONEY!
I'M SURE YOU CAN SPARE SOME FOR YOUR OWN DAUGHTER, CAN'T YOU?
AND YOU THOUGHT ALL OF THIS WAS APPROPRIATE TO DISCUSS IN FRONT OF THE CHILD?
I WANT TEN MILLION FOR A START.
OR WOULD YOU RATHER I GO PUBLIC WITH THIS?

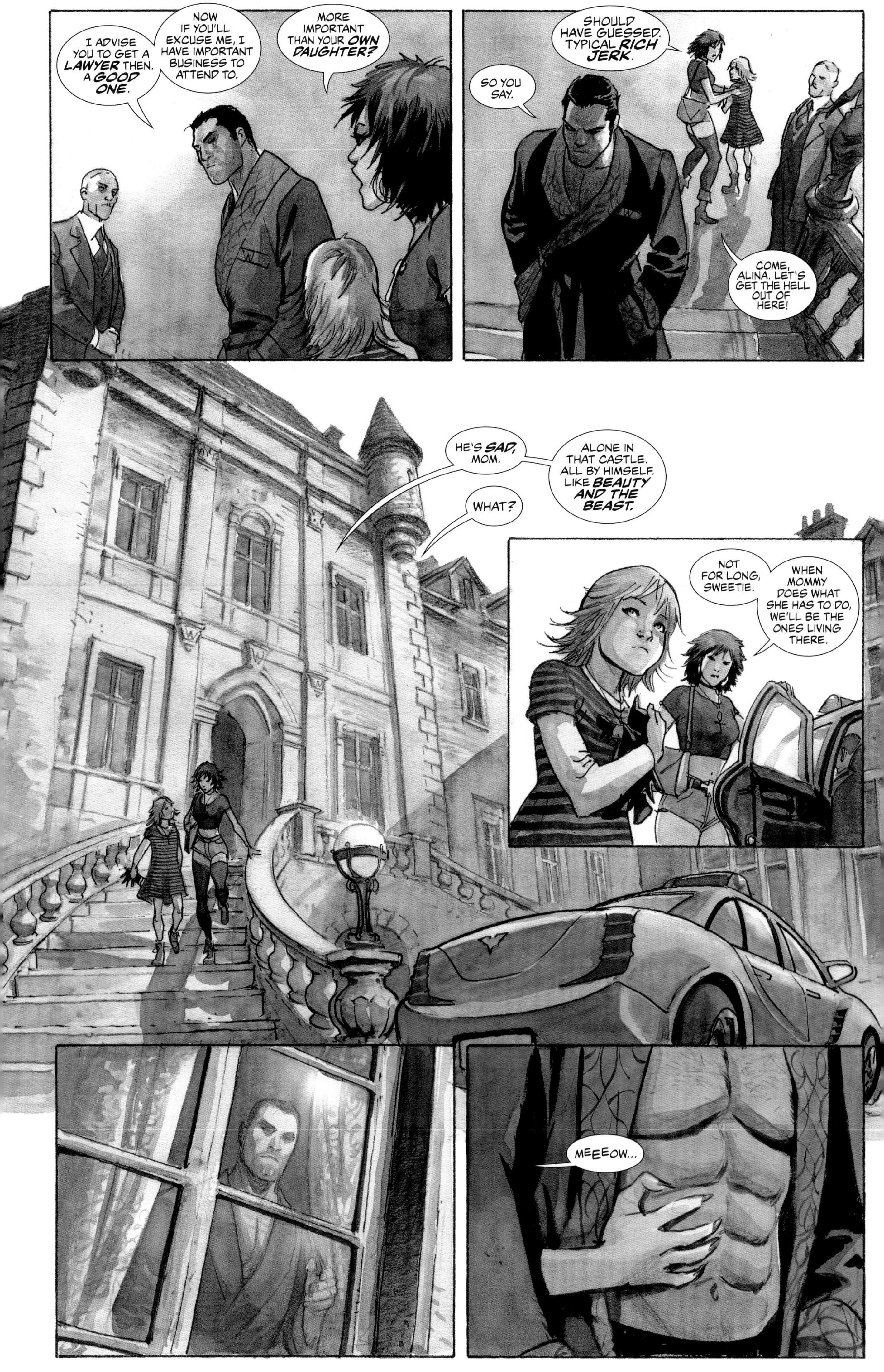
I ADVISE YOU TO GET A LAWYER THEN. A GOOD ONE.
NOW IF YOU'LL EXCUSE ME, I HAVE IMPORTANT BUSINESS TO ATTEND TO.
MORE IMPORTANT THAN YOUR OWN DAUGHTER?
SHOULD HAVE GUESSED. TYPICAL RICH JERK.
SO YOU SAY.
COME, ALINA. LET'S GET THE HELL OUT OF HERE!
HE'S SAD, MOM.
ALONE IN THAT CASTLE. ALL BY HIMSELF. LIKE BEAUTY AND THE BEAST.
WHAT?
NOT FOR LONG, SWEETIE.
WHEN MOMMY DOES WHAT SHE HAS TO DO, WE'LL BE THE ONES LIVING THERE.
MEEEOW...

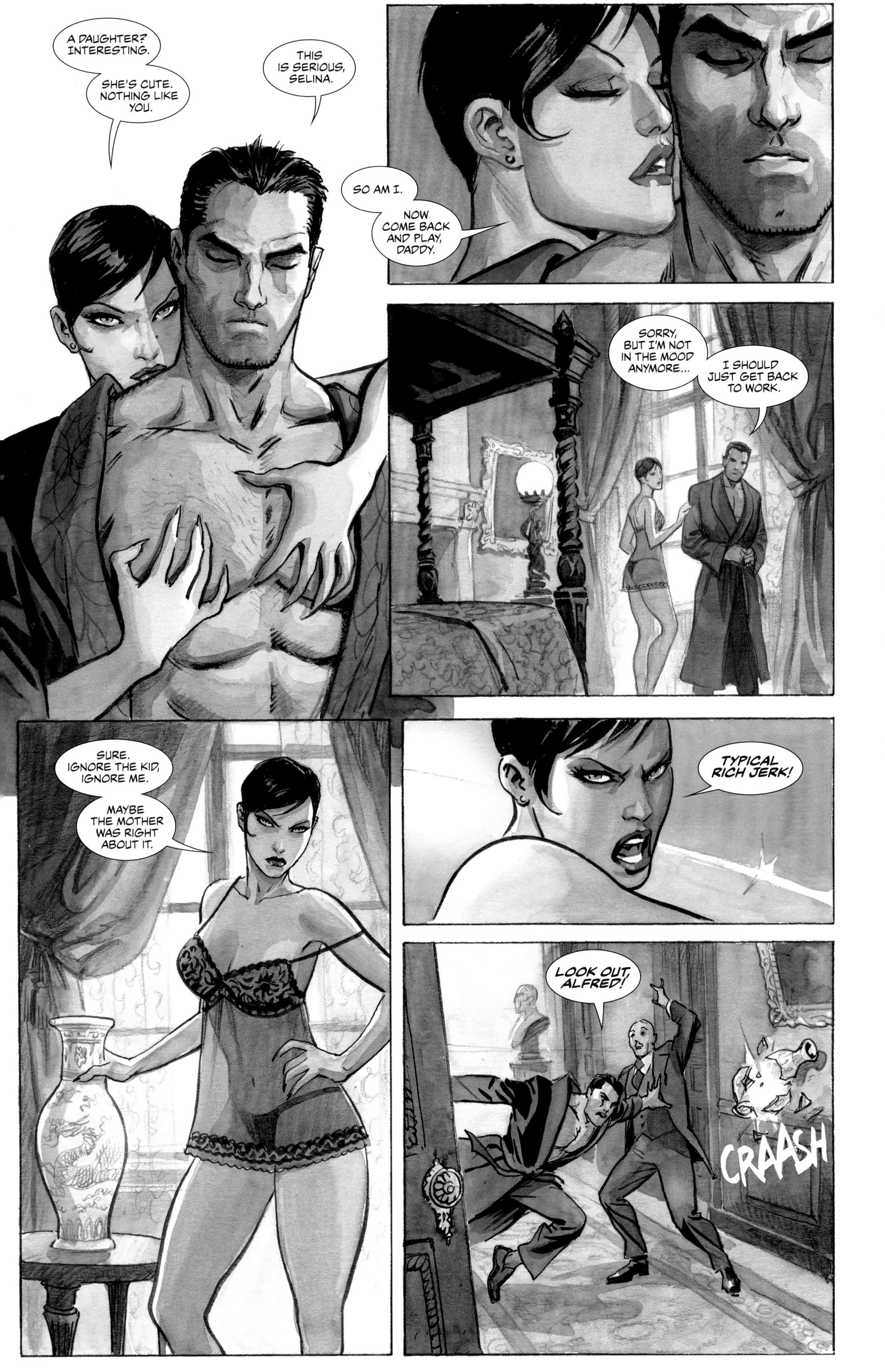

A DAUGHTER? INTERESTING.
SHE'S CUTE. NOTHING LIKE YOU.
THIS IS SERIOUS, SELINA.
SO AM I.
NOW COME BACK AND PLAY, DADDY.
SORRY, BUT I'M NOT IN THE MOOD ANYMORE...
I SHOULD JUST GET BACK TO WORK.
SURE. IGNORE THE KID, IGNORE ME.
MAYBE THE MOTHER WAS RIGHT ABOUT IT.
TYPICAL RICH JERK!
LOOK OUT, ALFRED!
CRAASH

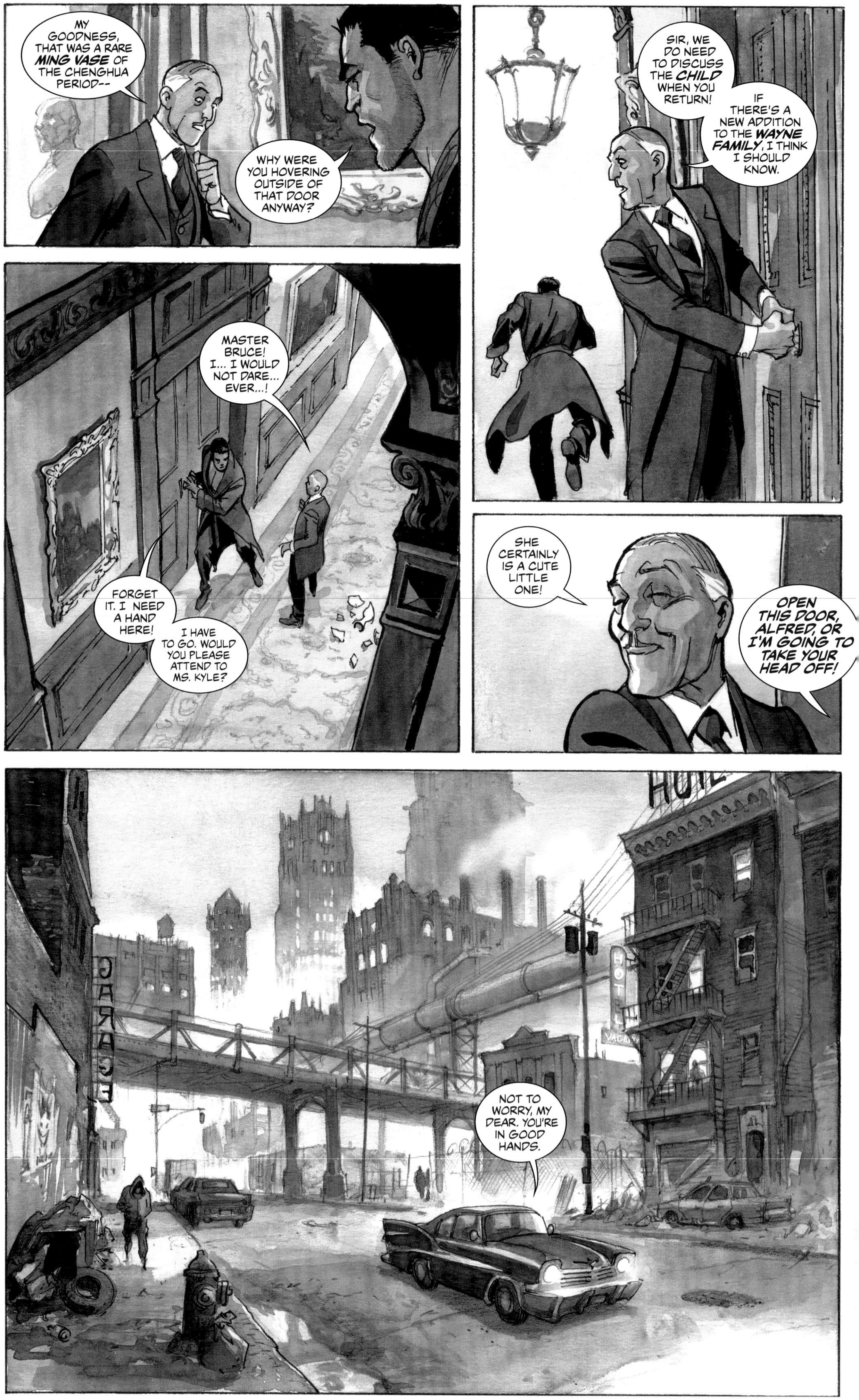

MY GOODNESS, THAT WAS A RARE MING VASE OF THE CHENGHUA PERIOD--
WHY WERE YOU HOVERING OUTSIDE OF THAT DOOR ANYWAY?
SIR, WE DO NEED TO DISCUSS THE CHILD WHEN YOU RETURN!
IF THERE'S A NEW ADDITION TO THE WAYNE FAMILY, I THINK I SHOULD KNOW.
MASTER BRUCE! I... I WOULD NOT DARE... EVER...!
FORGET IT. I NEED A HAND HERE!
I HAVE TO GO. WOULD YOU PLEASE ATTEND TO MS. KYLE?
SHE CERTAINLY IS A CUTE LITTLE ONE!
OPEN THIS DOOR, ALFRED, OR I'M GOING TO TAKE YOUR HEAD OFF!
GARAGE
HOTEL
NOT TO WORRY, MY DEAR. YOU'RE IN GOOD HANDS.

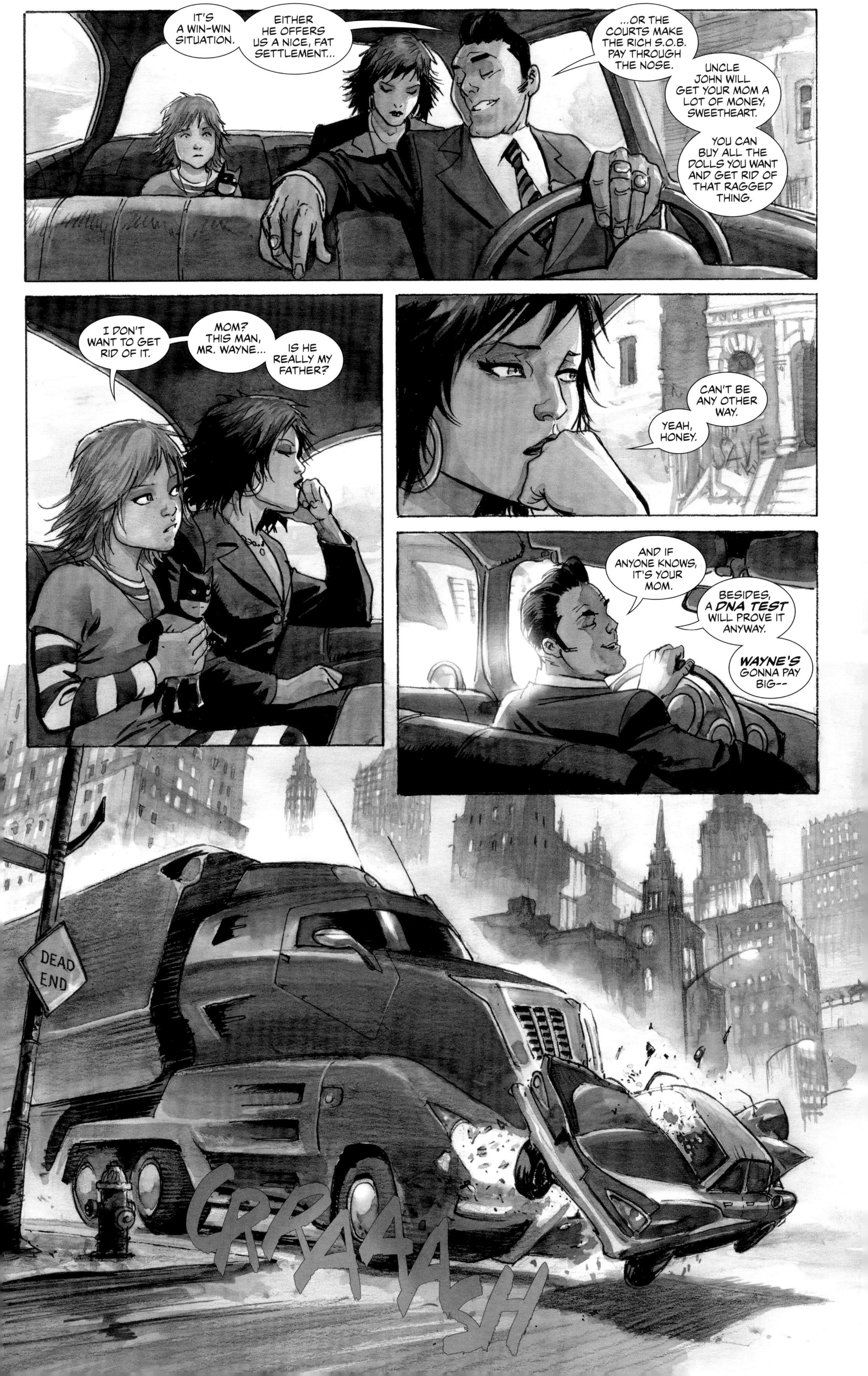
IT'S A WIN-WIN SITUATION.
EITHER HE OFFERS US A NICE, FAT SETTLEMENT...
...OR THE COURTS MAKE THE RICH S.O.B. PAY THROUGH THE NOSE.
UNCLE JOHN WILL GET YOUR MOM A LOT OF MONEY, SWEETHEART.
YOU CAN BUY ALL THE DOLLS YOU WANT AND GET RID OF THAT RAGGED THING.
I DON'T WANT TO GET RID OF IT.
MOM? THIS MAN, MR. WAYNE...
IS HE REALLY MY FATHER?
CAN'T BE ANY OTHER WAY.
YEAH, HONEY.
AND IF ANYONE KNOWS, IT'S YOUR MOM.
BESIDES, A DNA TEST WILL PROVE IT ANYWAY.
WAYNE'S GONNA PAY BIG--
DEAD END
GRRAAASH

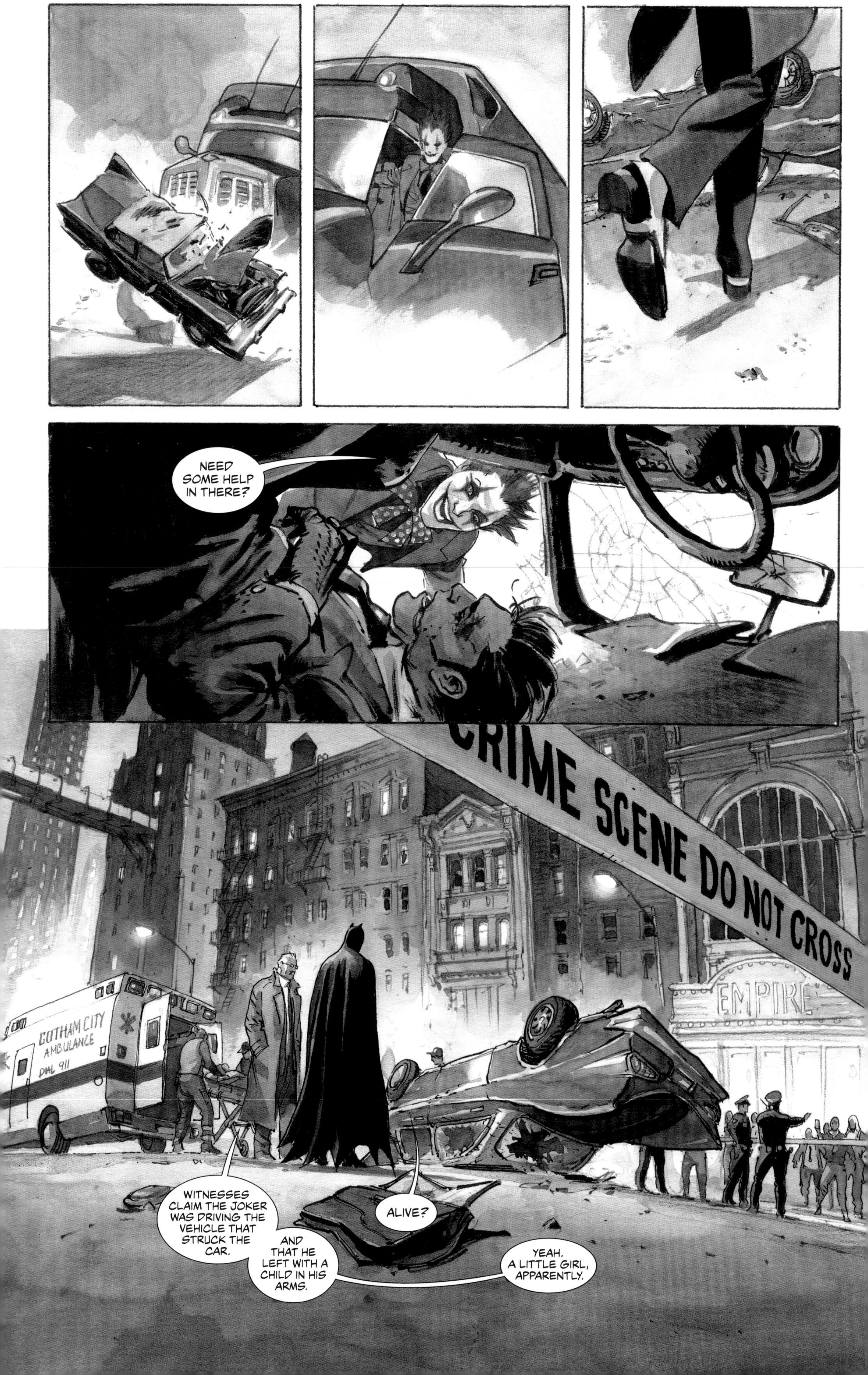
NEED SOME HELP IN THERE?
CRIME SCENE DO NOT CROSS
GOTHAM CITY AMBULANCE DIAL 911
EMPIRE
WITNESSES CLAIM THE JOKER WAS DRIVING THE VEHICLE THAT STRUCK THE CAR.
ALIVE?
AND THAT HE LEFT WITH A CHILD IN HIS ARMS.
YEAH. A LITTLE GIRL, APPARENTLY.

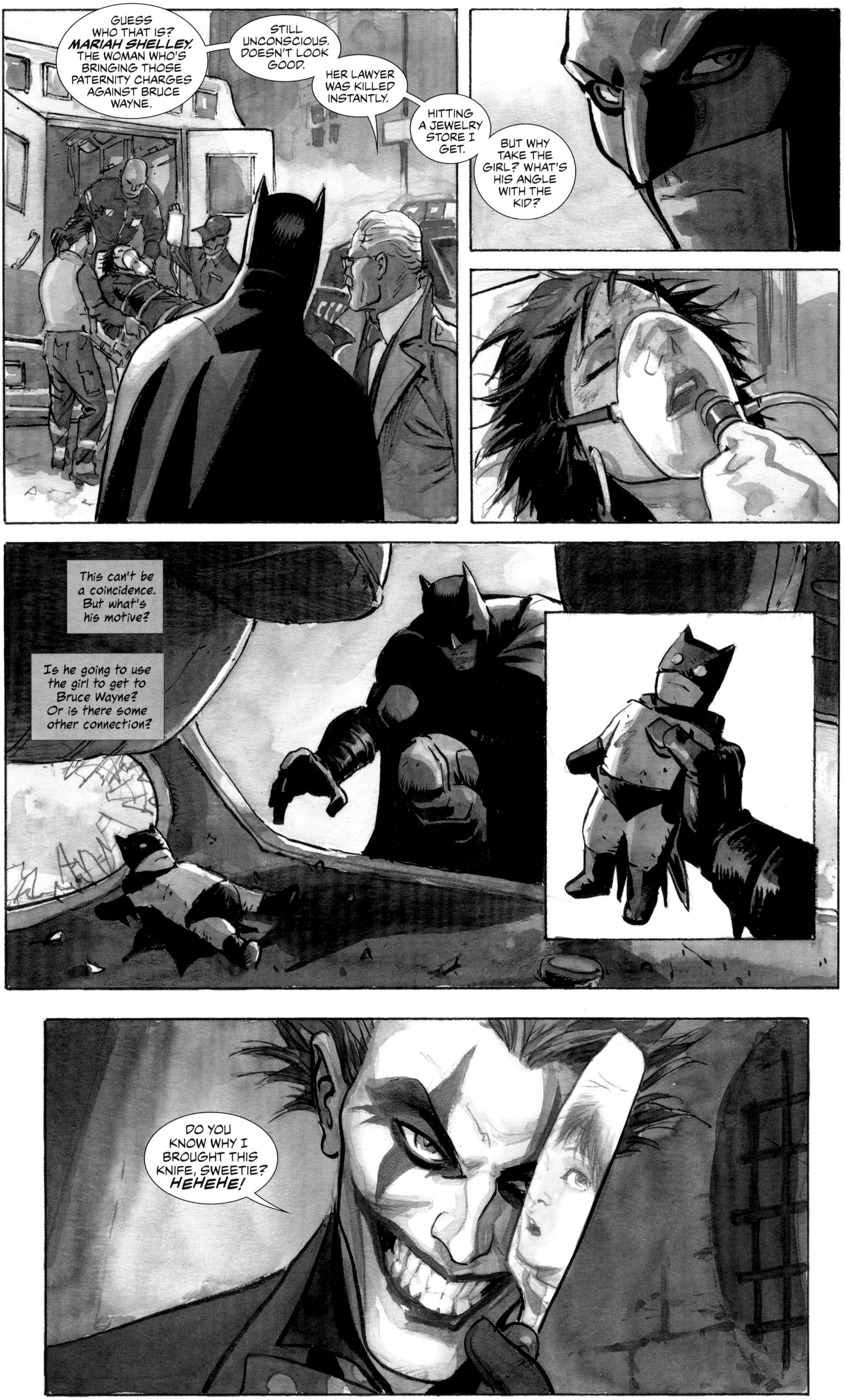
GUESS WHO THAT IS? MARIAH SHELLEY. THE WOMAN WHO'S BRINGING THOSE PATERNITY CHARGES AGAINST BRUCE WAYNE.
STILL UNCONSCIOUS. DOESN'T LOOK GOOD.
HER LAWYER WAS KILLED INSTANTLY.
HITTING A JEWELRY STORE I GET.
BUT WHY TAKE THE GIRL? WHAT'S HIS ANGLE WITH THE KID?
This can't be a coincidence. But what's his motive?
Is he going to use the girl to get to Bruce Wayne? Or is there some other connection?
DO YOU KNOW WHY I BROUGHT THIS KNIFE, SWEETIE? HEHEHE!

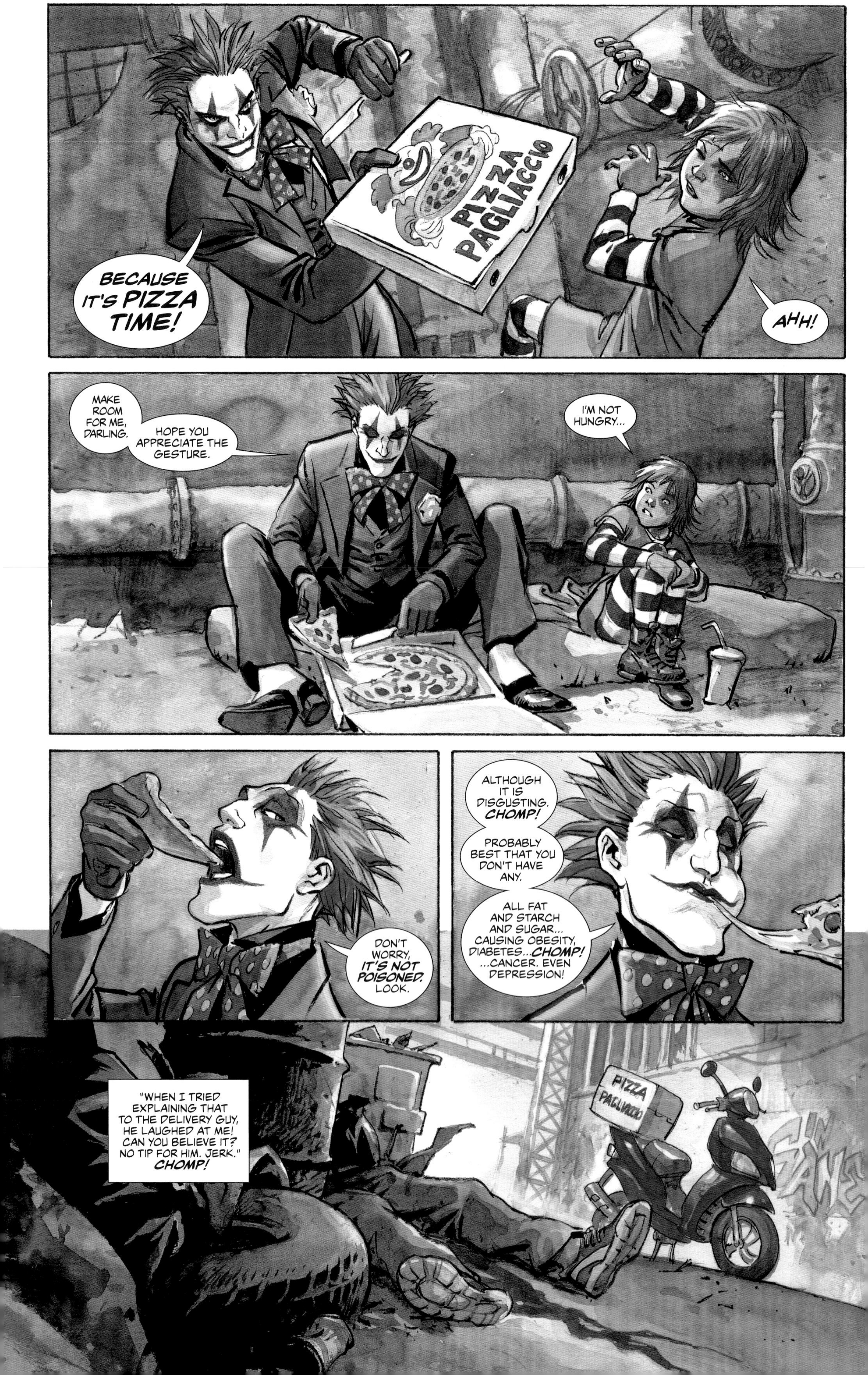
PIZZA PAGLIACCIO
BECAUSE IT'S PIZZA TIME!
AHH!
MAKE ROOM FOR ME, DARLING.
HOPE YOU APPRECIATE THE GESTURE.
I'M NOT HUNGRY...
DON'T WORRY, IT'S NOT POISONED. LOOK.
ALTHOUGH IT IS DISGUSTING. CHOMP!
PROBABLY BEST THAT YOU DON'T HAVE ANY.
ALL FAT AND STARCH AND SUGAR... CAUSING OBESITY, DIABETES...CHOMP! ...CANCER. EVEN DEPRESSION!
"WHEN I TRIED EXPLAINING THAT TO THE DELIVERY GUY, HE LAUGHED AT ME! CAN YOU BELIEVE IT? NO TIP FOR HIM. JERK." CHOMP!
PIZZA PAGLIACCIO

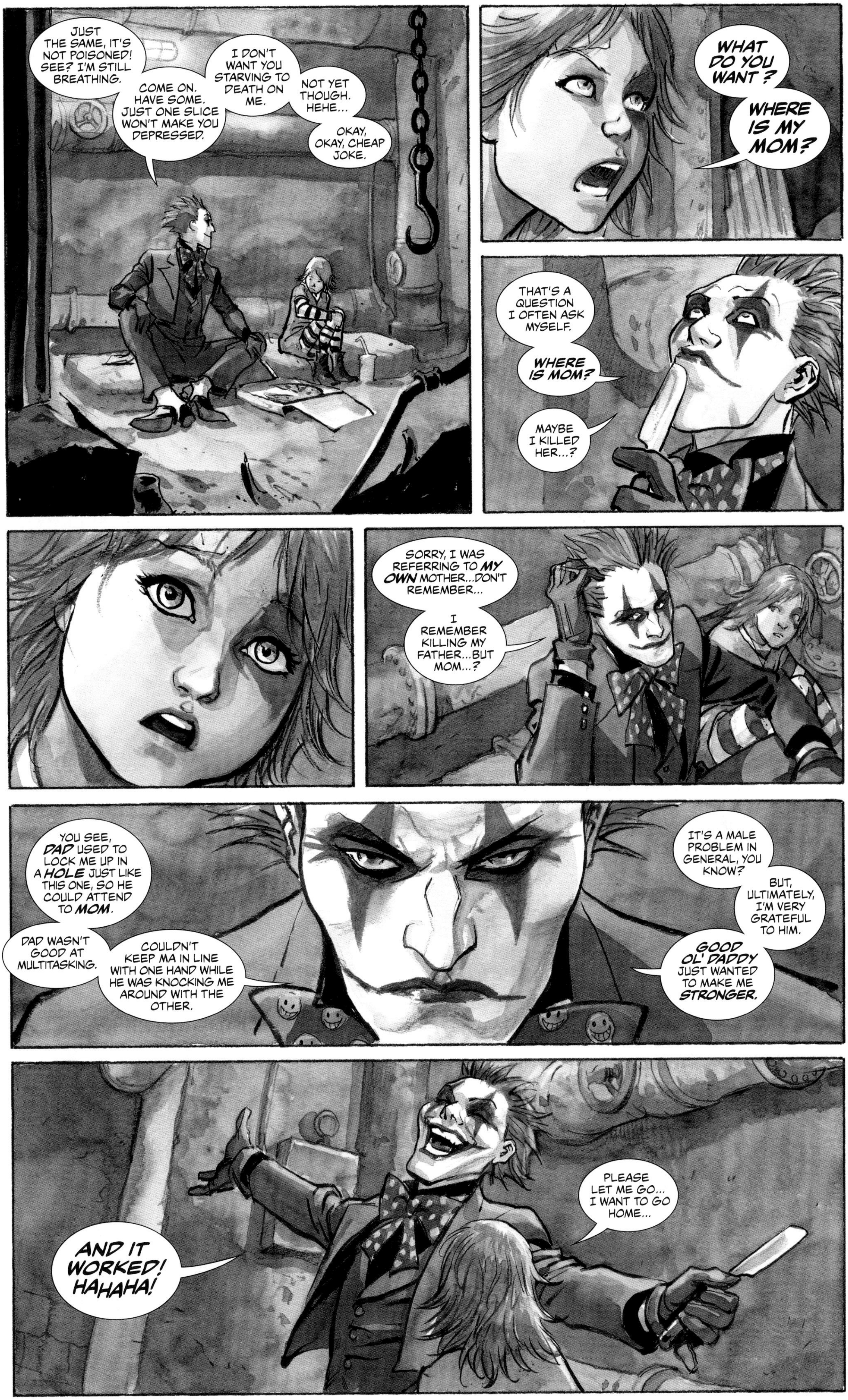

JUST THE SAME, IT'S NOT POISONED! SEE? I'M STILL BREATHING.
COME ON. HAVE SOME. JUST ONE SLICE WON'T MAKE YOU DEPRESSED.
I DON'T WANT YOU STARVING TO DEATH ON ME.
NOT YET THOUGH. HEHE...
OKAY, OKAY, CHEAP JOKE.
WHAT DO YOU WANT ?
WHERE IS MY MOM?
THAT'S A QUESTION I OFTEN ASK MYSELF.
WHERE IS MOM?
MAYBE I KILLED HER...?
SORRY, I WAS REFERRING TO MY OWN MOTHER...DON'T REMEMBER...
I REMEMBER KILLING MY FATHER...BUT MOM...?
YOU SEE, DAD USED TO LOCK ME UP IN A HOLE JUST LIKE THIS ONE, SO HE COULD ATTEND TO MOM.
DAD WASN'T GOOD AT MULTITASKING.
COULDN'T KEEP MA IN LINE WITH ONE HAND WHILE HE WAS KNOCKING ME AROUND WITH THE OTHER.
IT'S A MALE PROBLEM IN GENERAL, YOU KNOW?
BUT, ULTIMATELY, I'M VERY GRATEFUL TO HIM.
GOOD OL' DADDY JUST WANTED TO MAKE ME STRONGER.
AND IT WORKED! HAHAHA!
PLEASE LET ME GO... I WANT TO GO HOME...

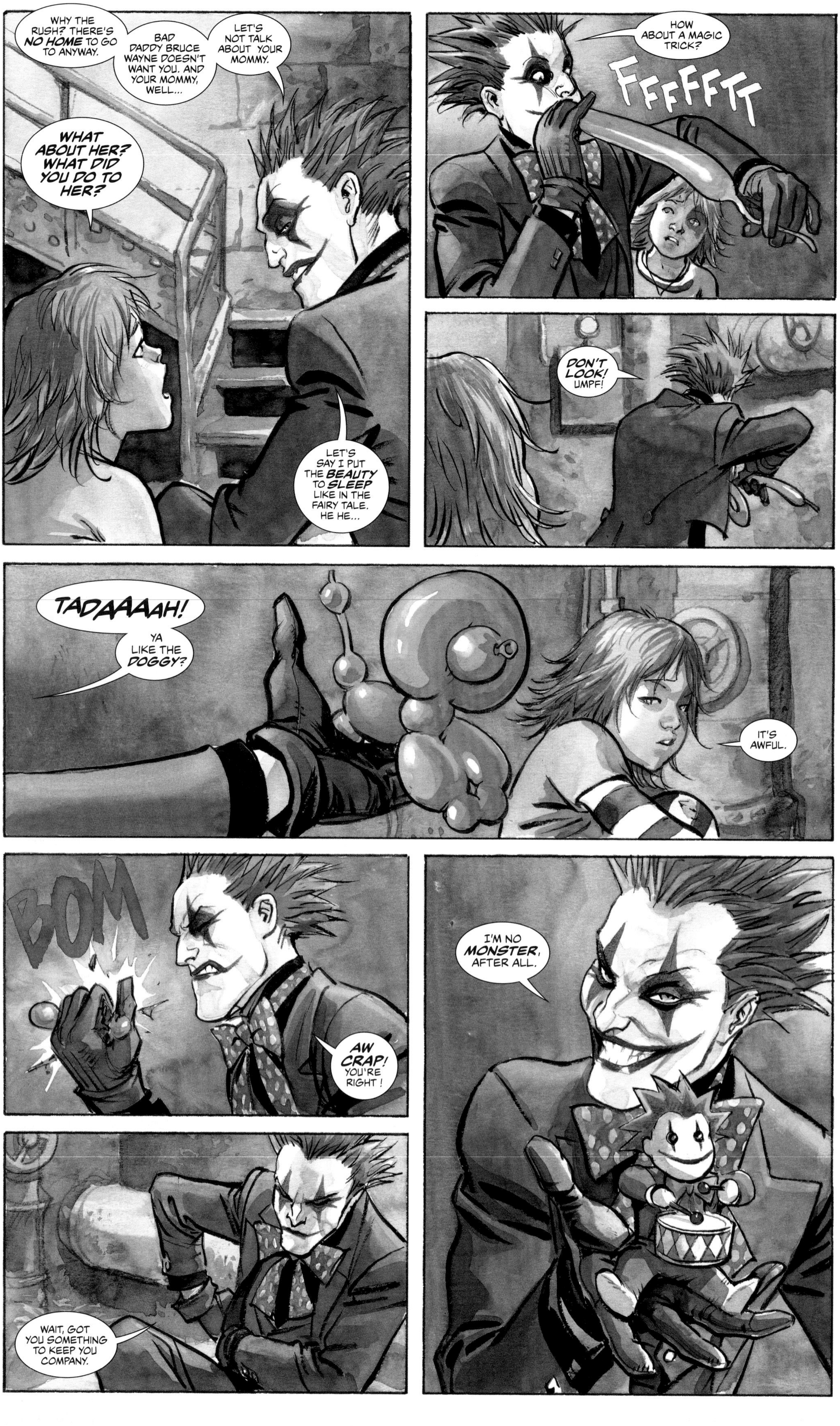
WHY THE RUSH? THERE'S NO HOME TO GO TO ANYWAY.
BAD DADDY BRUCE WAYNE DOESN'T WANT YOU. AND YOUR MOMMY, WELL...
LET'S NOT TALK ABOUT YOUR MOMMY.
WHAT ABOUT HER? WHAT DID YOU DO TO HER?
LET'S SAY I PUT THE BEAUTY TO SLEEP LIKE IN THE FAIRY TALE. HE HE...
HOW ABOUT A MAGIC TRICK?
FFFFFTT
DON'T LOOK! UMPF!
TADAAAAH!
YA LIKE THE DOGGY?
IT'S AWFUL.
BOM
AW CRAP! YOU'RE RIGHT!
WAIT, GOT YOU SOMETHING TO KEEP YOU COMPANY.
I'M NO MONSTER, AFTER ALL.

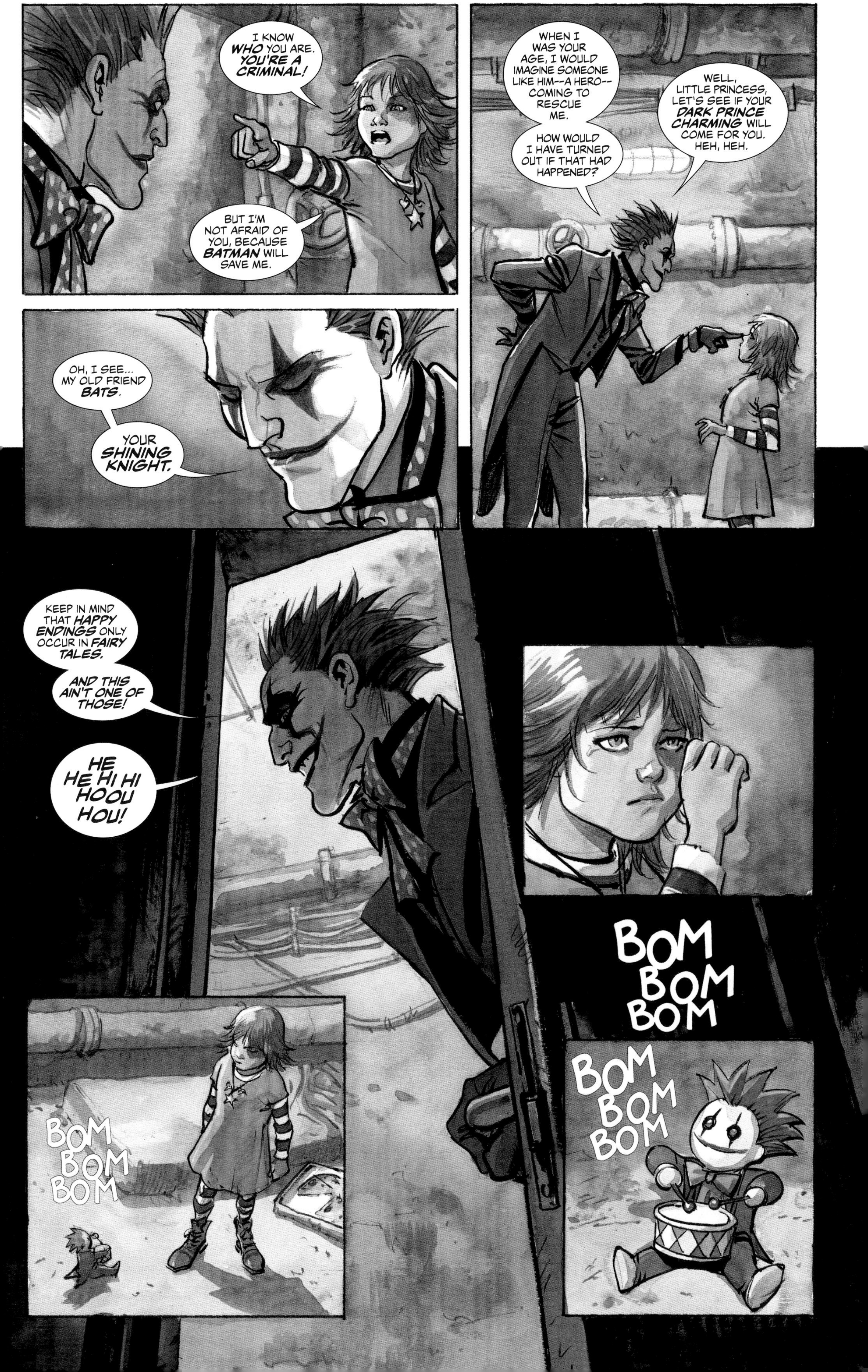
I KNOW WHO YOU ARE. YOU'RE A CRIMINAL!
BUT I'M NOT AFRAID OF YOU, BECAUSE BATMAN WILL SAVE ME.
OH, I SEE... MY OLD FRIEND BATS.
YOUR SHINING KNIGHT.
WHEN I WAS YOUR AGE, I WOULD IMAGINE SOMEONE LIKE HIM--A HERO--COMING TO RESCUE ME.
HOW WOULD I HAVE TURNED OUT IF THAT HAD HAPPENED?
WELL, LITTLE PRINCESS, LET'S SEE IF YOUR DARK PRINCE CHARMING WILL COME FOR YOU. HEH, HEH.
KEEP IN MIND THAT HAPPY ENDINGS ONLY OCCUR IN FAIRY TALES.
AND THIS AIN'T ONE OF THOSE!
HE HE HI HI HOOU HOU!
BOM BOM BOM
BOM BOM BOM
BOM BOM BOM

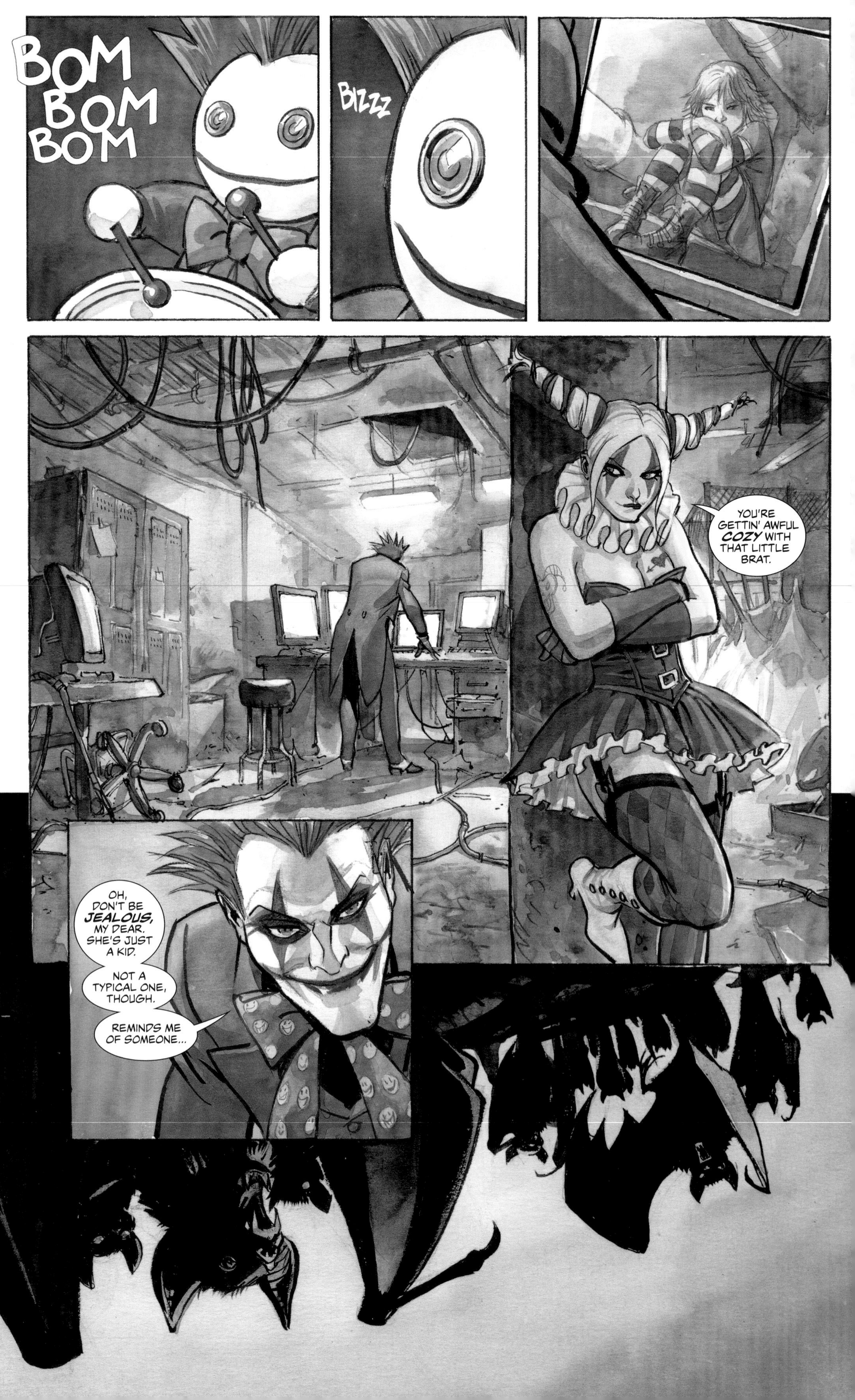
BOM
BOM
BOM
BIZZZ
YOU'RE GETTIN' AWFUL COZY WITH THAT LITTLE BRAT.
OH, DON'T BE JEALOUS, MY DEAR. SHE'S JUST A KID.
NOT A TYPICAL ONE, THOUGH.
REMINDS ME OF SOMEONE...

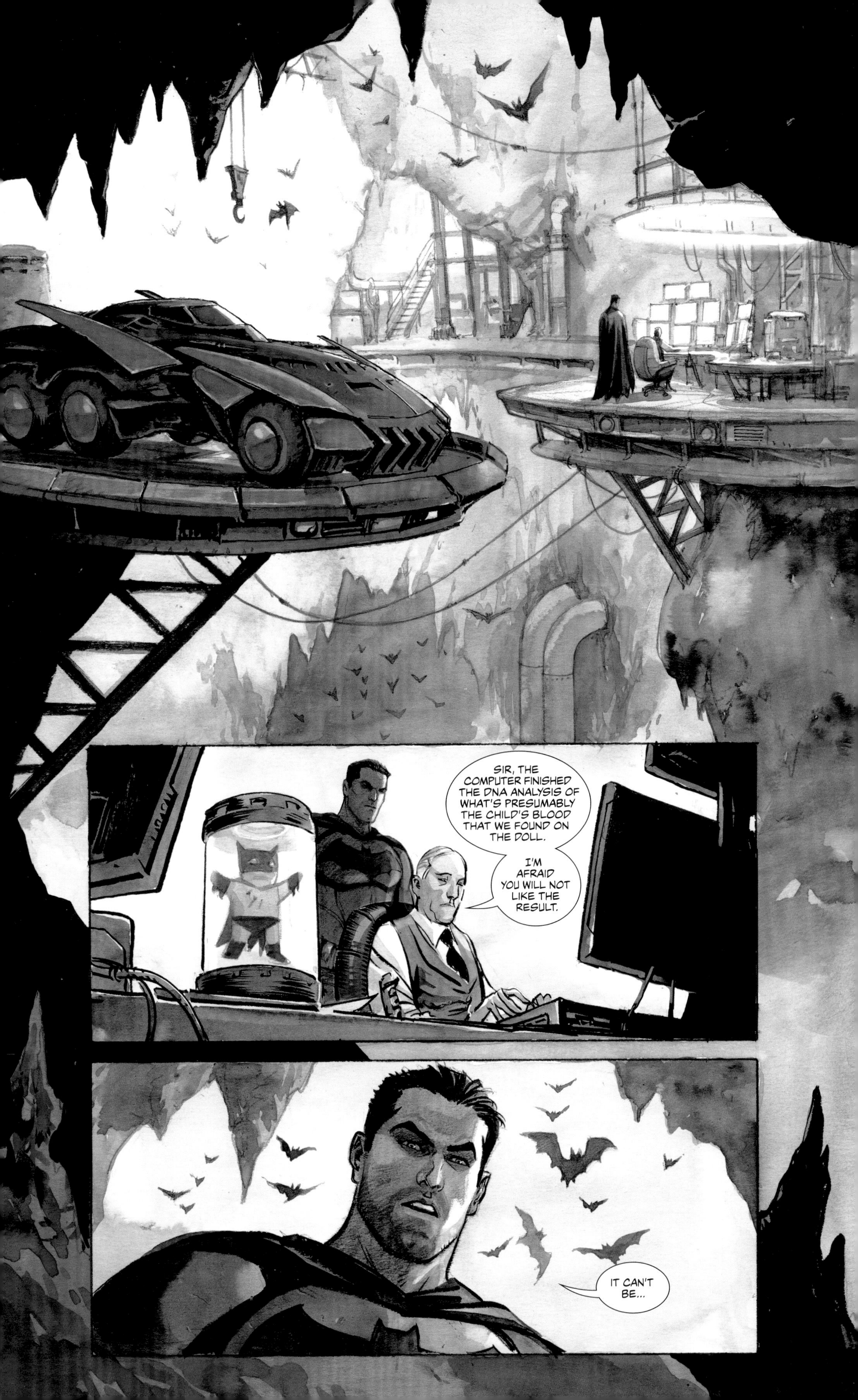
SIR, THE COMPUTER FINISHED THE DNA ANALYSIS OF WHAT'S PRESUMABLY THE CHILD'S BLOOD THAT WE FOUND ON THE DOLL.
I'M AFRAID YOU WILL NOT LIKE THE RESULT.
IT CAN'T BE...

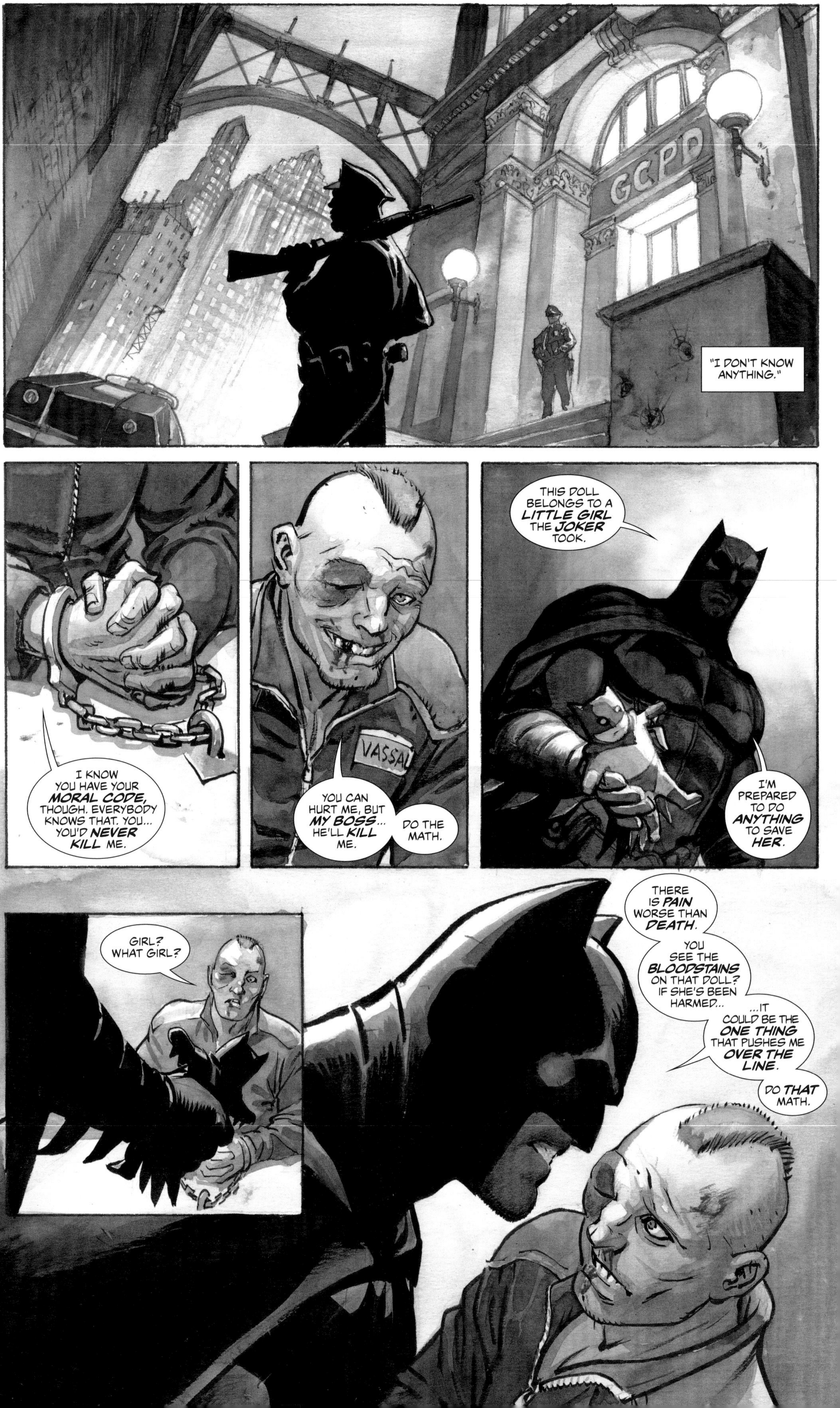
GCPD
"I DON'T KNOW ANYTHING."
I KNOW YOU HAVE YOUR MORAL CODE, THOUGH. EVERYBODY KNOWS THAT. YOU... YOU'D NEVER KILL ME.
VASSAL
YOU CAN HURT ME, BUT MY BOSS... HE'LL KILL ME.
DO THE MATH.
THIS DOLL BELONGS TO A LITTLE GIRL THE JOKER TOOK.
I'M PREPARED TO DO ANYTHING TO SAVE HER.
GIRL? WHAT GIRL?
THERE IS PAIN WORSE THAN DEATH.
YOU SEE THE BLOODSTAINS ON THAT DOLL? IF SHE'S BEEN HARMED...
...IT COULD BE THE ONE THING THAT PUSHES ME OVER THE LINE.
DO THAT MATH.

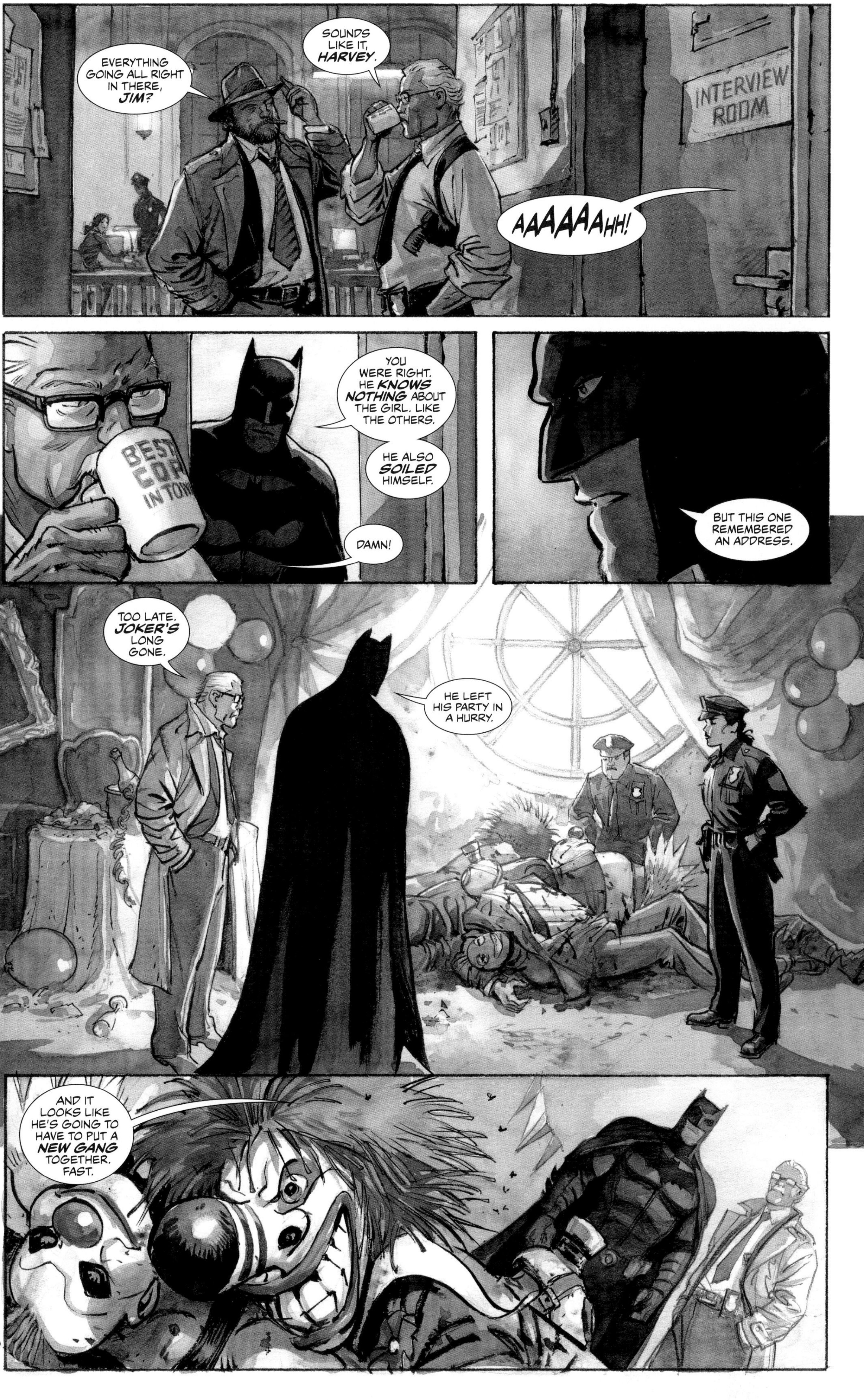
EVERYTHING GOING ALL RIGHT IN THERE, JIM?
SOUNDS LIKE IT, HARVEY.
INTERVIEW ROOM
AAAAAAHH!
YOU WERE RIGHT. HE KNOWS NOTHING ABOUT THE GIRL. LIKE THE OTHERS.
HE ALSO SOILED HIMSELF.
DAMN!
BUT THIS ONE REMEMBERED AN ADDRESS.
TOO LATE. JOKER'S LONG GONE.
HE LEFT HIS PARTY IN A HURRY.
AND IT LOOKS LIKE HE'S GOING TO HAVE TO PUT A NEW GANG TOGETHER. FAST.

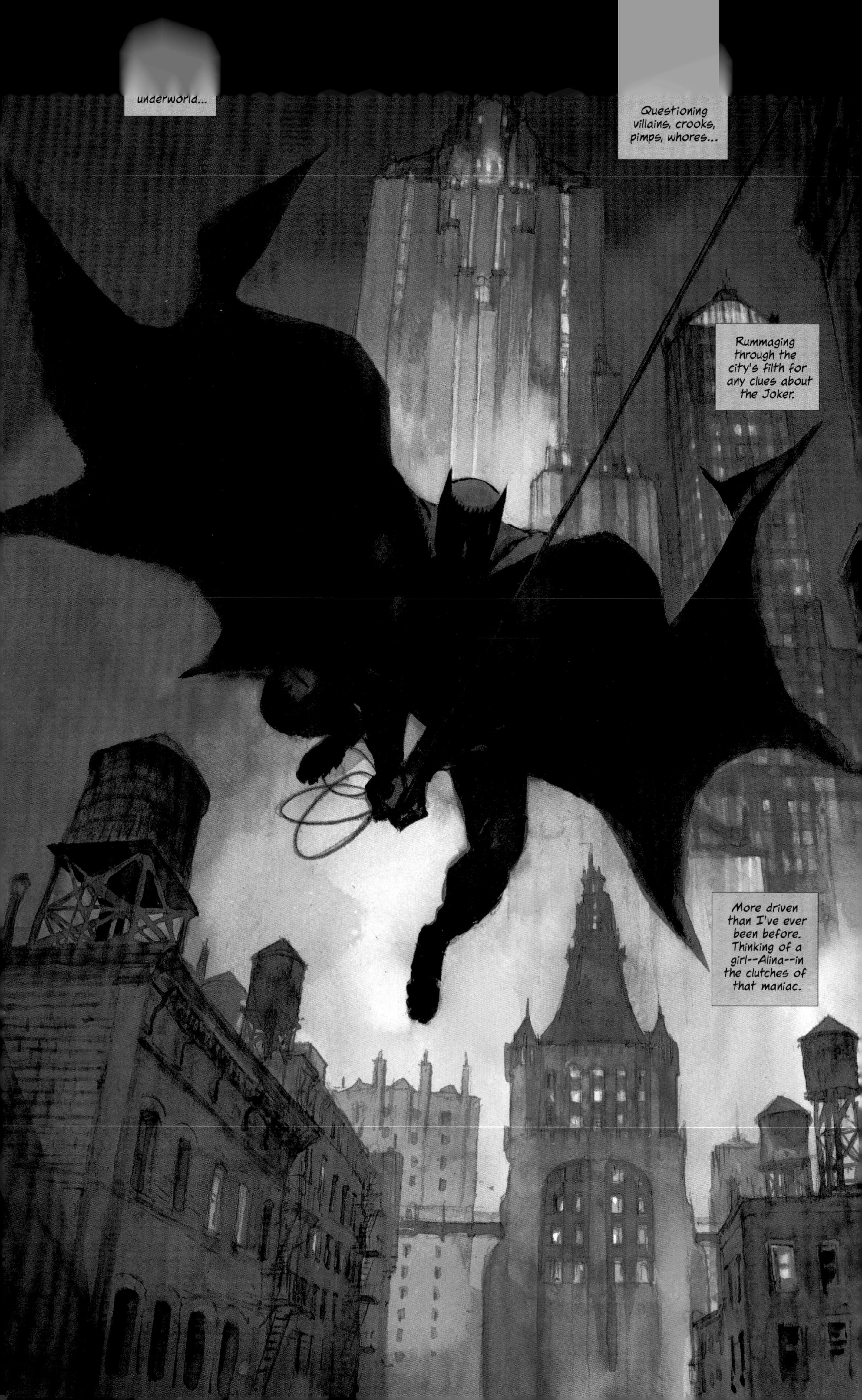
underworld...
Questioning villains, crooks, pimps, whores...
Rummaging through the city's filth for any clues about the Joker.
More driven than I've ever been before. Thinking of a girl--Alina--in the clutches of that maniac.

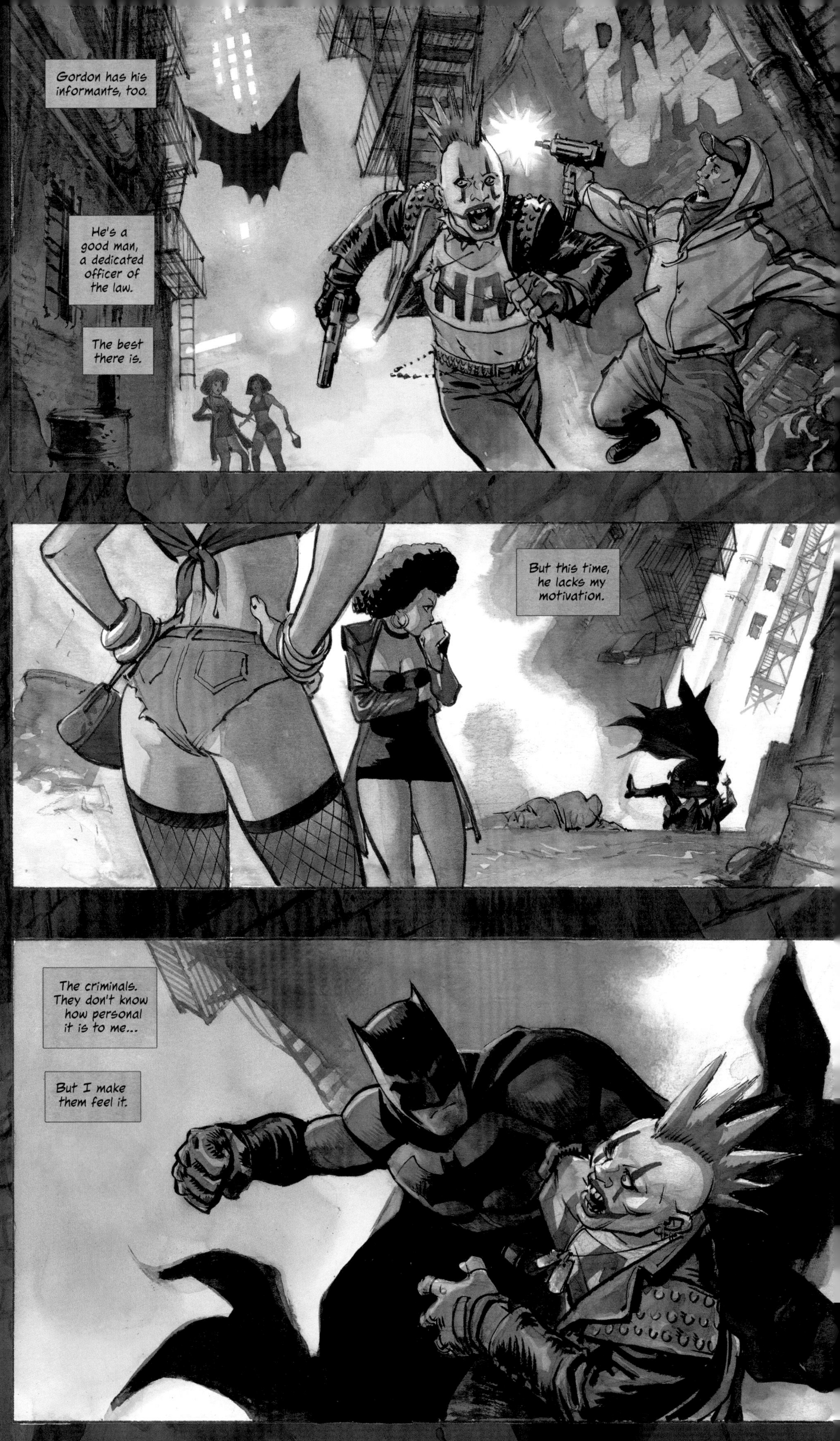
Gordon has his informants, too.
He's a good man, a dedicated officer of the law.
The best there is.
But this time, he lacks my motivation.
The criminals. They don't know how personal it is to me...
But I make them feel it.

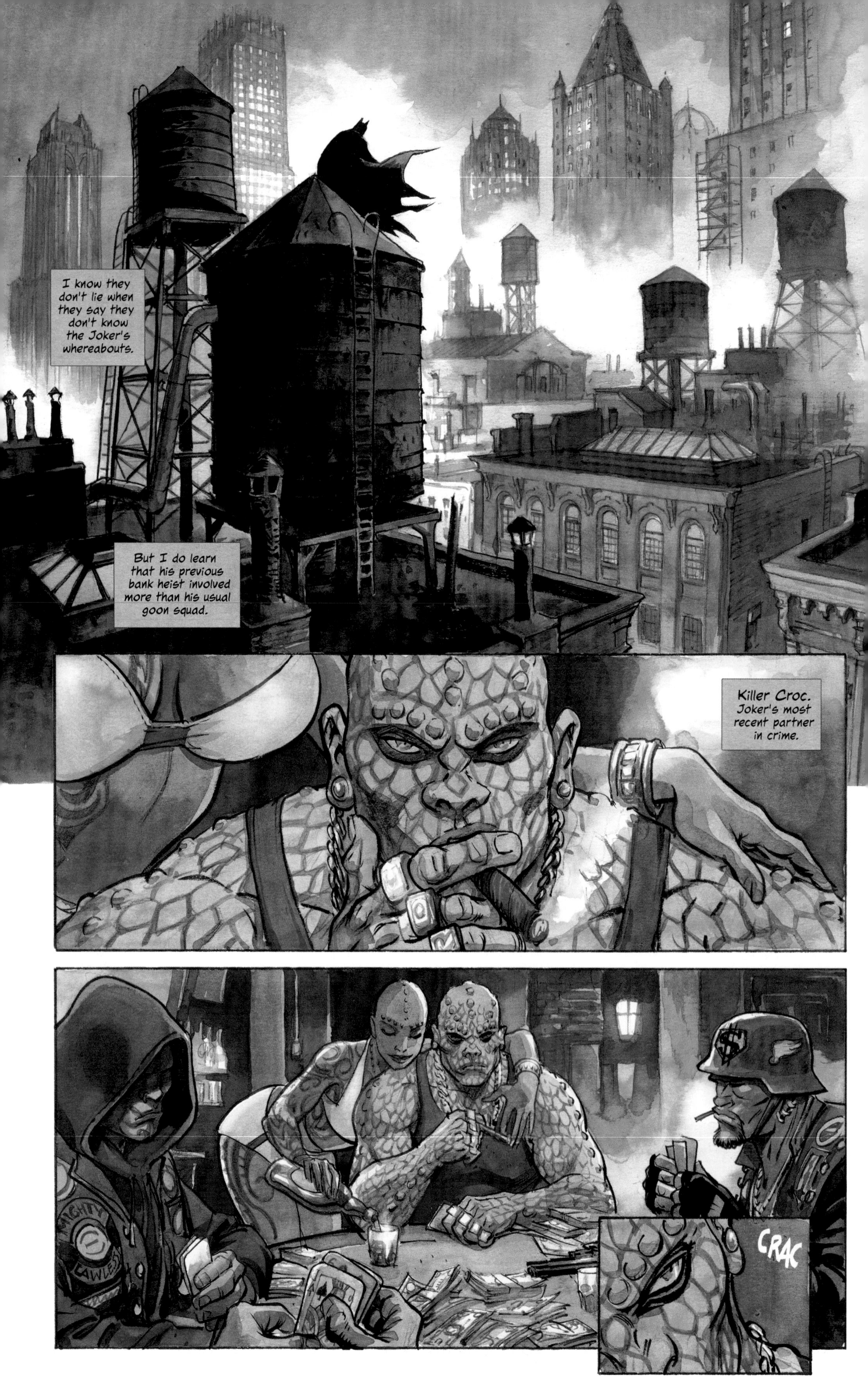

I know they don't lie when they say they don't know the Joker's whereabouts.
But I do learn that his previous bank heist involved more than his usual goon squad.
Killer Croc. Joker's most recent partner in crime.
MIGHTY
LAWLESS
CRAC

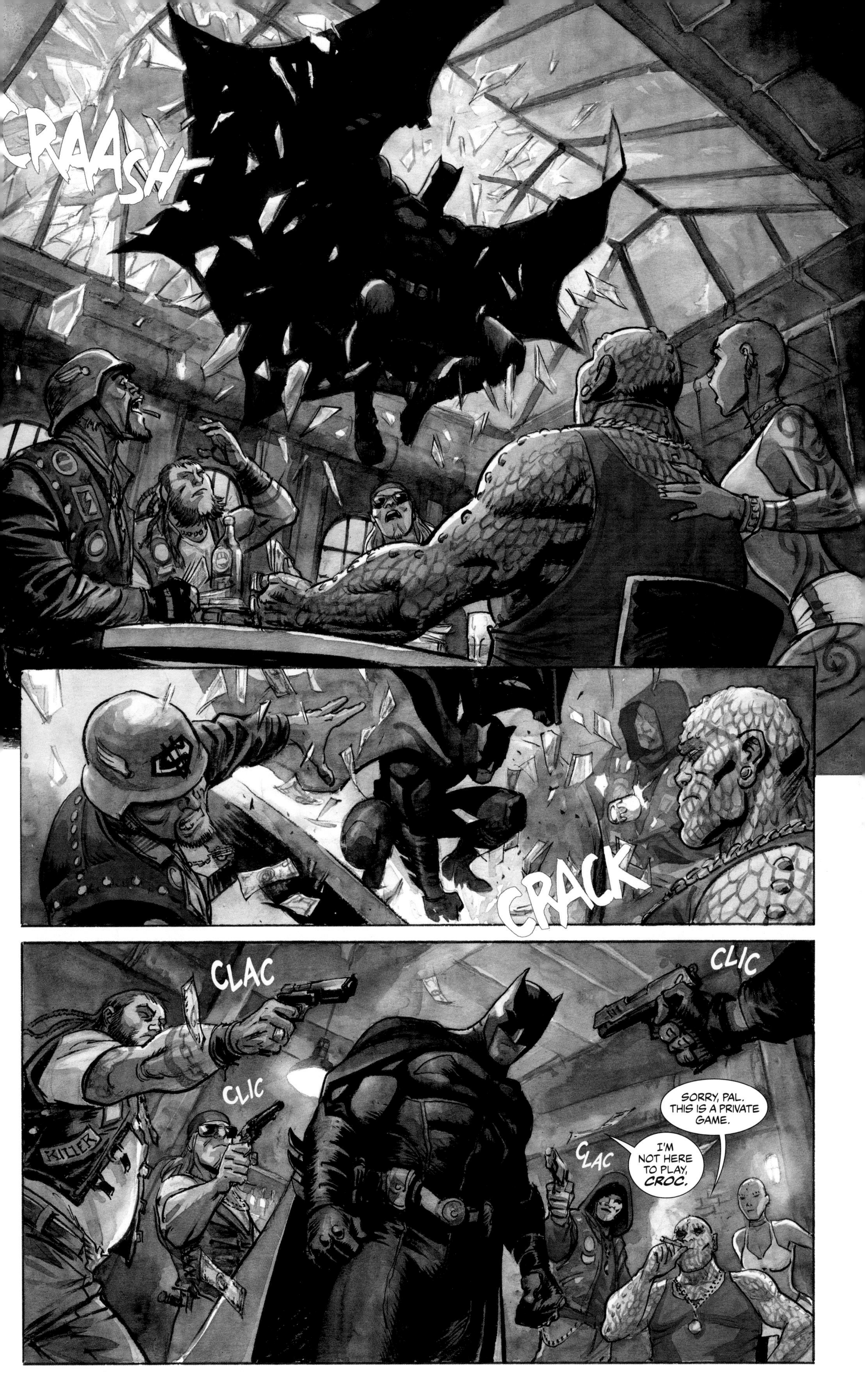
CRAASH
CRACK
CLAC
CLIC
CLIC
SORRY, PAL. THIS IS A PRIVATE GAME.
CLAC
I'M NOT HERE TO PLAY, CROC.

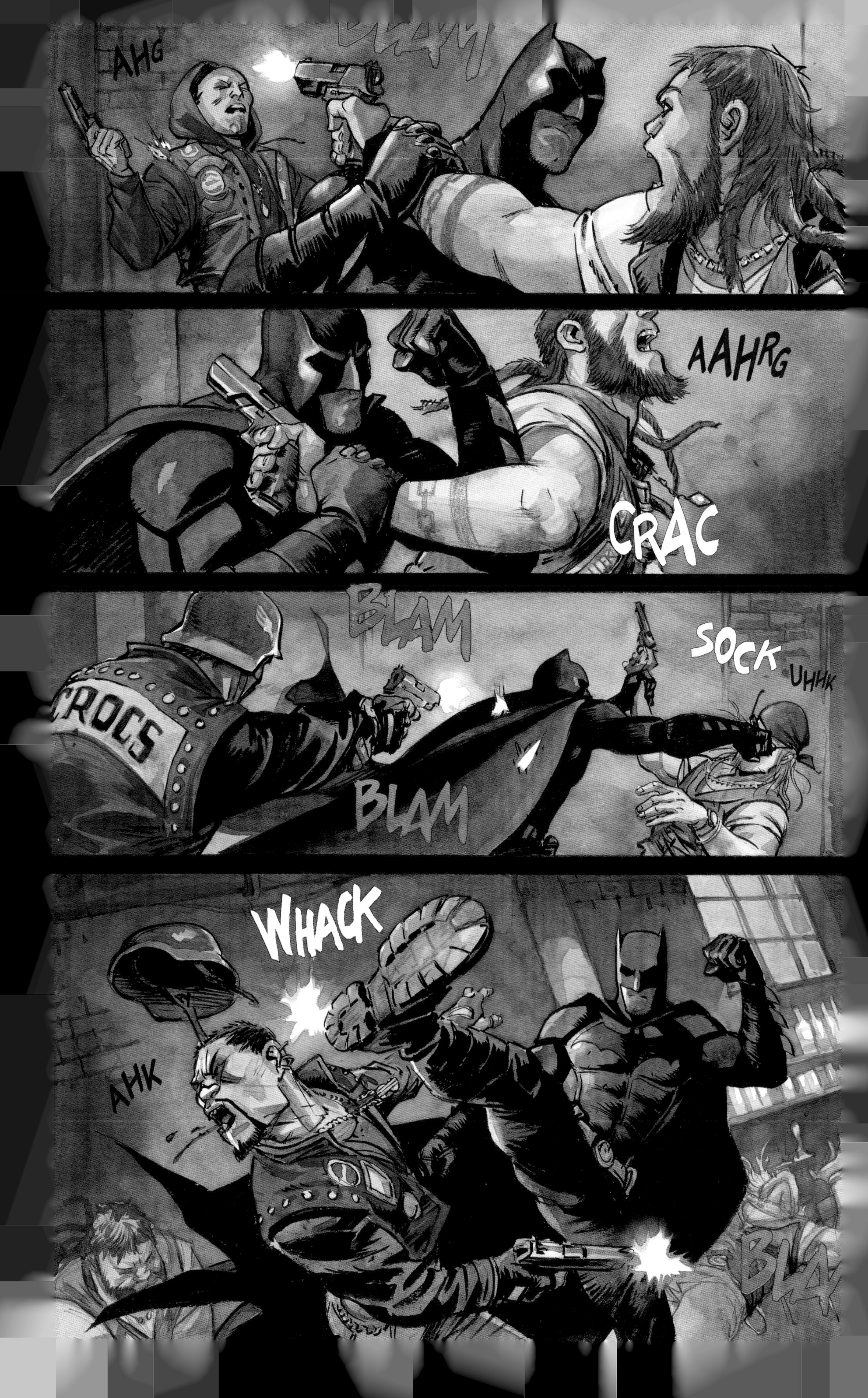
AHG
AAHRG
CRAC
BLAM
SOCK
UHHK
CROCS
BLAM
WHACK
AHK

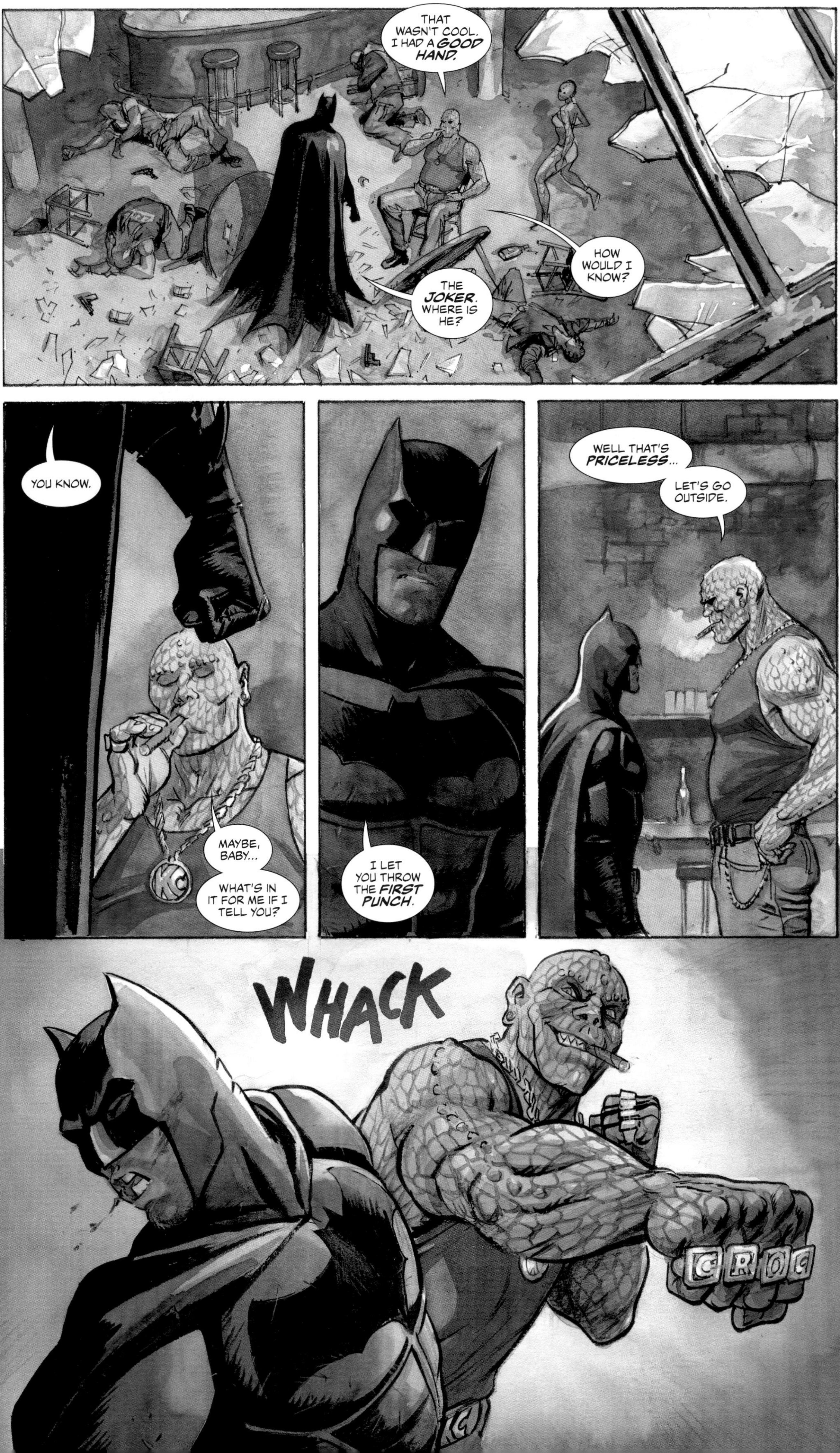
THAT WASN'T COOL. I HAD A GOOD HAND.
THE JOKER. WHERE IS HE?
HOW WOULD I KNOW?
YOU KNOW.
MAYBE, BABY...
WHAT'S IN IT FOR ME IF I TELL YOU?
I LET YOU THROW THE FIRST PUNCH.
WELL THAT'S PRICELESS...
LET'S GO OUTSIDE.
WHACK
CROC

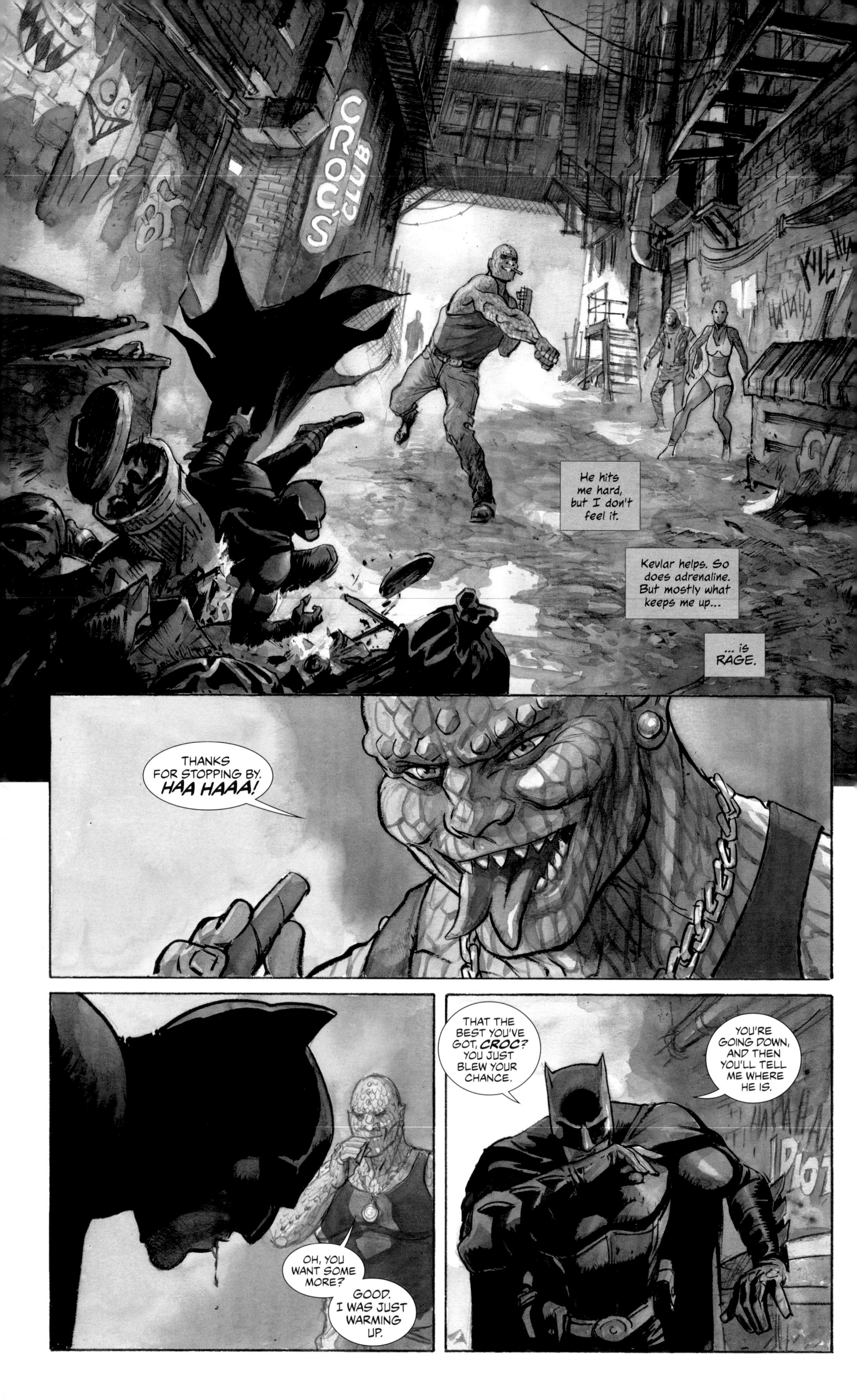
CROC'S CLUB
He hits me hard, but I don't feel it.
Kevlar helps. So does adrenaline. But mostly what keeps me up...
... is RAGE.
THANKS FOR STOPPING BY. HAA HAAA!
OH, YOU WANT SOME MORE?
GOOD. I WAS JUST WARMING UP.
THAT THE BEST YOU'VE GOT, CROC? YOU JUST BLEW YOUR CHANCE.
YOU'RE GOING DOWN, AND THEN YOU'LL TELL ME WHERE HE IS.

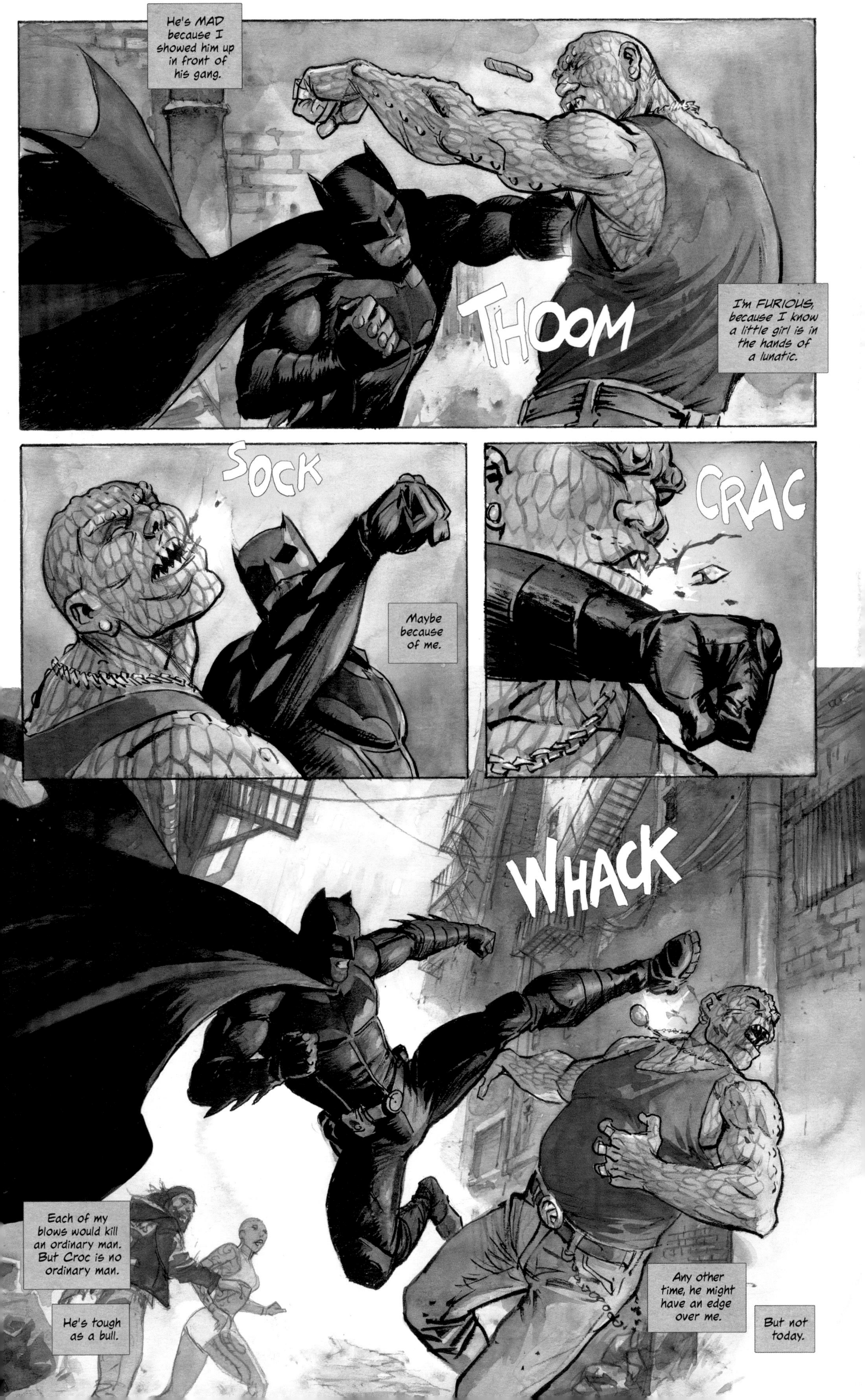
He's MAD because I showed him up in front of his gang.
THOOM
I'm FURIOUS, because I know a little girl is in the hands of a lunatic.
SOCK
Maybe because of me.
CRAC
WHACK
Each of my blows would kill an ordinary man. But Croc is no ordinary man.
He's tough as a bull.
Any other time, he might have an edge over me.
But not today.

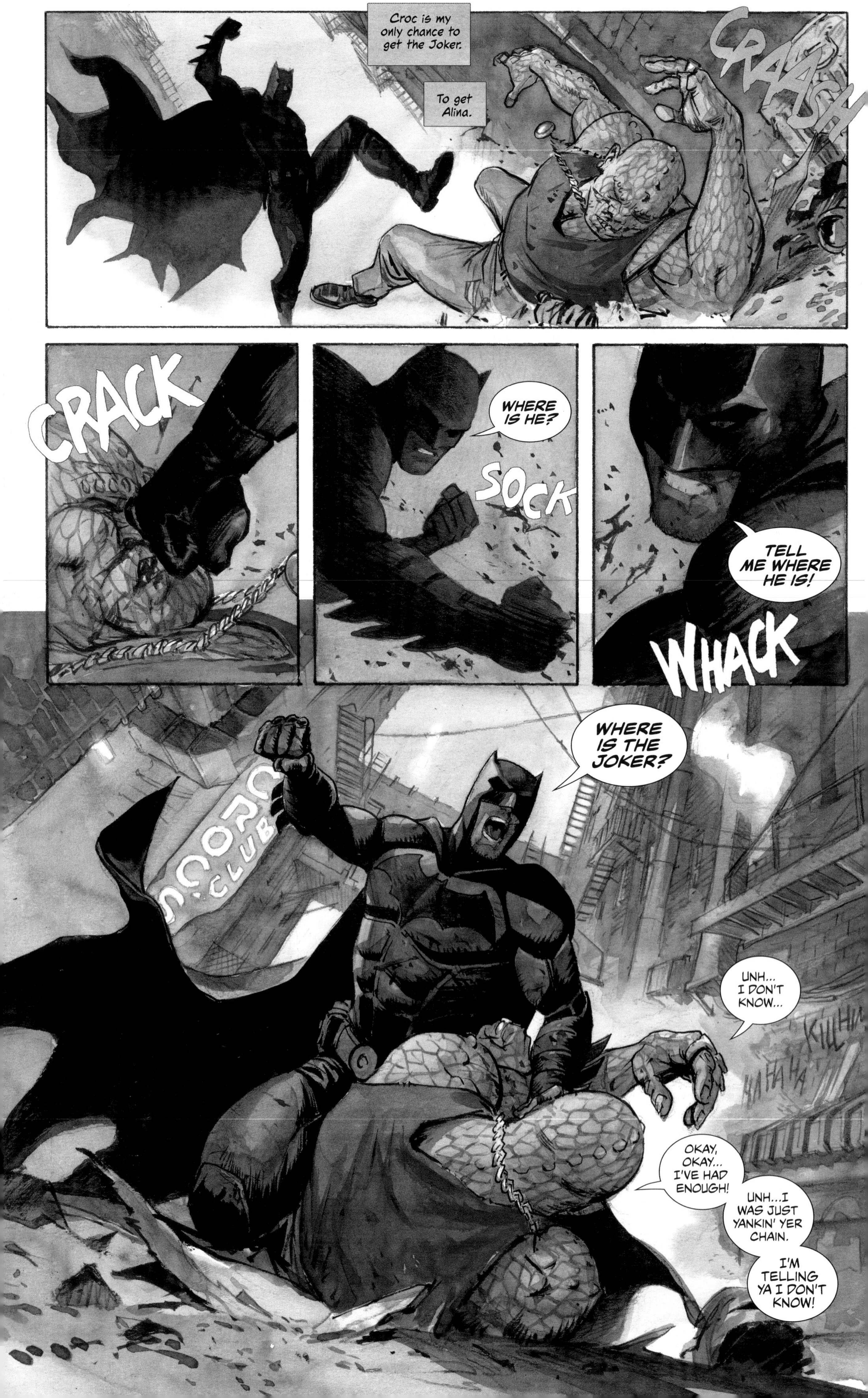
Croc is my only chance to get the Joker.
To get Alina.
CRAASH
CRACK
WHERE IS HE?
SOCK
TELL ME WHERE HE IS!
WHACK
WHERE IS THE JOKER?
UNH... I DON'T KNOW...
OKAY, OKAY... I'VE HAD ENOUGH!
UNH...I WAS JUST YANKIN' YER CHAIN.
I'M TELLING YA I DON'T KNOW!

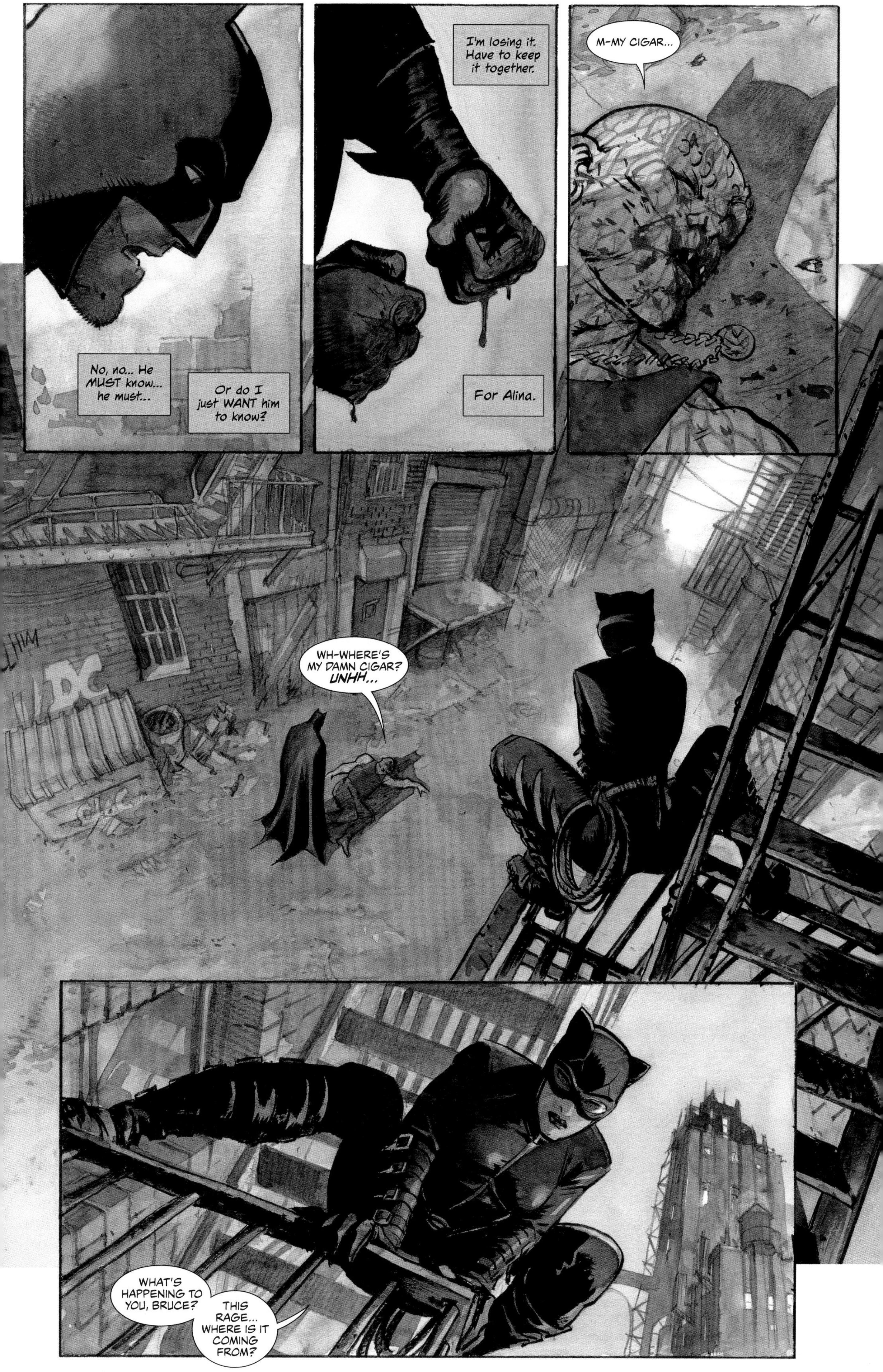
No, no... He MUST know... he must...
Or do I just WANT him to know?
I'm losing it. Have to keep it together.
For Alina.
M-MY CIGAR...
WH-WHERE'S MY DAMN CIGAR? UNHH...
WHAT'S HAPPENING TO YOU, BRUCE?
THIS RAGE... WHERE IS IT COMING FROM?

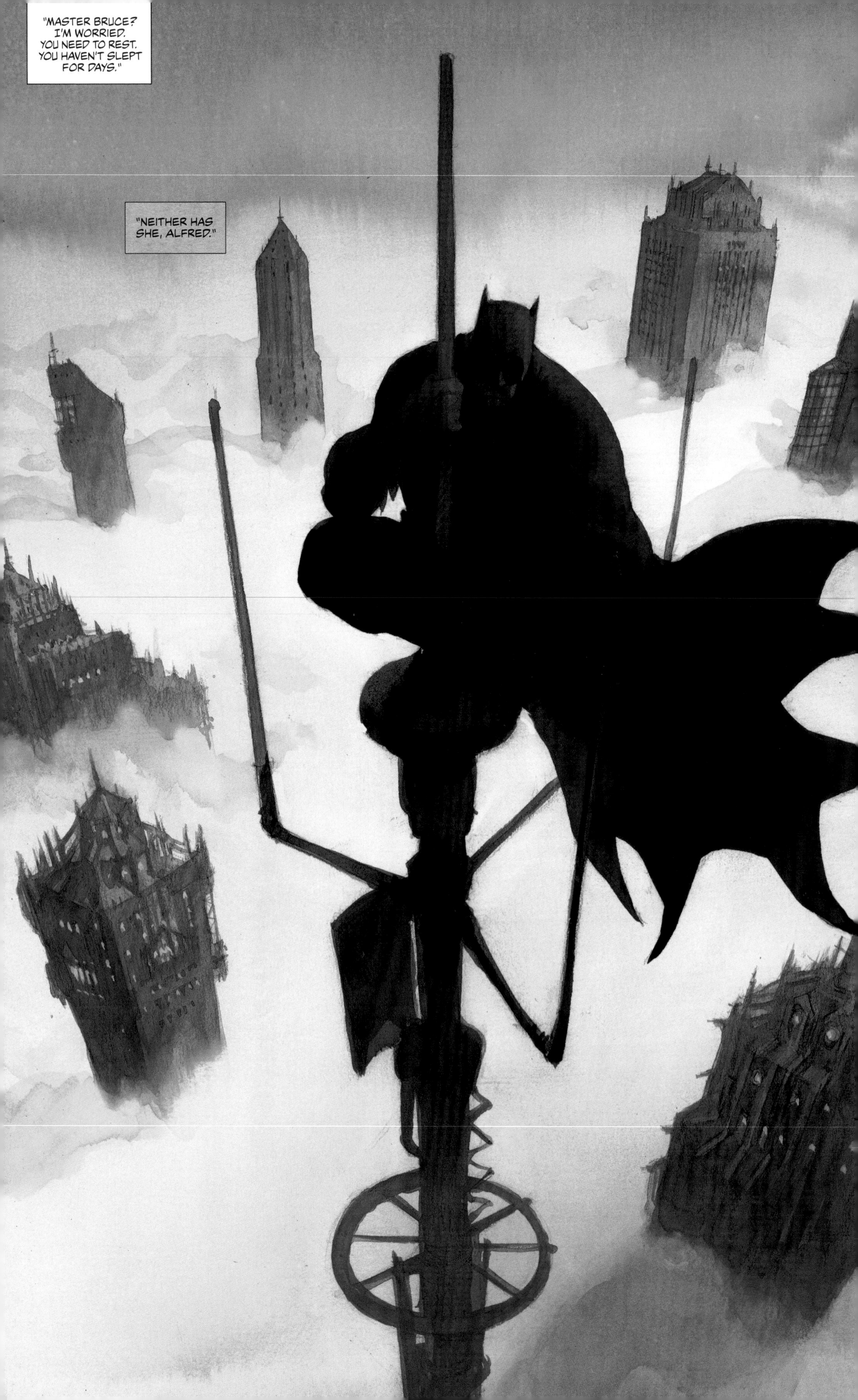
"MASTER BRUCE? I'M WORRIED. YOU NEED TO REST. YOU HAVEN'T SLEPT FOR DAYS."
"NEITHER HAS SHE, ALFRED."

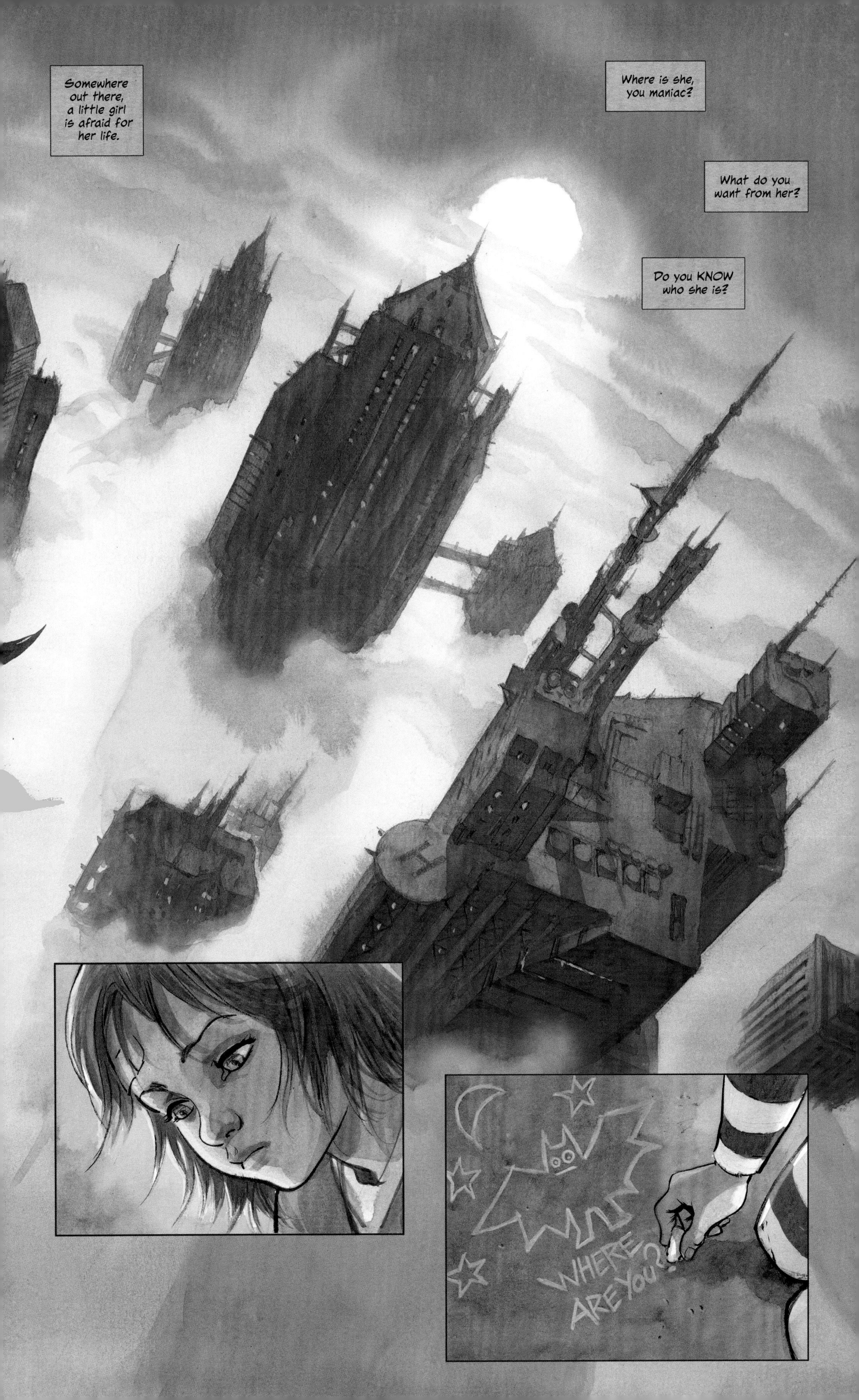

Somewhere out there, a little girl is afraid for her life.
Where is she, you maniac?
What do you want from her?
Do you KNOW who she is?
WHERE ARE YOU?

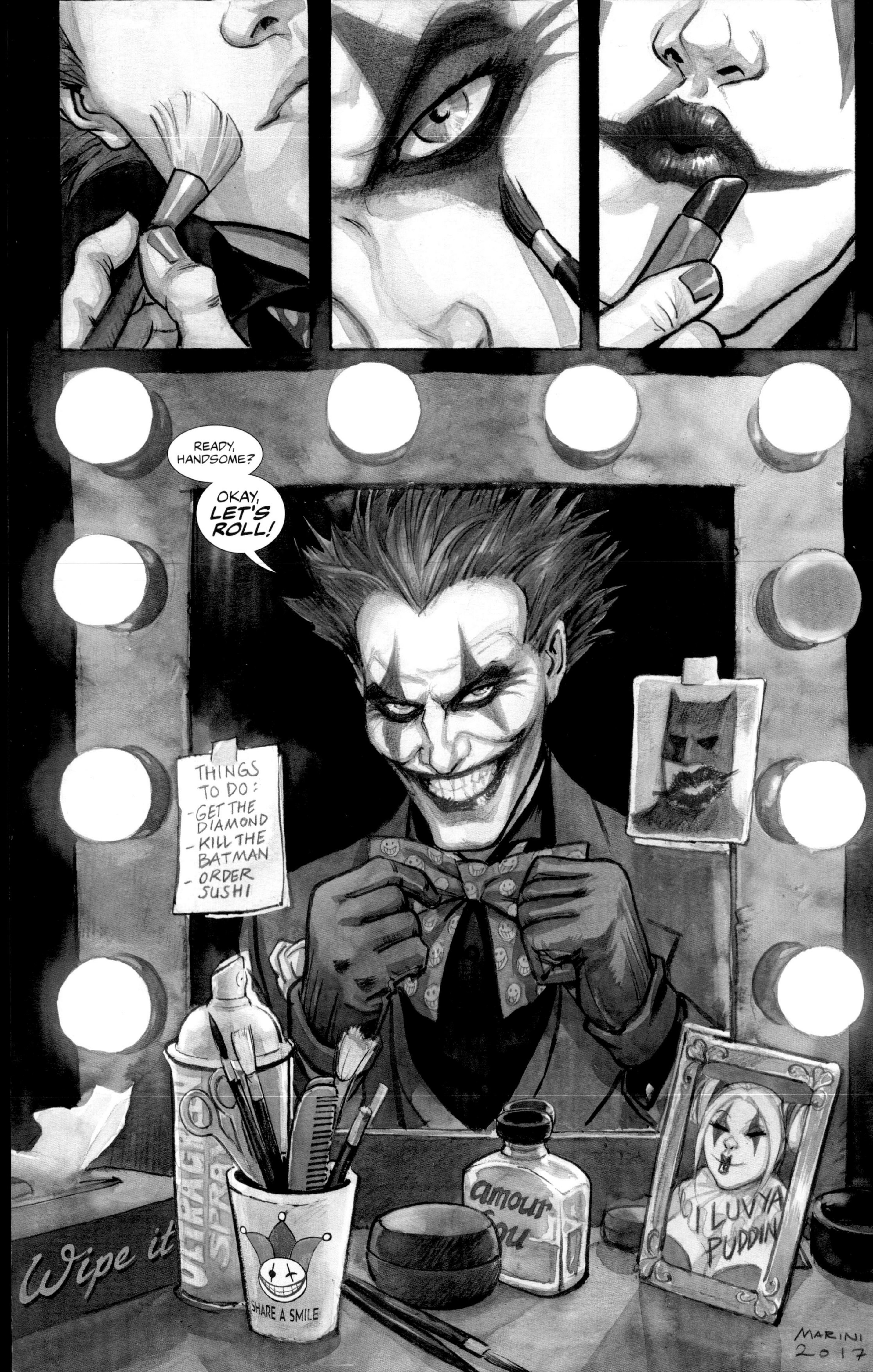
READY, HANDSOME?
OKAY, LET'S ROLL!
THINGS TO DO: - GET THE DIAMOND - KILL THE BATMAN - ORDER SUSHI
Wipe it
amour fou
SHARE A SMILE
I LUV YA PUDDIN
MARINI 2017

"Happy endings
only occur in fairy tales.
And this ain't one of those."

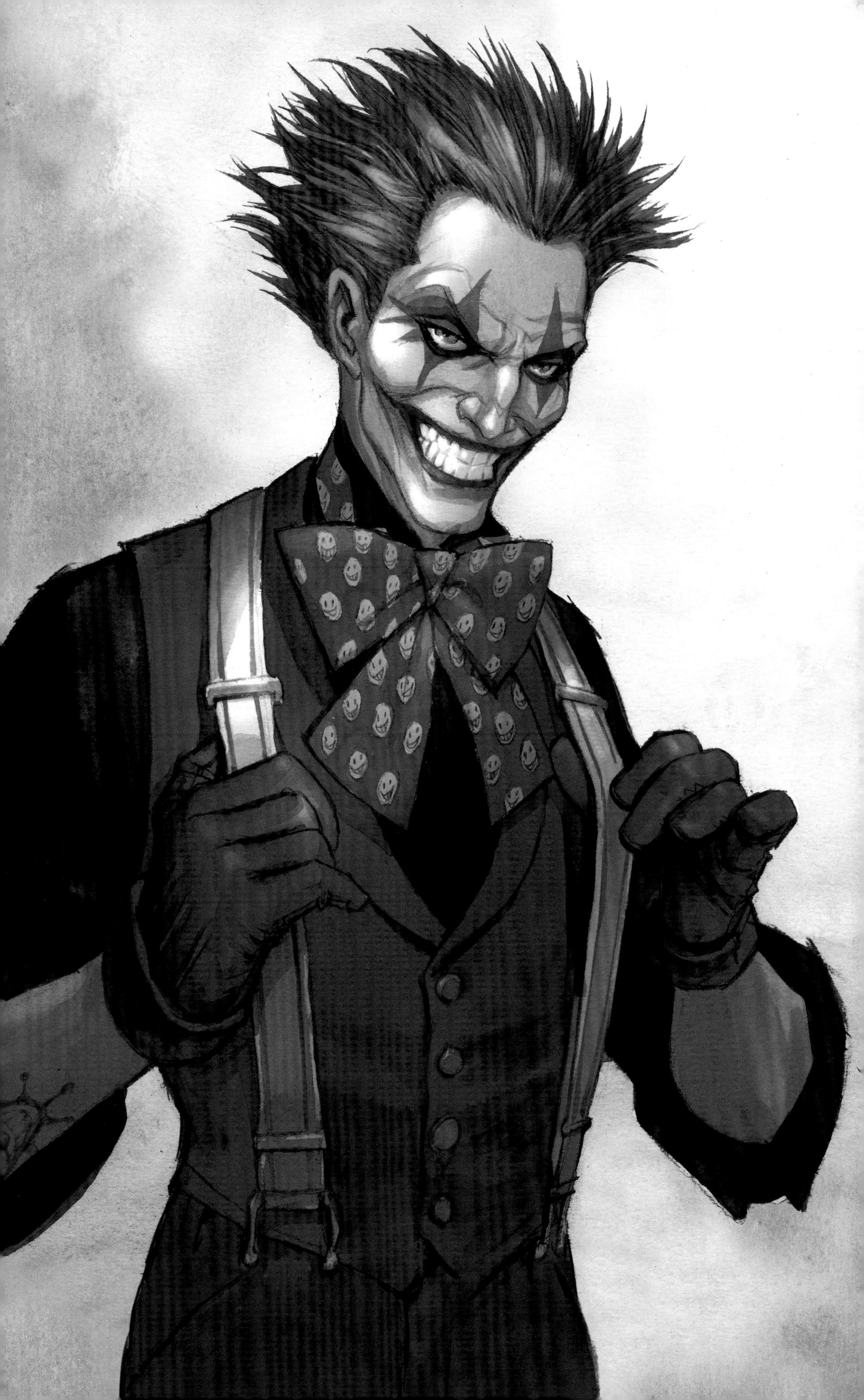

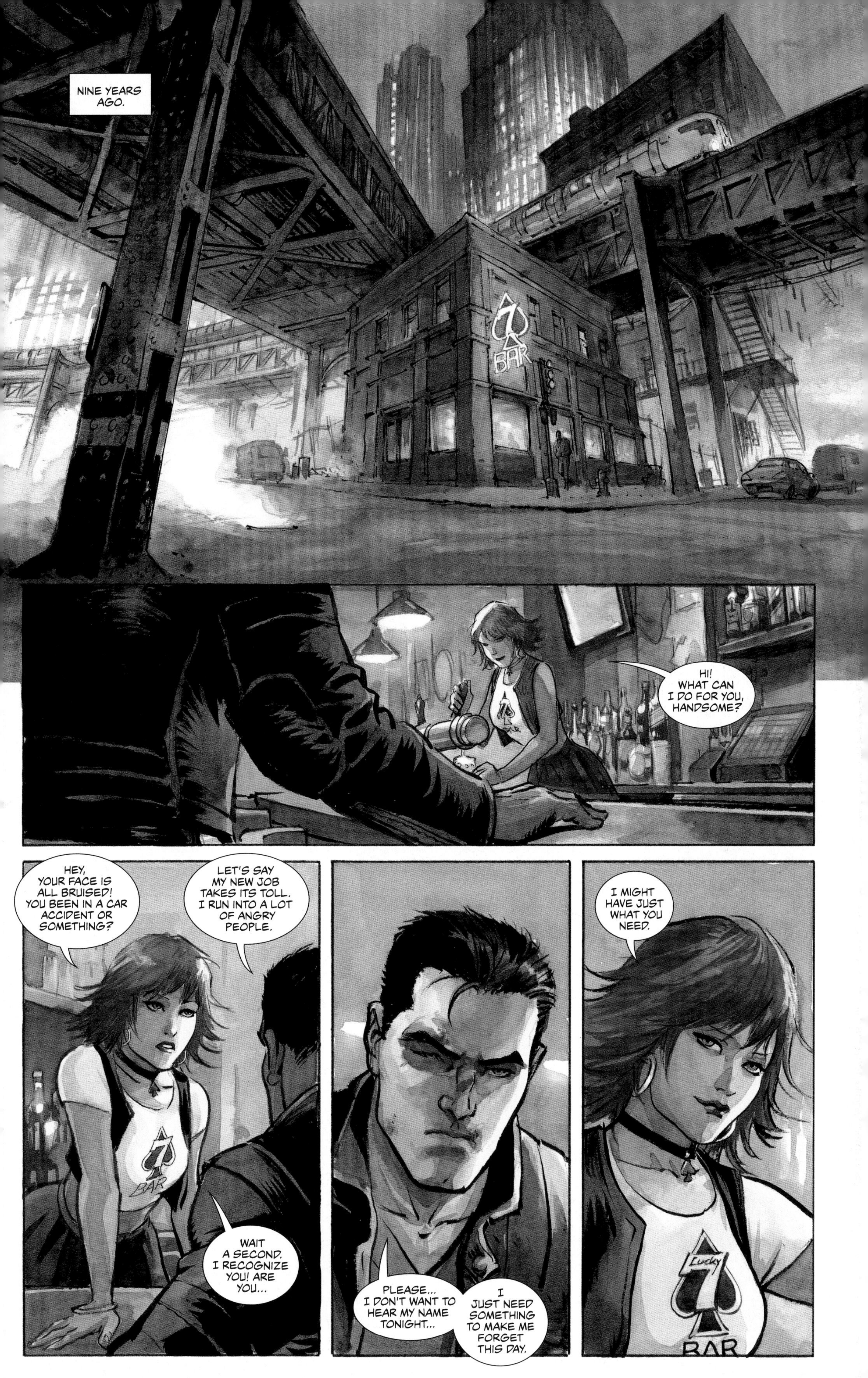
NINE YEARS AGO.
7 BAR
HI! WHAT CAN I DO FOR YOU, HANDSOME?
HEY, YOUR FACE IS ALL BRUISED! YOU BEEN IN A CAR ACCIDENT OR SOMETHING?
LET'S SAY MY NEW JOB TAKES ITS TOLL. I RUN INTO A LOT OF ANGRY PEOPLE.
WAIT A SECOND. I RECOGNIZE YOU! ARE YOU...
PLEASE... I DON'T WANT TO HEAR MY NAME TONIGHT...
I JUST NEED SOMETHING TO MAKE ME FORGET THIS DAY.
I MIGHT HAVE JUST WHAT YOU NEED.
Lucky 7 BAR

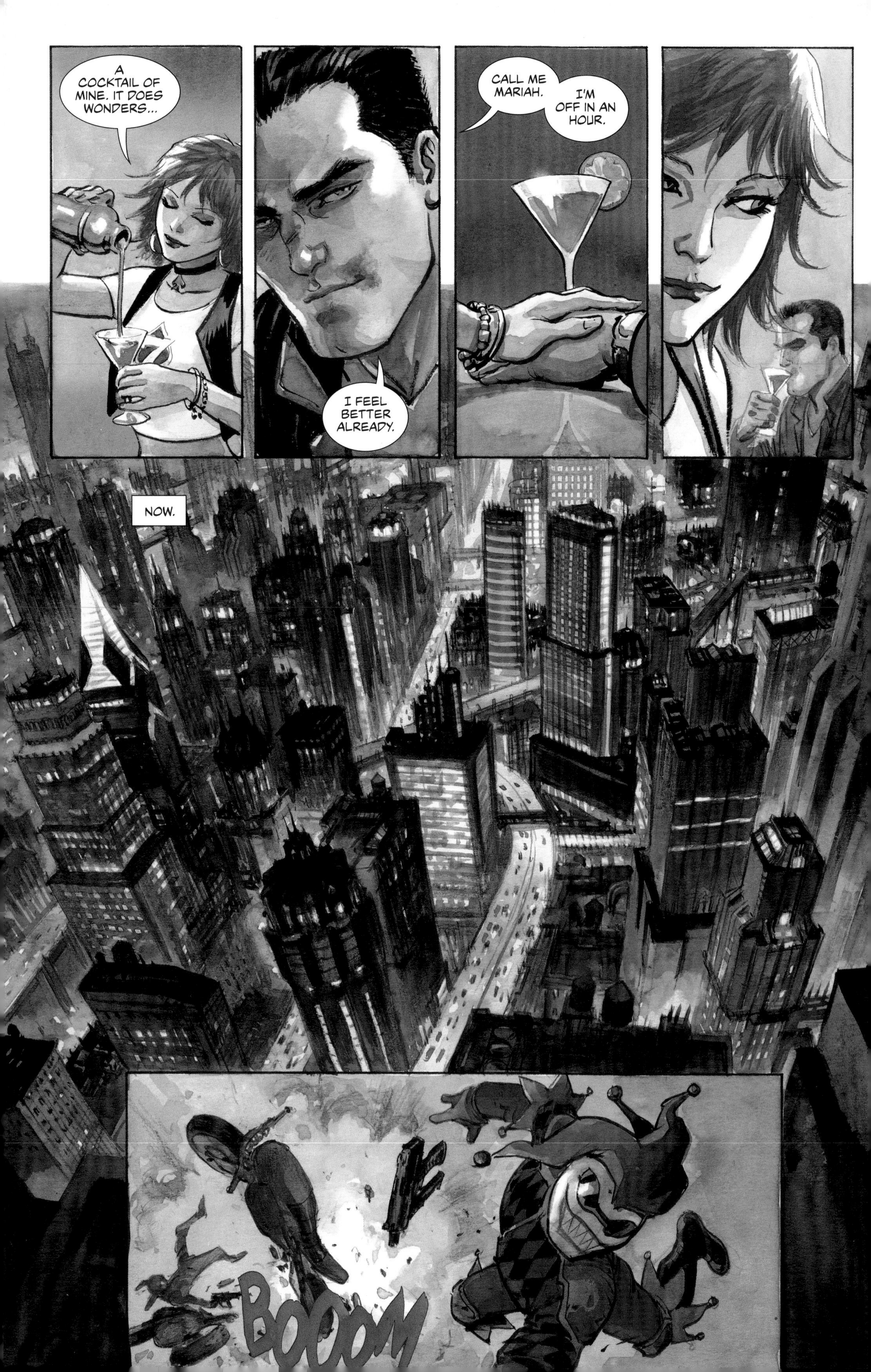
A COCKTAIL OF MINE. IT DOES WONDERS...
I FEEL BETTER ALREADY.
CALL ME MARIAH.
I'M OFF IN AN HOUR.
NOW.
BOOOM

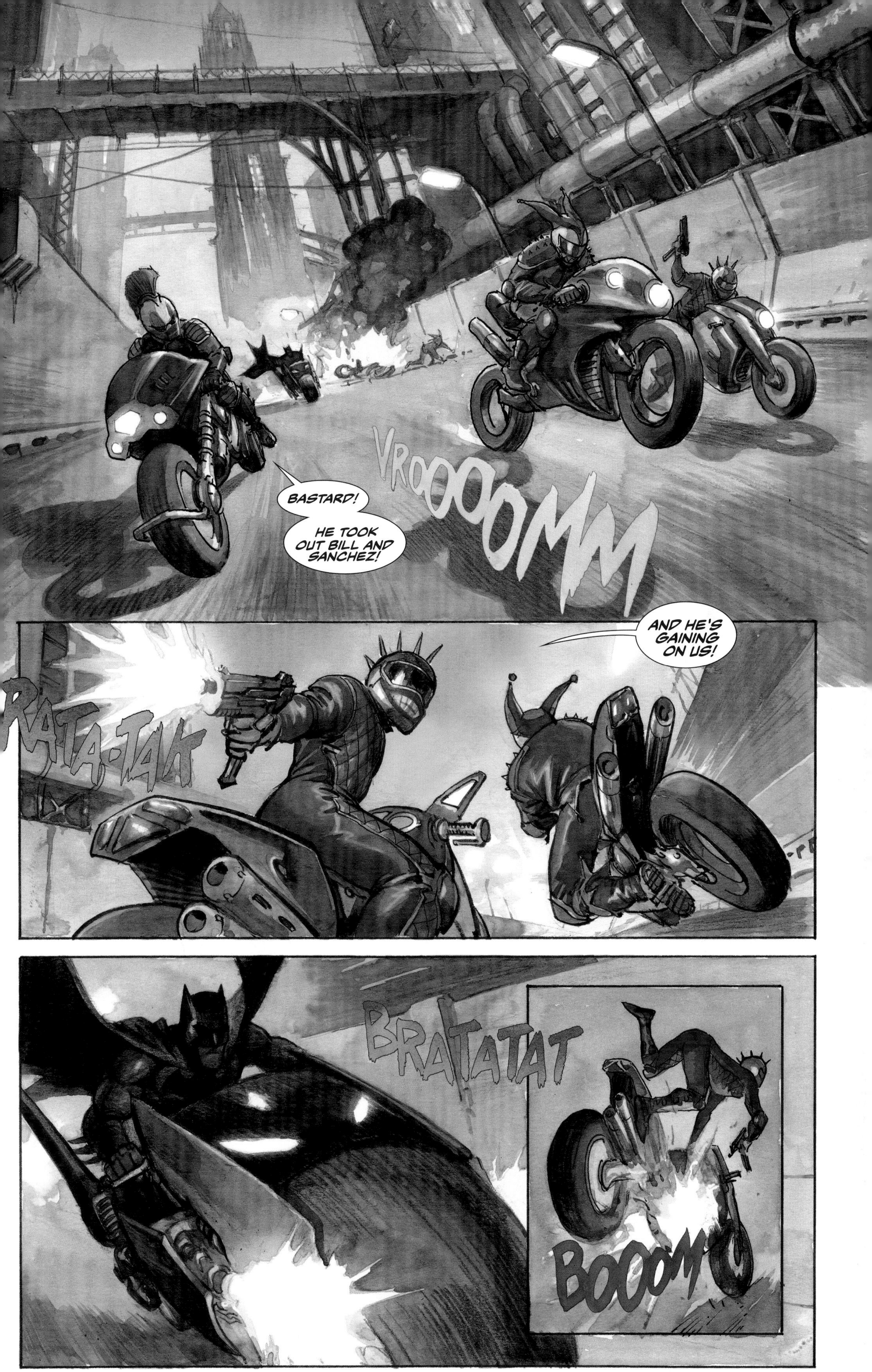
BASTARD!
HE TOOK OUT BILL AND SANCHEZ!
VROOOOOMM
AND HE'S GAINING ON US!
RATA-TAK
BRATATAT
BOOOM

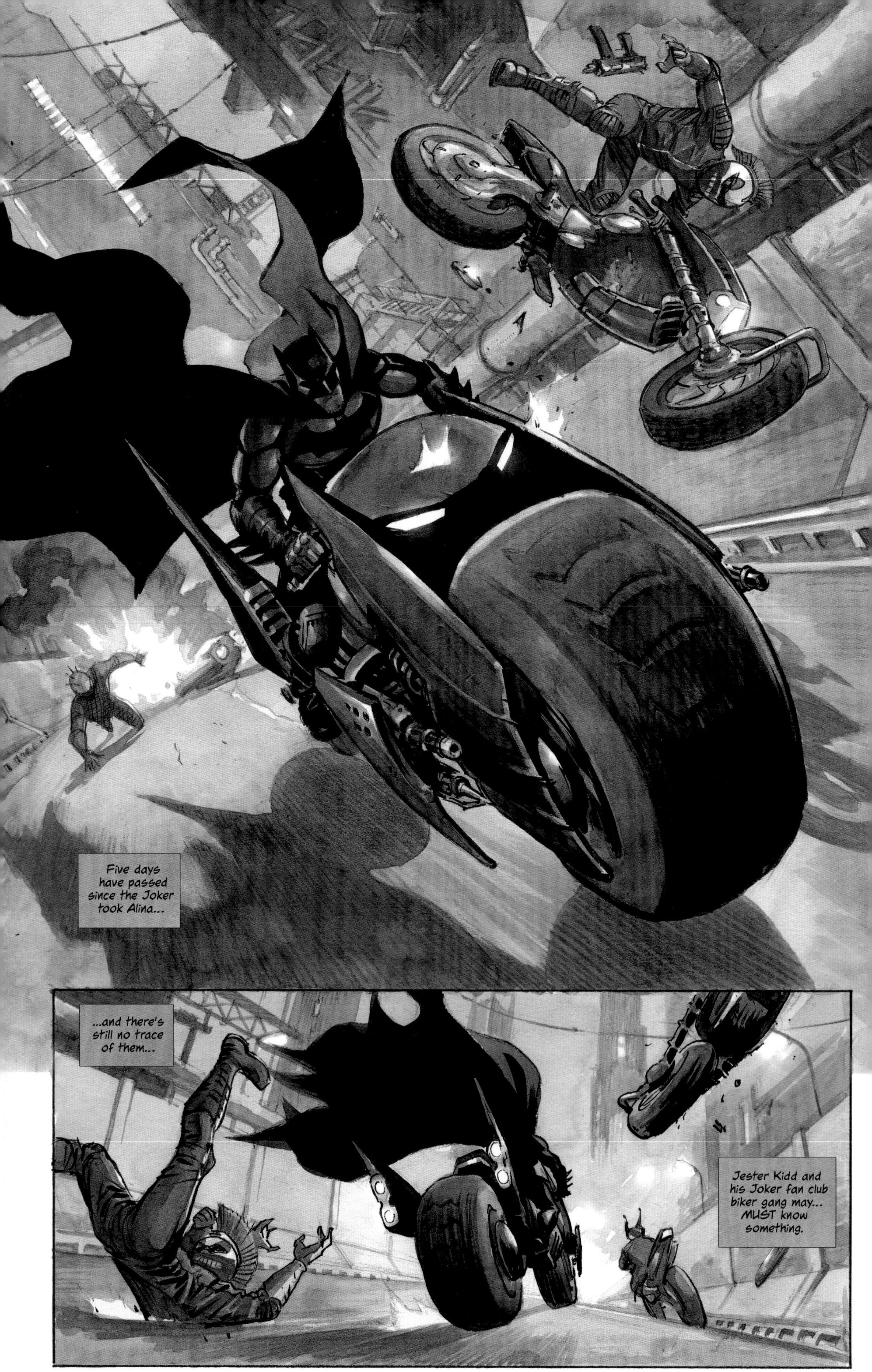
Five days have passed since the Joker took Alina...
...and there's still no trace of them...
Jester Kidd and his Joker fan club biker gang may... MUST know something.

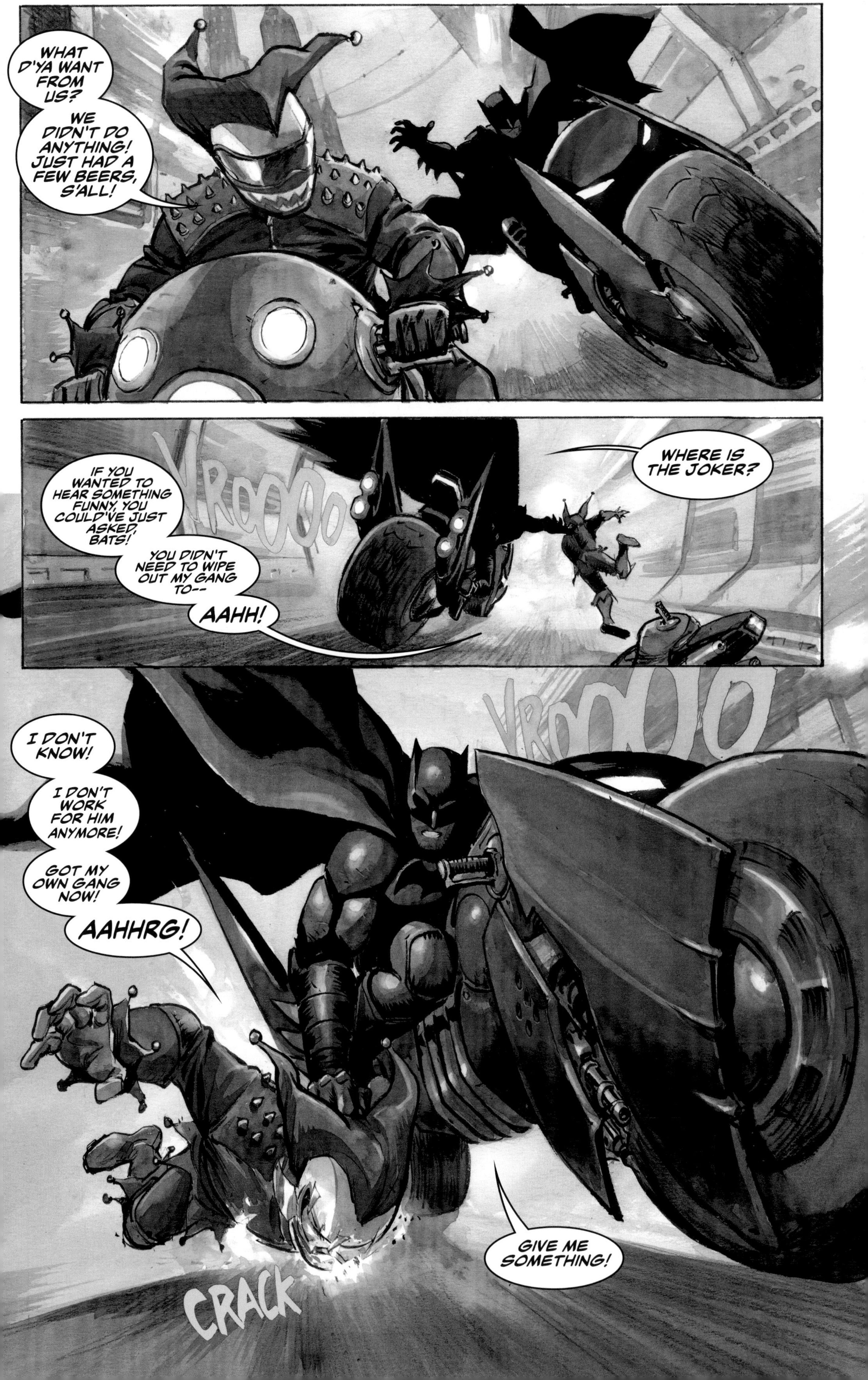
WHAT D'YA WANT FROM US?
WE DIDN'T DO ANYTHING! JUST HAD A FEW BEERS, S'ALL!
VROOOO
WHERE IS THE JOKER?
IF YOU WANTED TO HEAR SOMETHING FUNNY, YOU COULD'VE JUST ASKED, BATS!
YOU DIDN'T NEED TO WIPE OUT MY GANG TO--
AAHH!
VROOOO
I DON'T KNOW!
I DON'T WORK FOR HIM ANYMORE!
GOT MY OWN GANG NOW!
AAHHRG!
GIVE ME SOMETHING!
CRACK

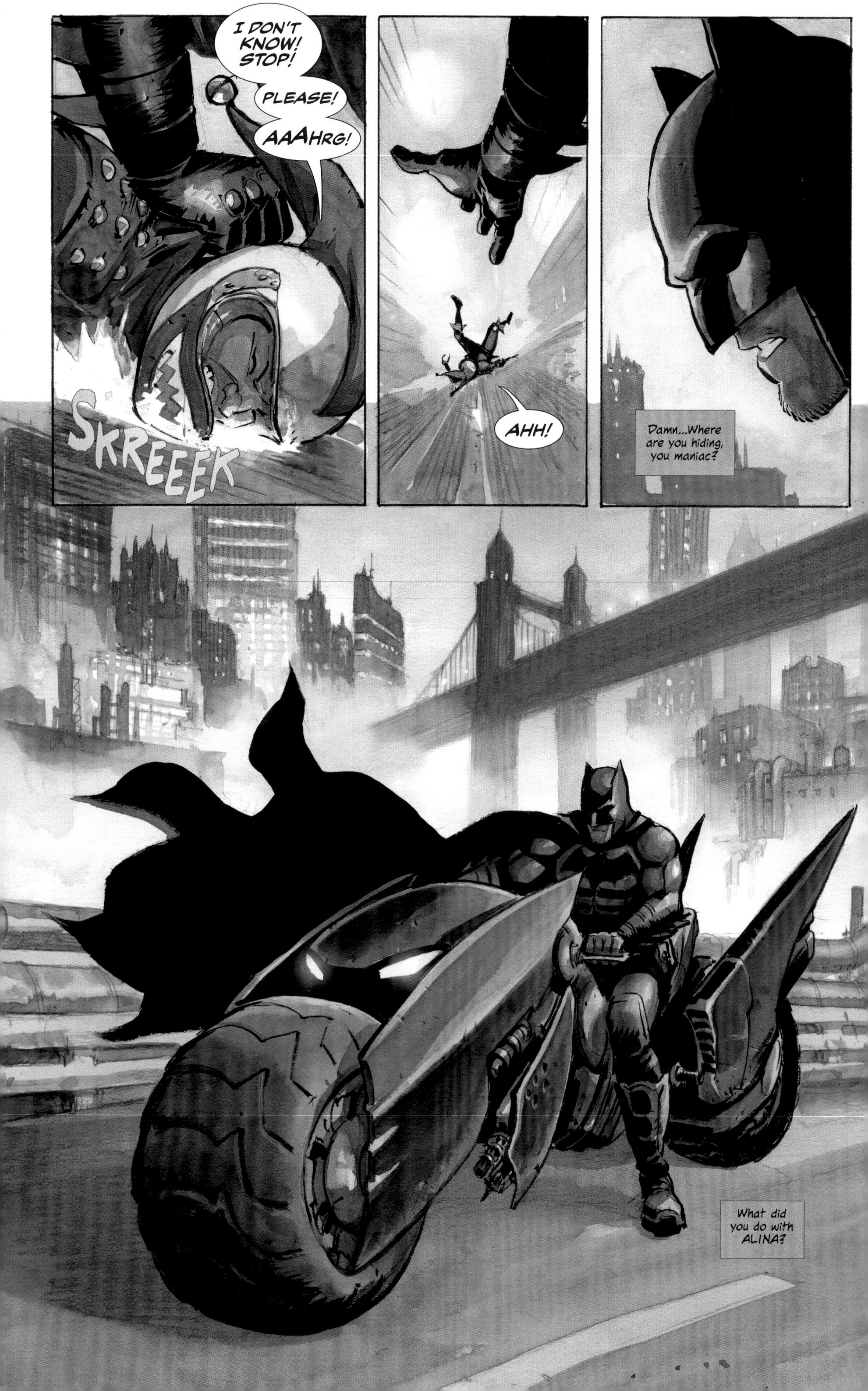
I DON'T KNOW! STOP!
PLEASE!
AAAHRG!
SKREEEEK
AHH!
Damn...Where are you hiding, you maniac?
What did you do with ALINA?

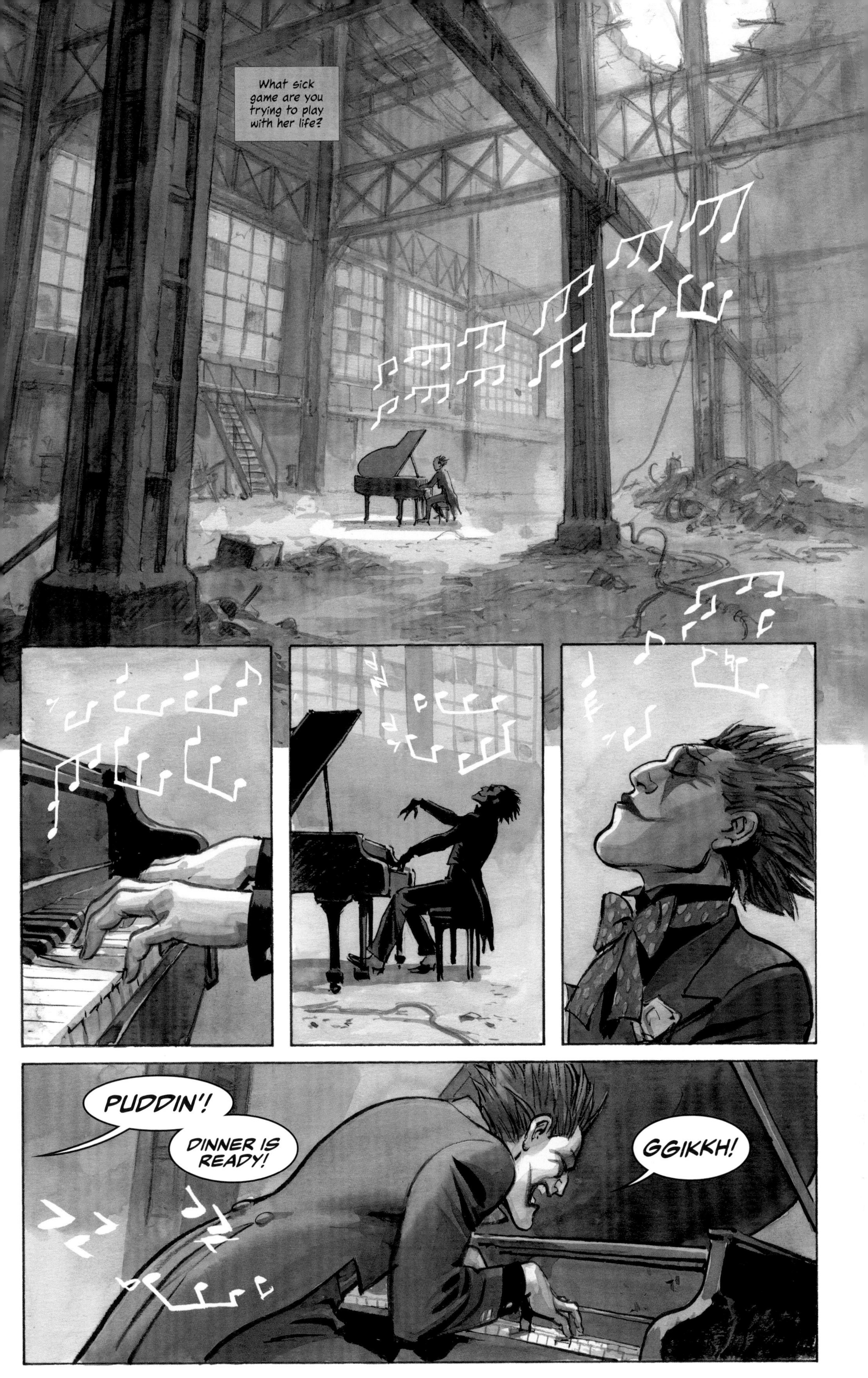
What sick game are you trying to play with her life?
PUDDIN'!
DINNER IS READY!
GGIKKH!

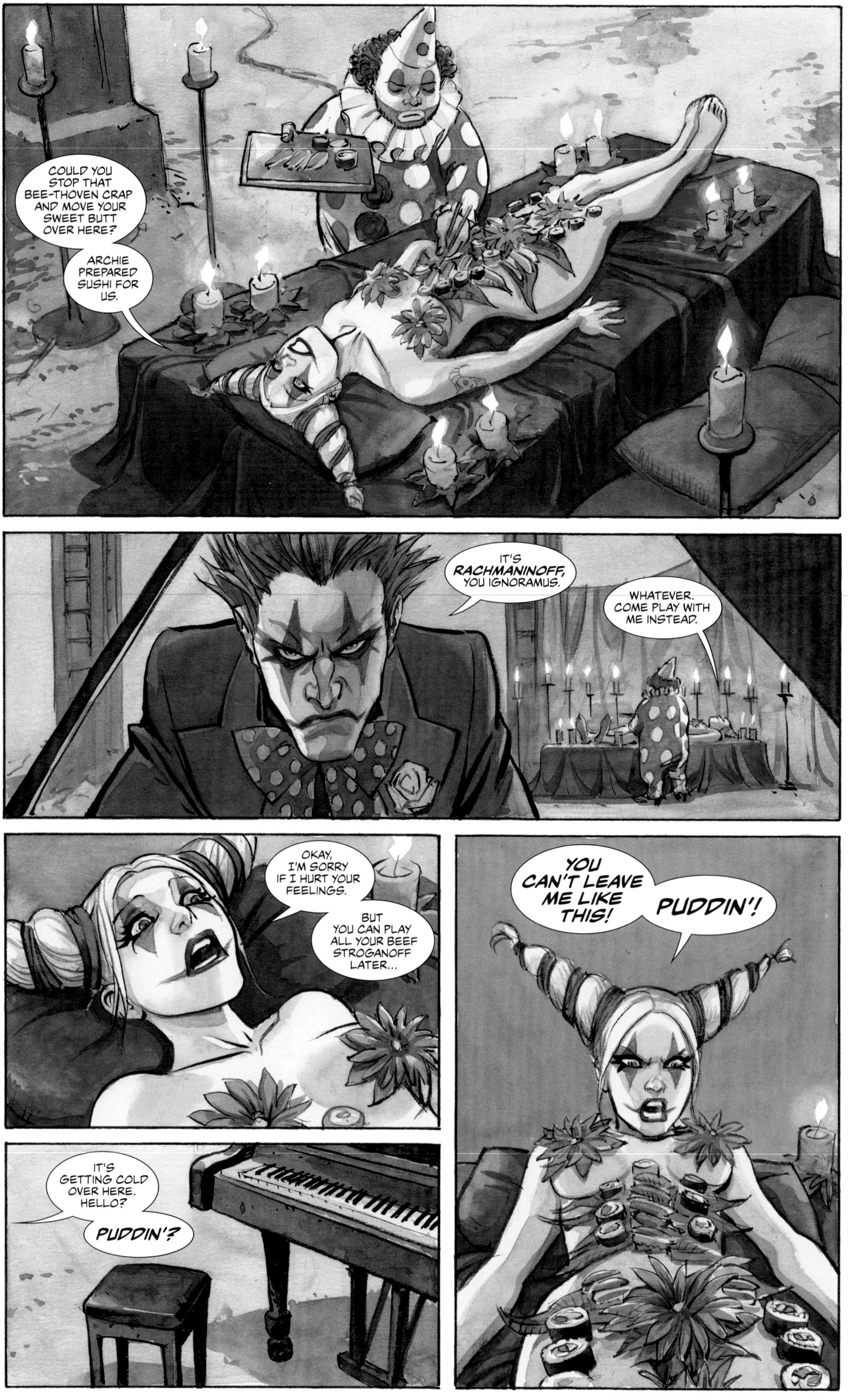
COULD YOU STOP THAT BEE-THOVEN CRAP AND MOVE YOUR SWEET BUTT OVER HERE?
ARCHIE PREPARED SUSHI FOR US.
IT'S *RACHMANINOFF,* YOU IGNORAMUS.
WHATEVER. COME PLAY WITH ME INSTEAD.
OKAY, I'M SORRY IF I HURT YOUR FEELINGS.
BUT YOU CAN PLAY ALL YOUR BEEF STROGANOFF LATER...
IT'S GETTING COLD OVER HERE. HELLO?
PUDDIN'?
YOU CAN'T LEAVE ME LIKE THIS!
PUDDIN'!

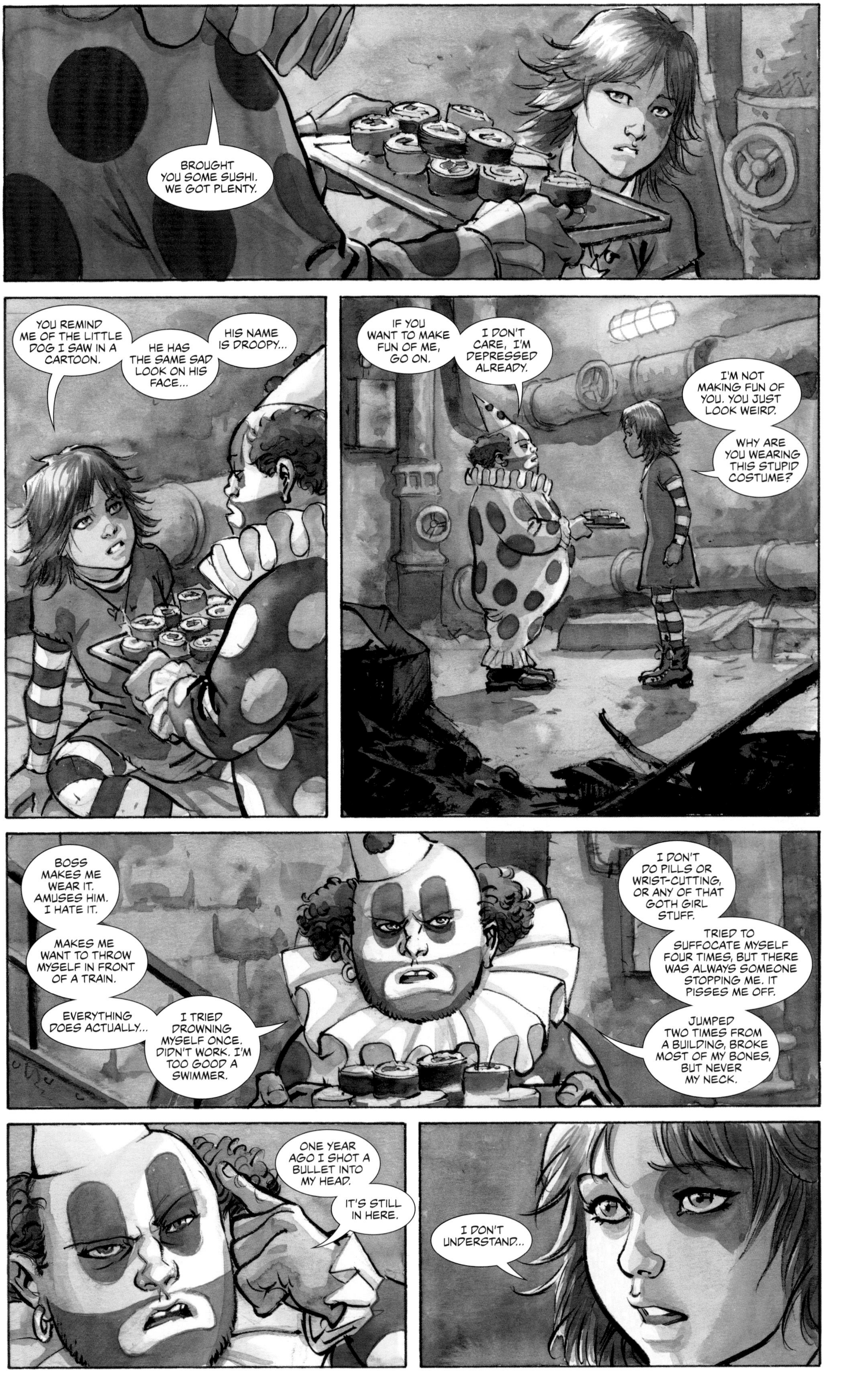
BROUGHT YOU SOME SUSHI. WE GOT PLENTY.
YOU REMIND ME OF THE LITTLE DOG I SAW IN A CARTOON.
HE HAS THE SAME SAD LOOK ON HIS FACE...
HIS NAME IS DROOPY...
IF YOU WANT TO MAKE FUN OF ME, GO ON.
I DON'T CARE, I'M DEPRESSED ALREADY.
I'M NOT MAKING FUN OF YOU. YOU JUST LOOK WEIRD.
WHY ARE YOU WEARING THIS STUPID COSTUME?
BOSS MAKES ME WEAR IT. AMUSES HIM. I HATE IT.
MAKES ME WANT TO THROW MYSELF IN FRONT OF A TRAIN.
EVERYTHING DOES ACTUALLY...
I TRIED DROWNING MYSELF ONCE. DIDN'T WORK. I'M TOO GOOD A SWIMMER.
I DON'T DO PILLS OR WRIST-CUTTING, OR ANY OF THAT GOTH GIRL STUFF.
TRIED TO SUFFOCATE MYSELF FOUR TIMES, BUT THERE WAS ALWAYS SOMEONE STOPPING ME. IT PISSES ME OFF.
JUMPED TWO TIMES FROM A BUILDING, BROKE MOST OF MY BONES, BUT NEVER MY NECK.
ONE YEAR AGO I SHOT A BULLET INTO MY HEAD.
IT'S STILL IN HERE.
I DON'T UNDERSTAND...

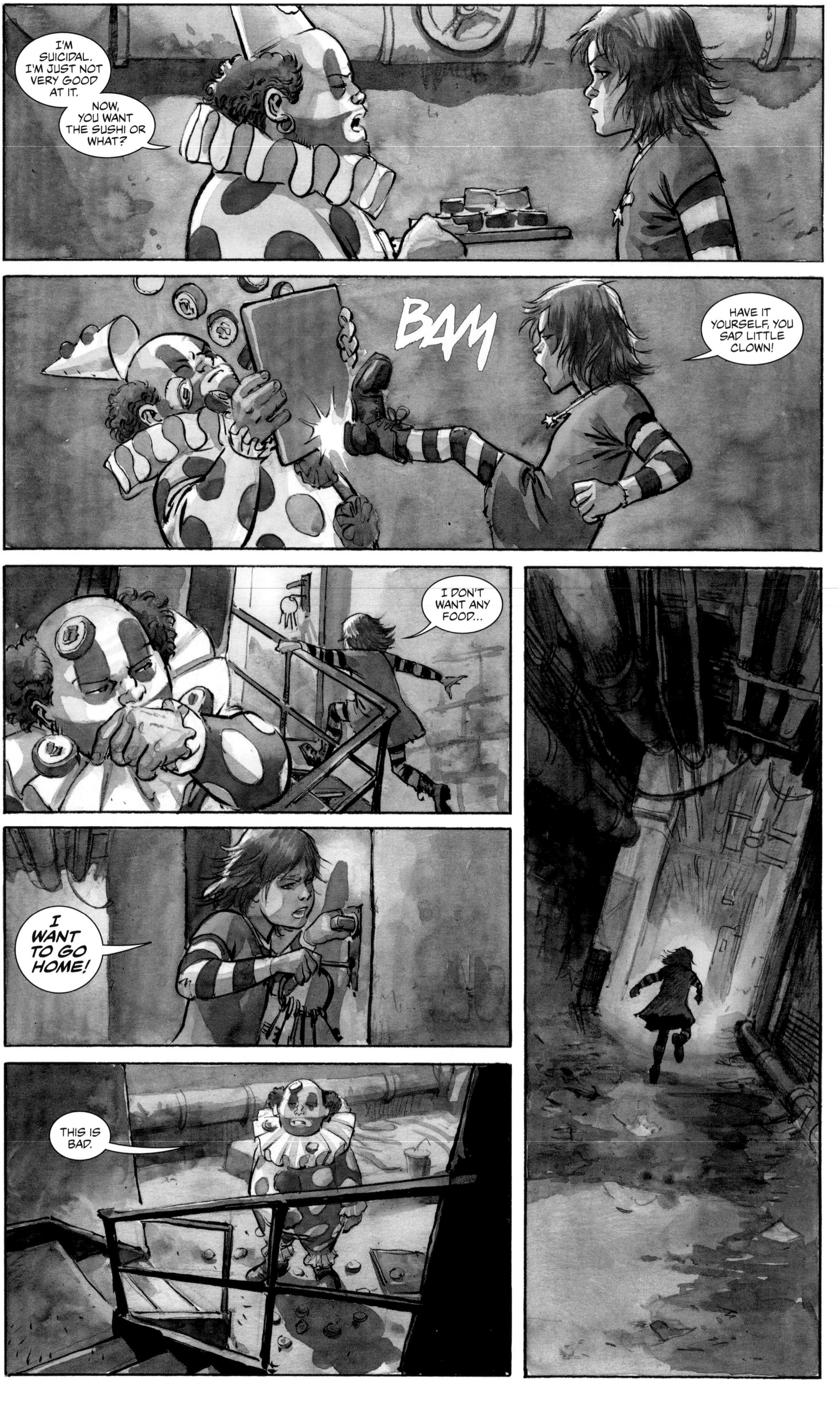
I'M SUICIDAL. I'M JUST NOT VERY GOOD AT IT.
NOW, YOU WANT THE SUSHI OR WHAT?
BAM
HAVE IT YOURSELF, YOU SAD LITTLE CLOWN!
I DON'T WANT ANY FOOD...
I WANT TO GO HOME!
THIS IS BAD.

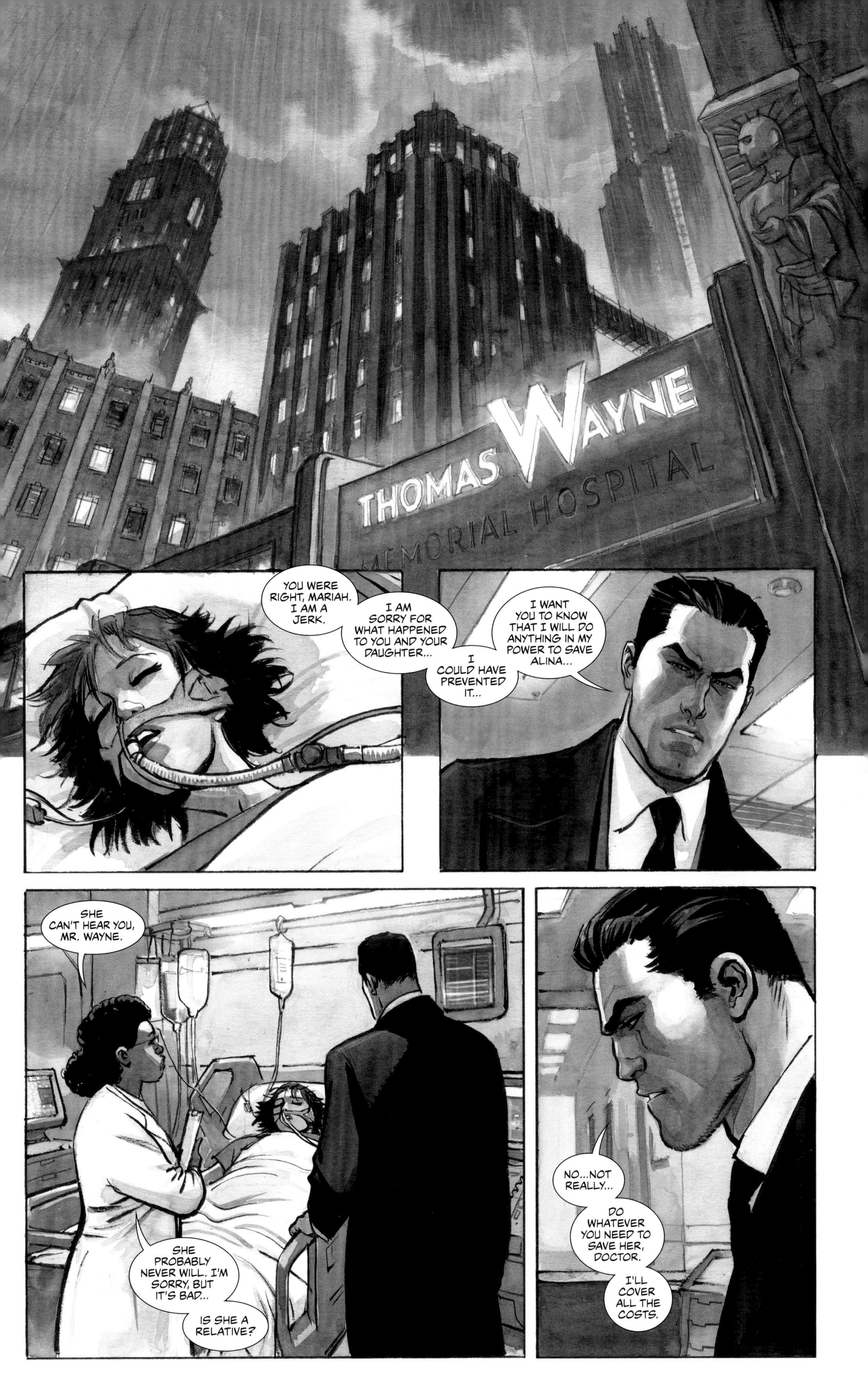
THOMAS WAYNE
MEMORIAL HOSPITAL
YOU WERE RIGHT, MARIAH. I AM A JERK.
I AM SORRY FOR WHAT HAPPENED TO YOU AND YOUR DAUGHTER...
I COULD HAVE PREVENTED IT...
I WANT YOU TO KNOW THAT I WILL DO ANYTHING IN MY POWER TO SAVE ALINA...
SHE CAN'T HEAR YOU, MR. WAYNE.
SHE PROBABLY NEVER WILL. I'M SORRY, BUT IT'S BAD...
IS SHE A RELATIVE?
NO...NOT REALLY...
DO WHATEVER YOU NEED TO SAVE HER, DOCTOR.
I'LL COVER ALL THE COSTS.

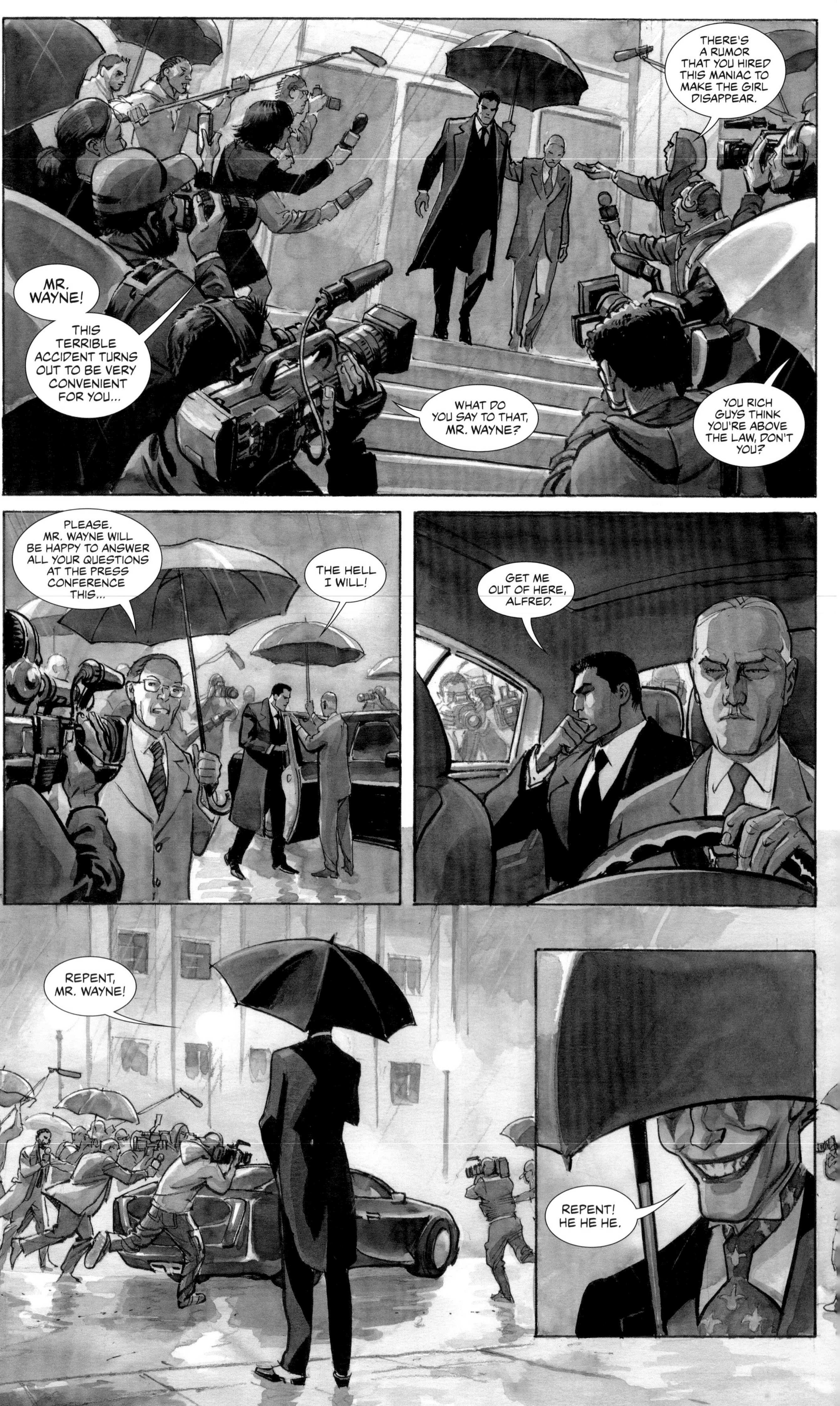
THERE'S A RUMOR THAT YOU HIRED THIS MANIAC TO MAKE THE GIRL DISAPPEAR.
MR. WAYNE!
THIS TERRIBLE ACCIDENT TURNS OUT TO BE VERY CONVENIENT FOR YOU...
WHAT DO YOU SAY TO THAT, MR. WAYNE?
YOU RICH GUYS THINK YOU'RE ABOVE THE LAW, DON'T YOU?
PLEASE. MR. WAYNE WILL BE HAPPY TO ANSWER ALL YOUR QUESTIONS AT THE PRESS CONFERENCE THIS...
THE HELL I WILL!
GET ME OUT OF HERE, ALFRED.
REPENT, MR. WAYNE!
REPENT! HE HE HE.

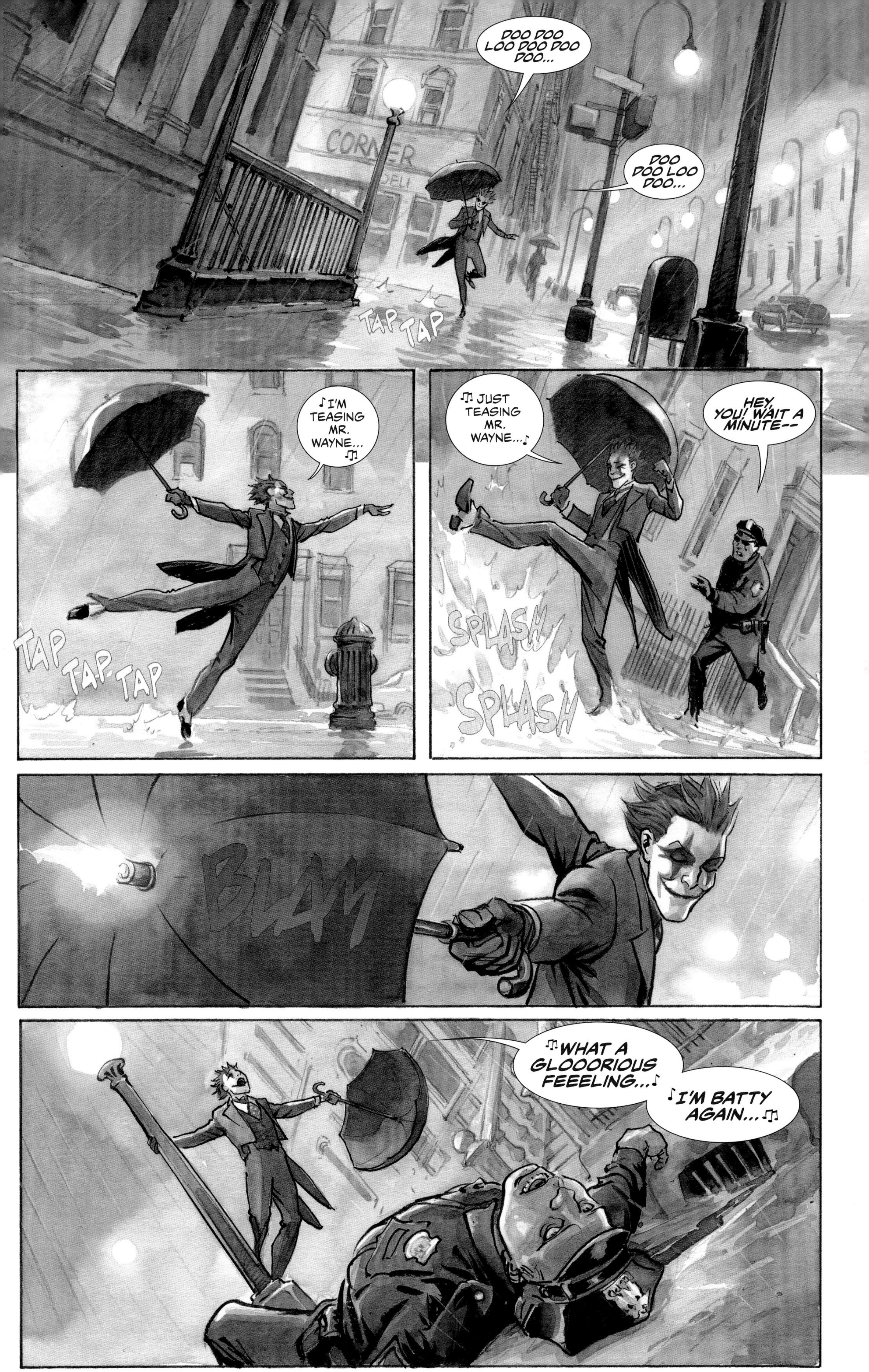
DOO DOO LOO DOO DOO DOO...
DOO DOO LOO DOO...
CORNER
DELI
TAP TAP
♪I'M TEASING MR. WAYNE... ♫
TAP TAP TAP
♫ JUST TEASING MR. WAYNE...♪
HEY, YOU! WAIT A MINUTE--
SPLASH
SPLASH
BLAM
♫WHAT A GLOOORIOUS FEEELING...♪
♪I'M BATTY AGAIN...♫

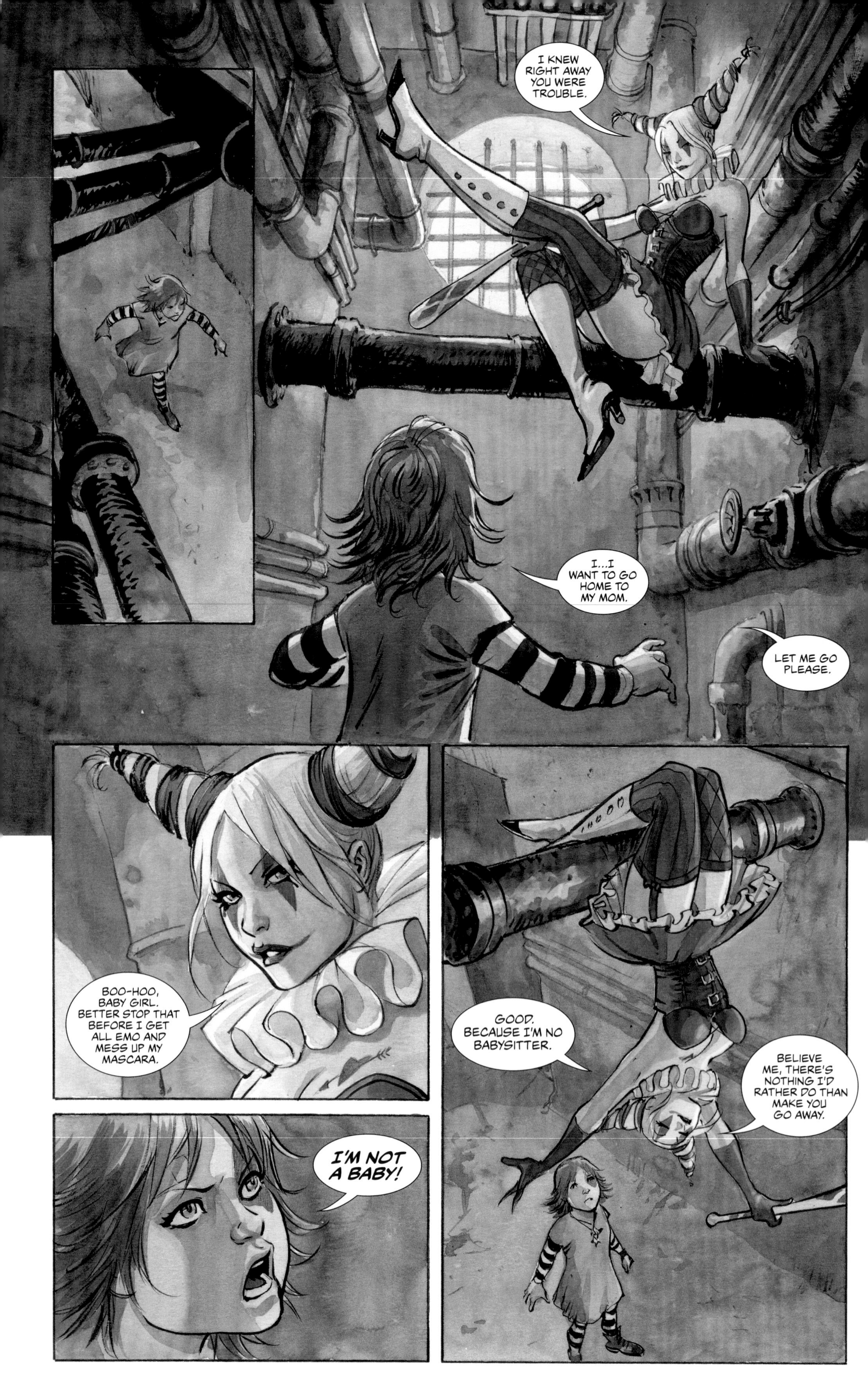
I KNEW RIGHT AWAY YOU WERE TROUBLE.
I...I WANT TO GO HOME TO MY MOM.
LET ME GO PLEASE.
BOO-HOO, BABY GIRL. BETTER STOP THAT BEFORE I GET ALL EMO AND MESS UP MY MASCARA.
I'M NOT A BABY!
GOOD. BECAUSE I'M NO BABYSITTER.
BELIEVE ME, THERE'S NOTHING I'D RATHER DO THAN MAKE YOU GO AWAY.

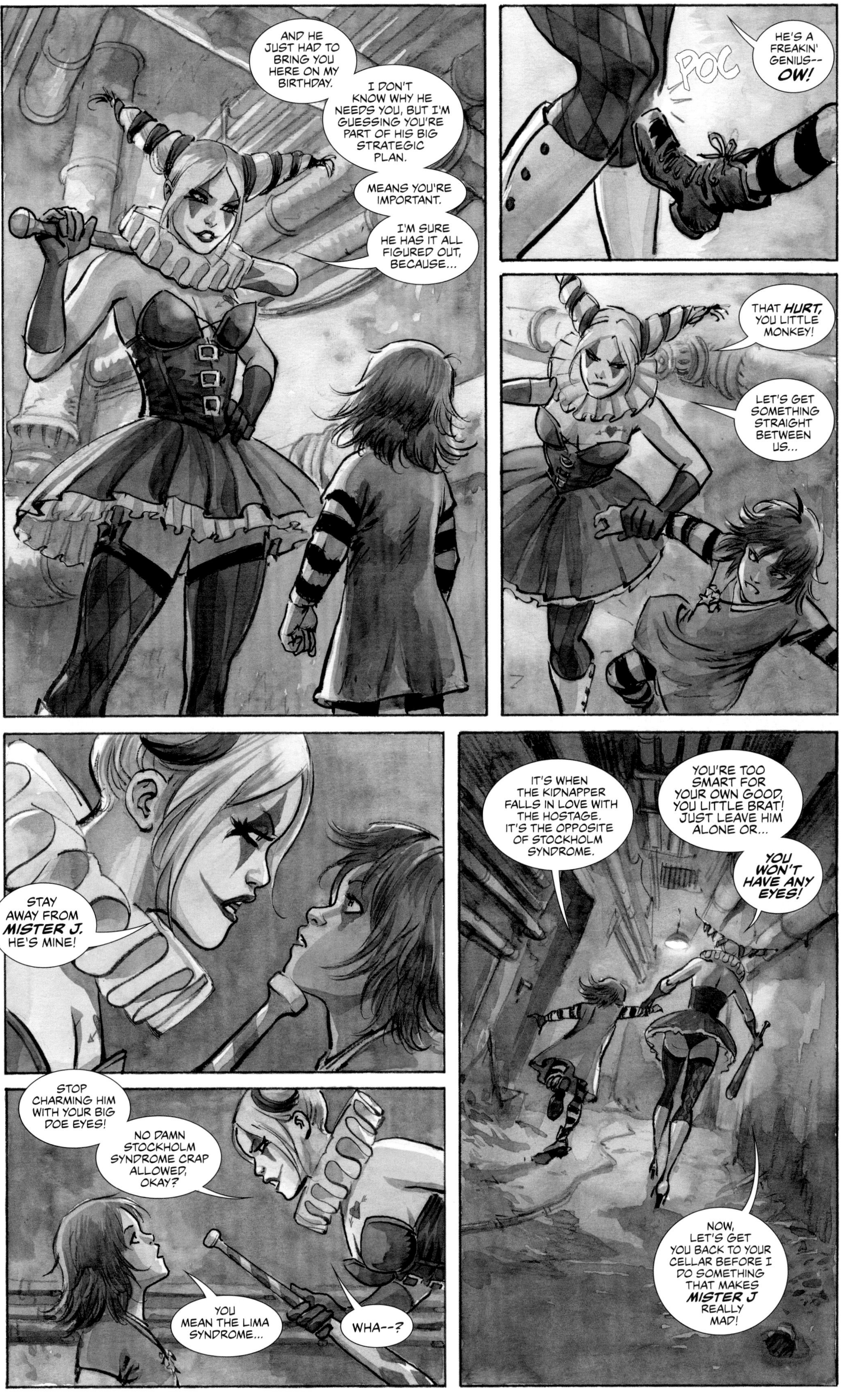
AND HE JUST HAD TO BRING YOU HERE ON MY BIRTHDAY.
I DON'T KNOW WHY HE NEEDS YOU, BUT I'M GUESSING YOU'RE PART OF HIS BIG STRATEGIC PLAN.
MEANS YOU'RE IMPORTANT.
I'M SURE HE HAS IT ALL FIGURED OUT, BECAUSE...
POC
HE'S A FREAKIN' GENIUS-- OW!
THAT HURT, YOU LITTLE MONKEY!
LET'S GET SOMETHING STRAIGHT BETWEEN US...
STAY AWAY FROM MISTER J. HE'S MINE!
STOP CHARMING HIM WITH YOUR BIG DOE EYES!
NO DAMN STOCKHOLM SYNDROME CRAP ALLOWED, OKAY?
YOU MEAN THE LIMA SYNDROME...
WHA--?
IT'S WHEN THE KIDNAPPER FALLS IN LOVE WITH THE HOSTAGE. IT'S THE OPPOSITE OF STOCKHOLM SYNDROME.
YOU'RE TOO SMART FOR YOUR OWN GOOD, YOU LITTLE BRAT! JUST LEAVE HIM ALONE OR...
YOU WON'T HAVE ANY EYES!
NOW, LET'S GET YOU BACK TO YOUR CELLAR BEFORE I DO SOMETHING THAT MAKES MISTER J REALLY MAD!

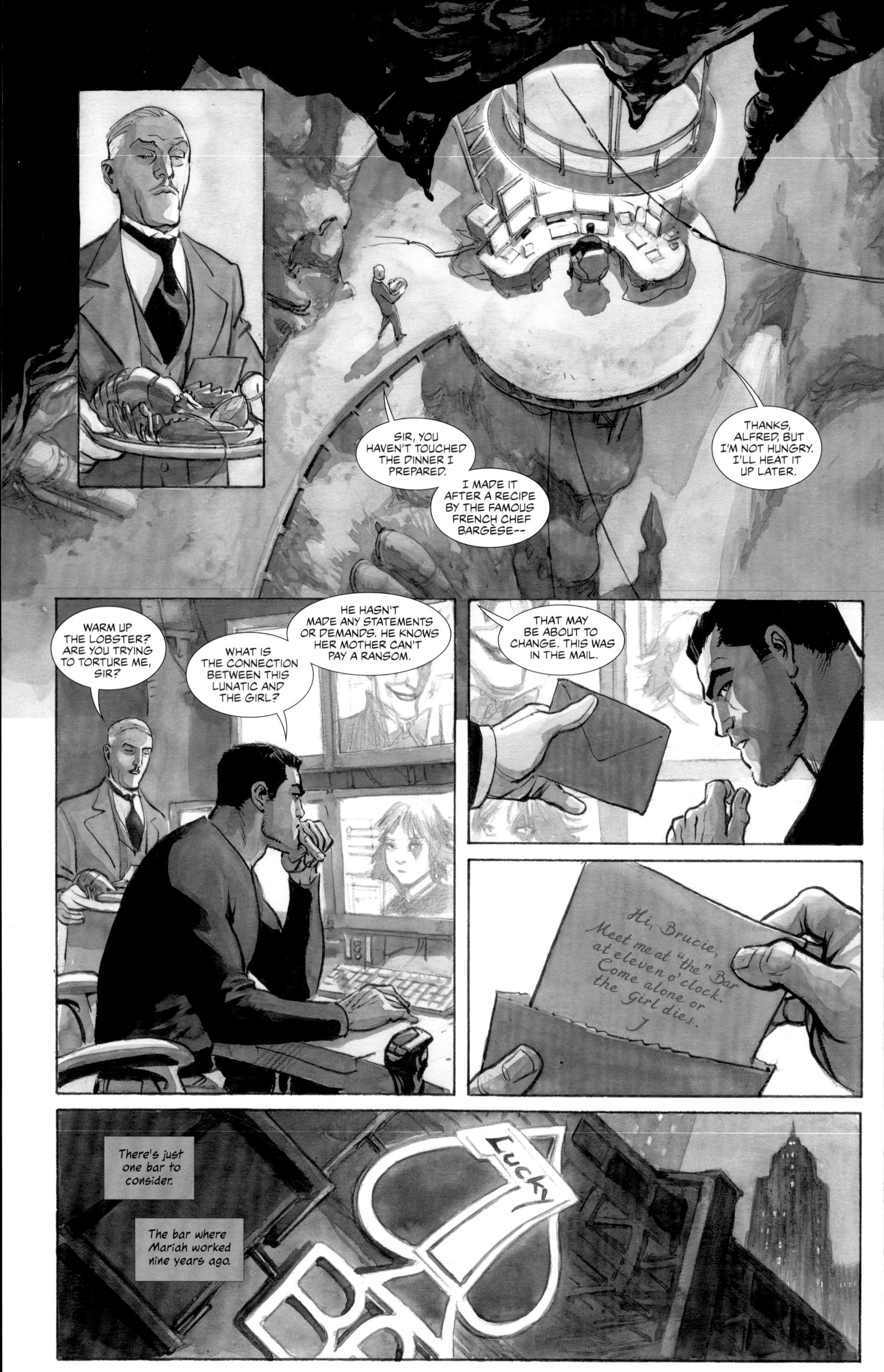
SIR, YOU HAVEN'T TOUCHED THE DINNER I PREPARED.
I MADE IT AFTER A RECIPE BY THE FAMOUS FRENCH CHEF BARGÈSE--
THANKS, ALFRED, BUT I'M NOT HUNGRY. I'LL HEAT IT UP LATER.
WARM UP THE LOBSTER? ARE YOU TRYING TO TORTURE ME, SIR?
WHAT IS THE CONNECTION BETWEEN THIS LUNATIC AND THE GIRL?
HE HASN'T MADE ANY STATEMENTS OR DEMANDS. HE KNOWS HER MOTHER CAN'T PAY A RANSOM.
THAT MAY BE ABOUT TO CHANGE. THIS WAS IN THE MAIL.
Hi, Brucie, Meet me at "the" Bar at eleven o'clock. Come alone or the Girl dies. J
There's just one bar to consider.
The bar where Mariah worked nine years ago.
Lucky

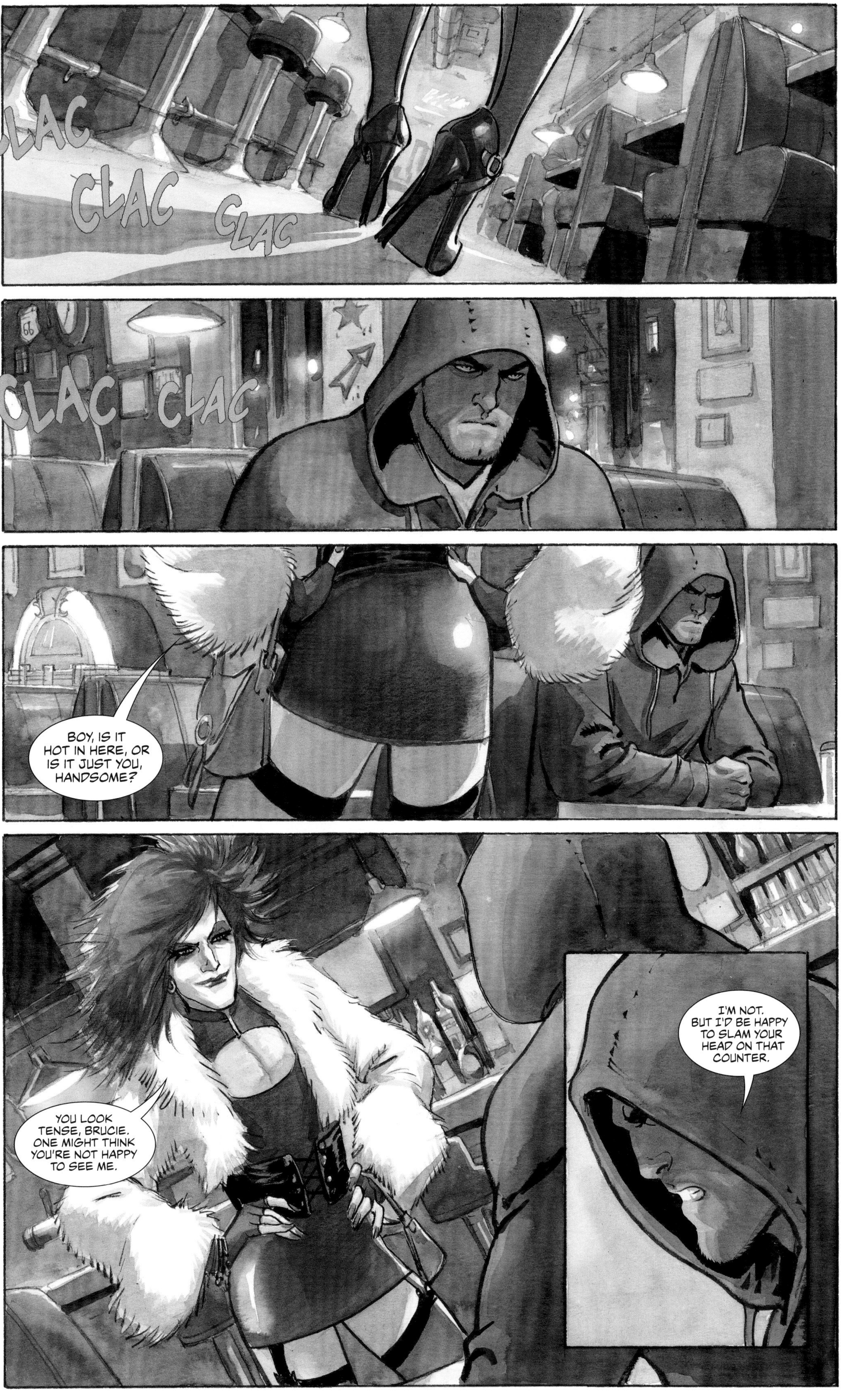
CLAC
CLAC
CLAC
CLAC
CLAC
BOY, IS IT HOT IN HERE, OR IS IT JUST YOU, HANDSOME?
YOU LOOK TENSE, BRUCIE. ONE MIGHT THINK YOU'RE NOT HAPPY TO SEE ME.
I'M NOT. BUT I'D BE HAPPY TO SLAM YOUR HEAD ON THAT COUNTER.

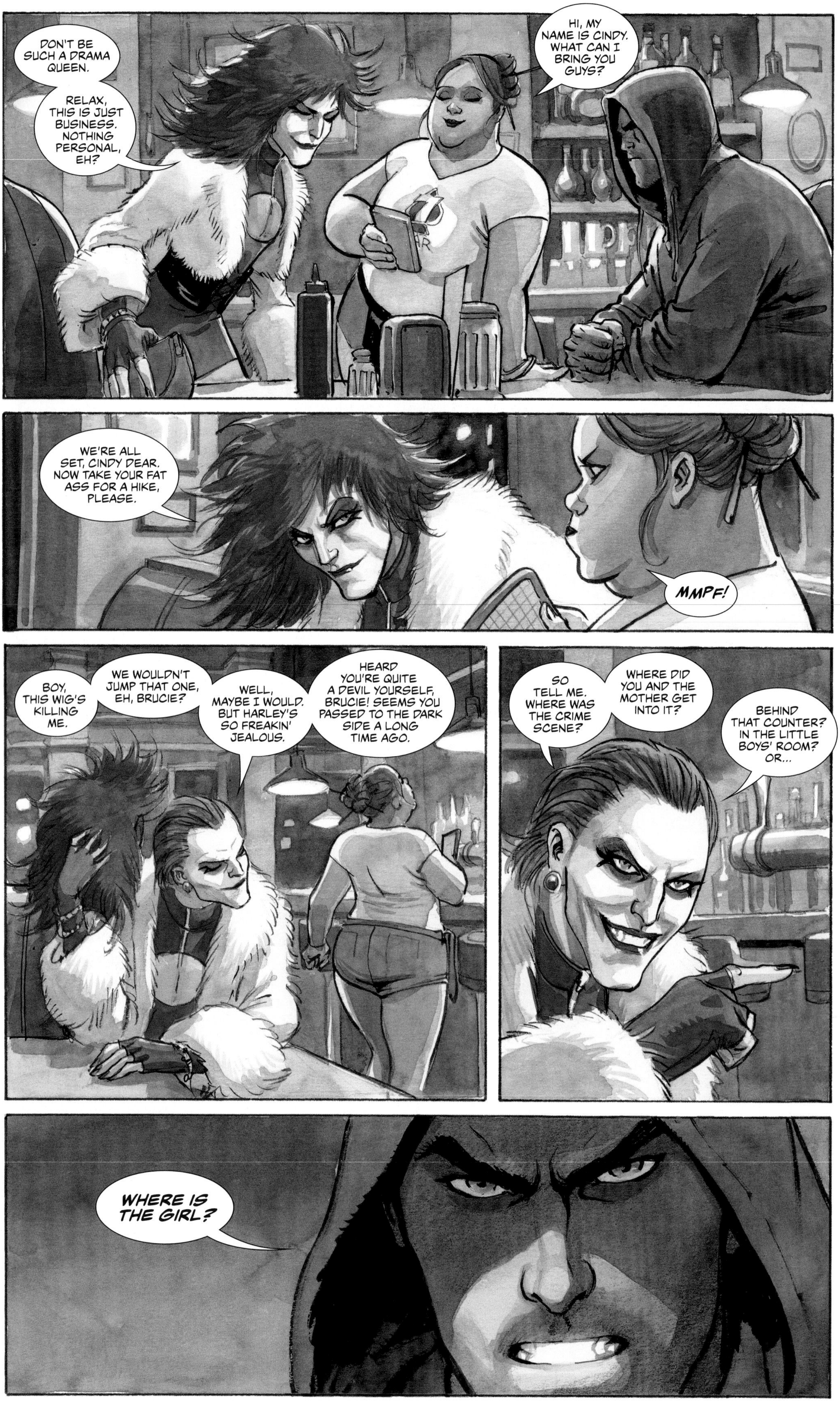
DON'T BE SUCH A DRAMA QUEEN.
RELAX, THIS IS JUST BUSINESS. NOTHING PERSONAL, EH?
HI, MY NAME IS CINDY. WHAT CAN I BRING YOU GUYS?
WE'RE ALL SET, CINDY DEAR. NOW TAKE YOUR FAT ASS FOR A HIKE, PLEASE.
MMPF!
BOY, THIS WIG'S KILLING ME.
WE WOULDN'T JUMP THAT ONE, EH, BRUCIE?
WELL, MAYBE I WOULD. BUT HARLEY'S SO FREAKIN' JEALOUS.
HEARD YOU'RE QUITE A DEVIL YOURSELF, BRUCIE! SEEMS YOU PASSED TO THE DARK SIDE A LONG TIME AGO.
SO TELL ME. WHERE WAS THE CRIME SCENE?
WHERE DID YOU AND THE MOTHER GET INTO IT?
BEHIND THAT COUNTER? IN THE LITTLE BOYS' ROOM? OR...
WHERE IS THE GIRL?

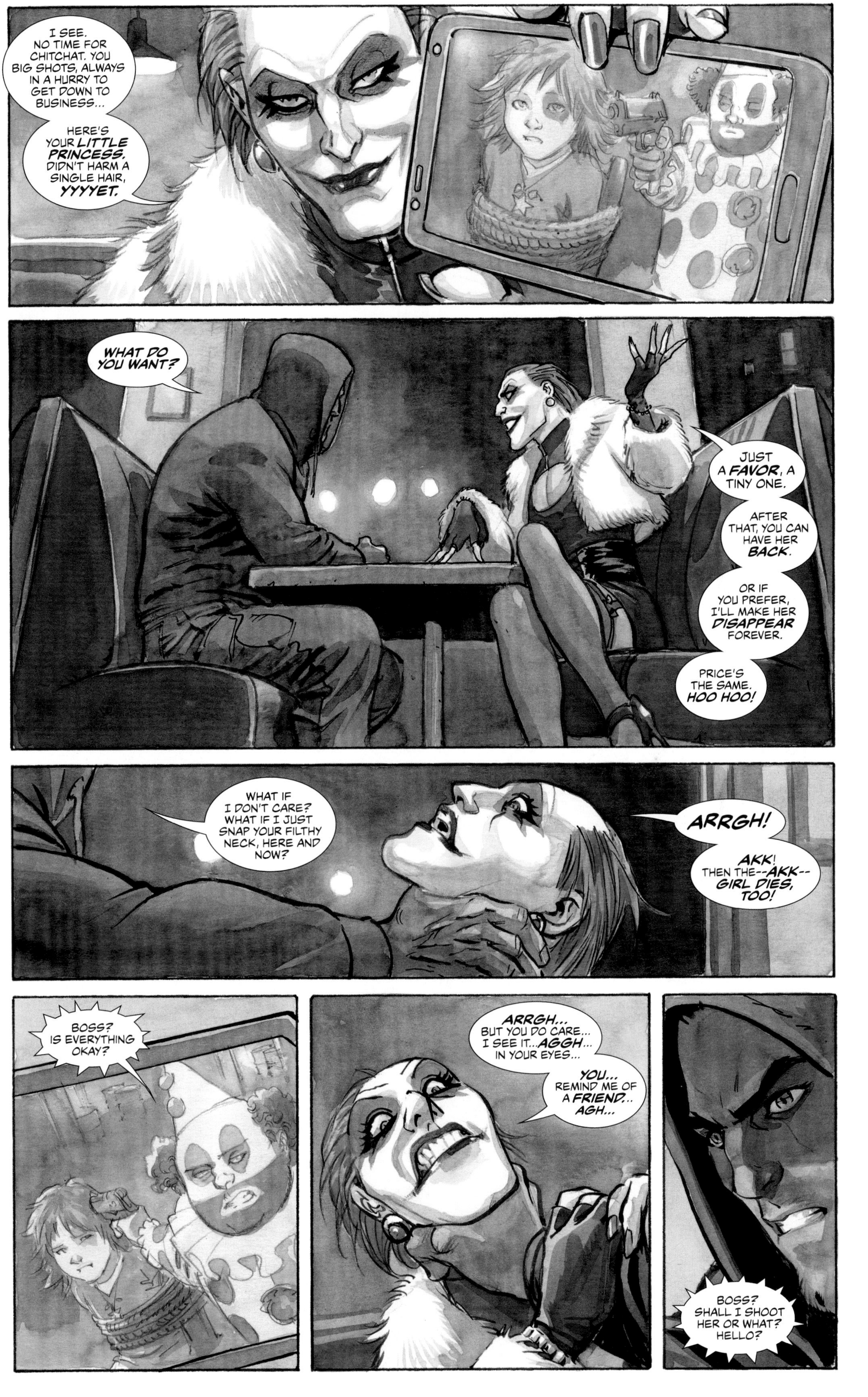
I SEE. NO TIME FOR CHITCHAT. YOU BIG SHOTS, ALWAYS IN A HURRY TO GET DOWN TO BUSINESS...
HERE'S YOUR LITTLE PRINCESS. DIDN'T HARM A SINGLE HAIR, YYYYET.
WHAT DO YOU WANT?
JUST A FAVOR, A TINY ONE.
AFTER THAT, YOU CAN HAVE HER BACK.
OR IF YOU PREFER, I'LL MAKE HER DISAPPEAR FOREVER.
PRICE'S THE SAME. HOO HOO!
WHAT IF I DON'T CARE? WHAT IF I JUST SNAP YOUR FILTHY NECK, HERE AND NOW?
ARRGH!
AKK! THEN THE--AKK--GIRL DIES, TOO!
BOSS? IS EVERYTHING OKAY?
ARRGH... BUT YOU DO CARE... I SEE IT...AGGH... IN YOUR EYES...
YOU... REMIND ME OF A FRIEND... AGH...
BOSS? SHALL I SHOOT HER OR WHAT? HELLO?

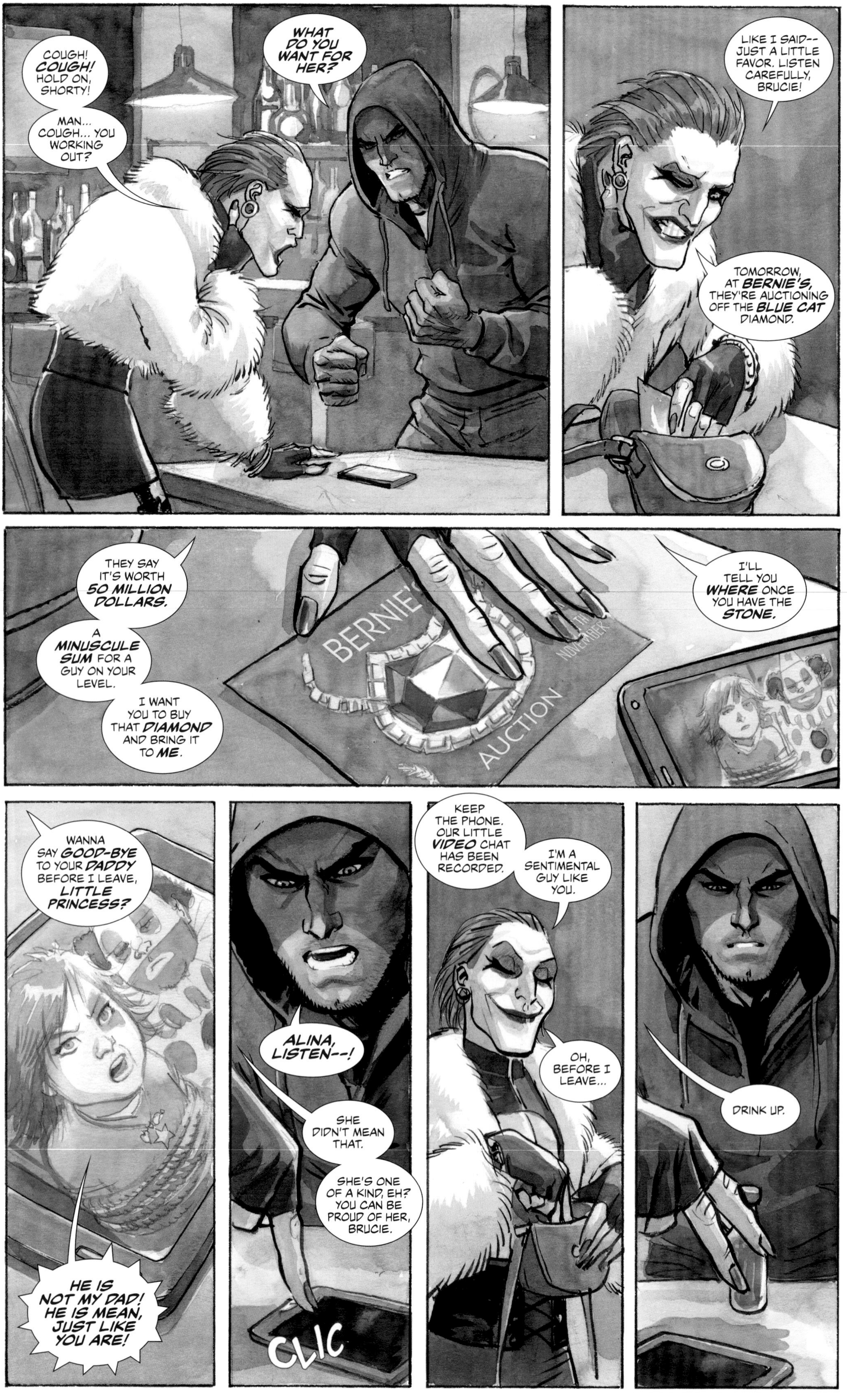
COUGH! COUGH! HOLD ON, SHORTY!
MAN... COUGH... YOU WORKING OUT?
WHAT DO YOU WANT FOR HER?
LIKE I SAID-- JUST A LITTLE FAVOR. LISTEN CAREFULLY, BRUCIE!
TOMORROW, AT BERNIE'S, THEY'RE AUCTIONING OFF THE BLUE CAT DIAMOND.
THEY SAY IT'S WORTH 50 MILLION DOLLARS.
A MINUSCULE SUM FOR A GUY ON YOUR LEVEL.
I WANT YOU TO BUY THAT DIAMOND AND BRING IT TO ME.
BERNIE'S
AUCTION
I'LL TELL YOU WHERE ONCE YOU HAVE THE STONE.
WANNA SAY GOOD-BYE TO YOUR DADDY BEFORE I LEAVE, LITTLE PRINCESS?
HE IS NOT MY DAD! HE IS MEAN, JUST LIKE YOU ARE!
ALINA, LISTEN--!
SHE DIDN'T MEAN THAT.
SHE'S ONE OF A KIND, EH? YOU CAN BE PROUD OF HER, BRUCIE.
CLIC
KEEP THE PHONE. OUR LITTLE VIDEO CHAT HAS BEEN RECORDED.
I'M A SENTIMENTAL GUY LIKE YOU.
OH, BEFORE I LEAVE...
DRINK UP.

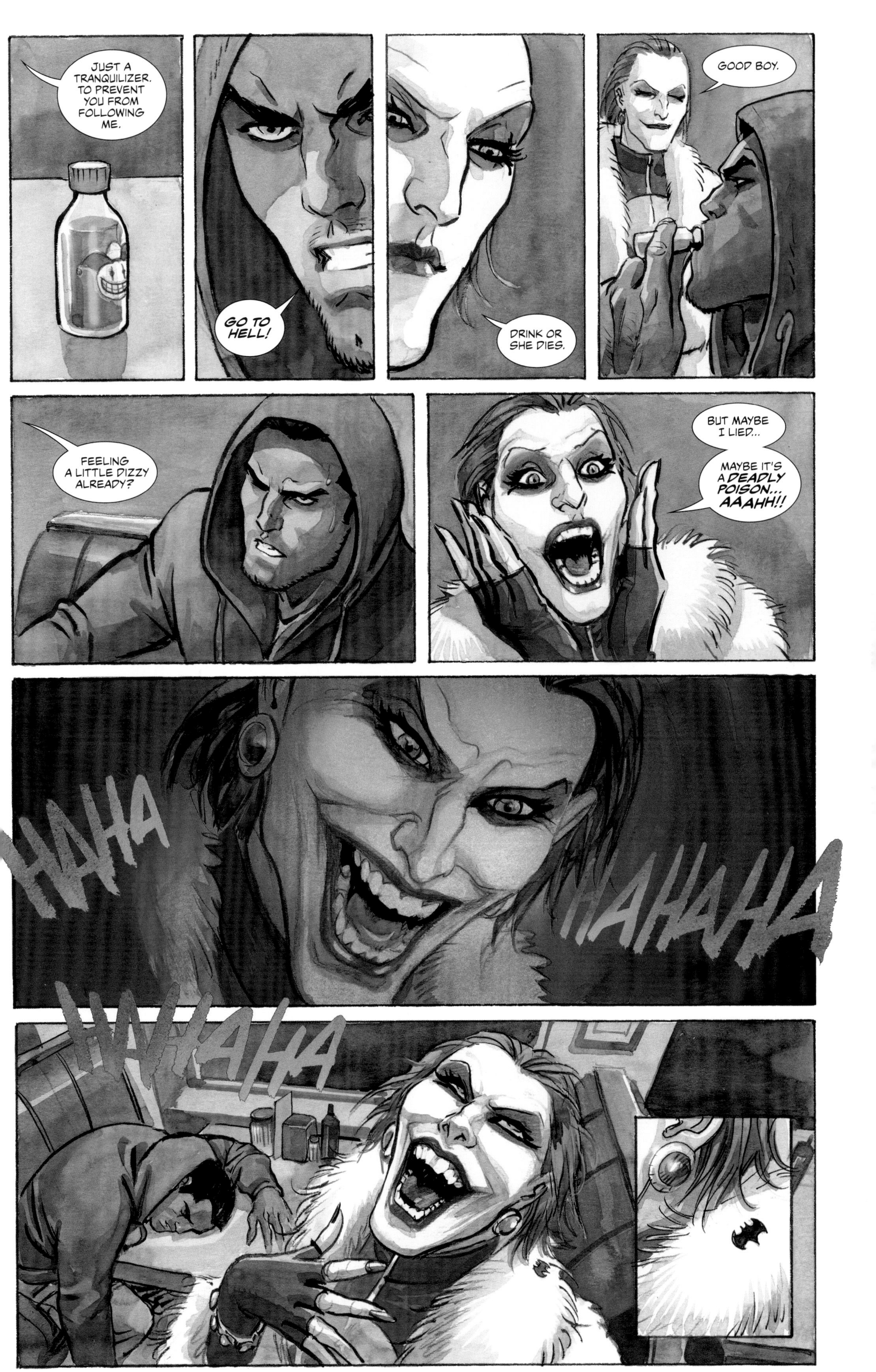
JUST A TRANQUILIZER. TO PREVENT YOU FROM FOLLOWING ME.
GO TO HELL!
DRINK OR SHE DIES.
GOOD BOY.
FEELING A LITTLE DIZZY ALREADY?
BUT MAYBE I LIED...
MAYBE IT'S A DEADLY POISON... AAAHH!!
HAHA
HAHAHA
HAHAHA

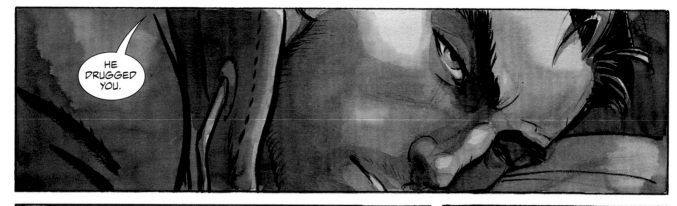

HE DRUGGED YOU.

I DRUGGED MYSELF ACTUALLY.

I BEG YOUR PARDON, SIR?

NEVER MIND. THANKS FOR PICKING ME UP.

I FOUND THIS IN THE ALLEY NEXT TO THE BAR. WE LOST HIM.

WHAT IF THE DRUG HAD BEEN LETHAL?

HE'S HOLDING ALL THE CARDS. IF HE REALLY WANTS THIS DIAMOND, I'M NO GOOD TO HIM DEAD.

"STILL, IT WAS QUITE THE RISK.

"LET'S JUST HOPE THERE ARE NO LINGERING EFFECTS AND THAT ALL HE GAVE YOU WAS A HEALTHY POWER NAP, SIR."

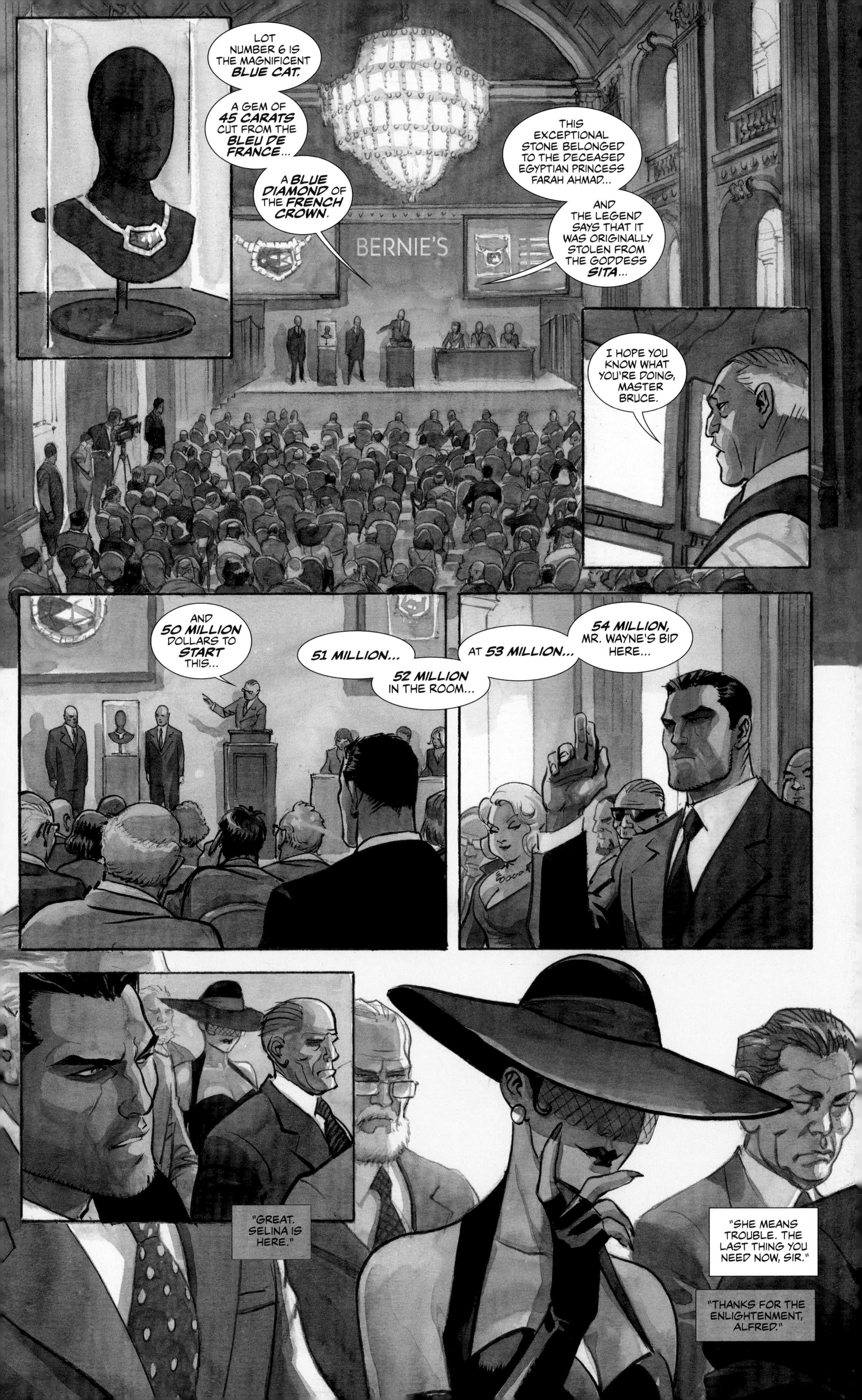
LOT NUMBER 6 IS THE MAGNIFICENT BLUE CAT.
A GEM OF 45 CARATS CUT FROM THE BLEU DE FRANCE...
A BLUE DIAMOND OF THE FRENCH CROWN.
THIS EXCEPTIONAL STONE BELONGED TO THE DECEASED EGYPTIAN PRINCESS FARAH AHMAD...
AND THE LEGEND SAYS THAT IT WAS ORIGINALLY STOLEN FROM THE GODDESS SITA...
BERNIE'S
I HOPE YOU KNOW WHAT YOU'RE DOING, MASTER BRUCE.
AND 50 MILLION DOLLARS TO START THIS...
51 MILLION...
52 MILLION IN THE ROOM...
AT 53 MILLION...
54 MILLION, MR. WAYNE'S BID HERE...
"GREAT. SELINA IS HERE."
"SHE MEANS TROUBLE. THE LAST THING YOU NEED NOW, SIR."
"THANKS FOR THE ENLIGHTENMENT, ALFRED."

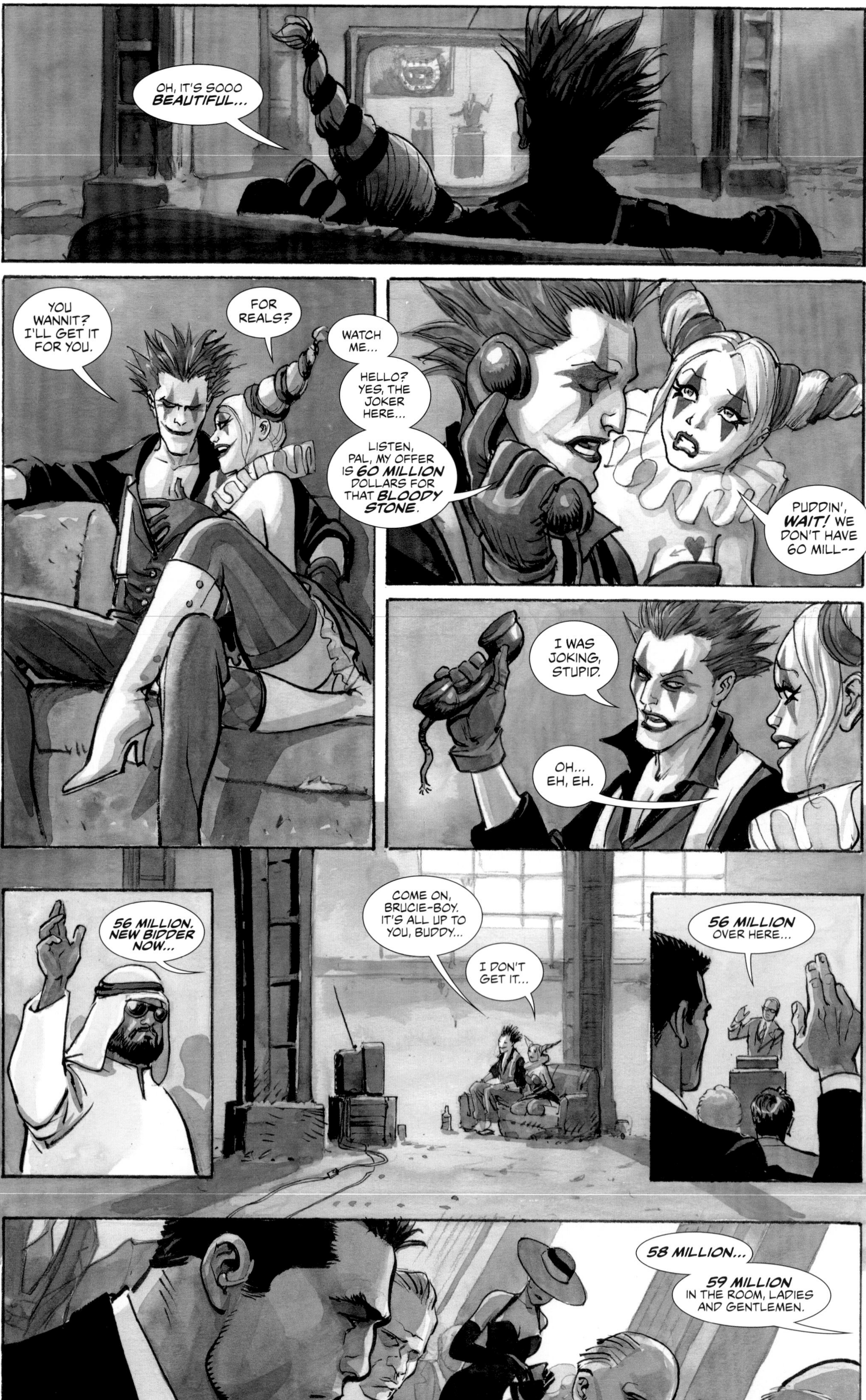
OH, IT'S SOOO BEAUTIFUL...
YOU WANNIT? I'LL GET IT FOR YOU.
FOR REALS?
WATCH ME...
HELLO? YES, THE JOKER HERE...
LISTEN, PAL, MY OFFER IS 60 MILLION DOLLARS FOR THAT BLOODY STONE.
PUDDIN', WAIT! WE DON'T HAVE 60 MILL--
I WAS JOKING, STUPID.
OH... EH, EH.
56 MILLION. NEW BIDDER NOW...
COME ON, BRUCIE-BOY. IT'S ALL UP TO YOU, BUDDY...
I DON'T GET IT...
56 MILLION OVER HERE...
58 MILLION...
59 MILLION IN THE ROOM, LADIES AND GENTLEMEN.

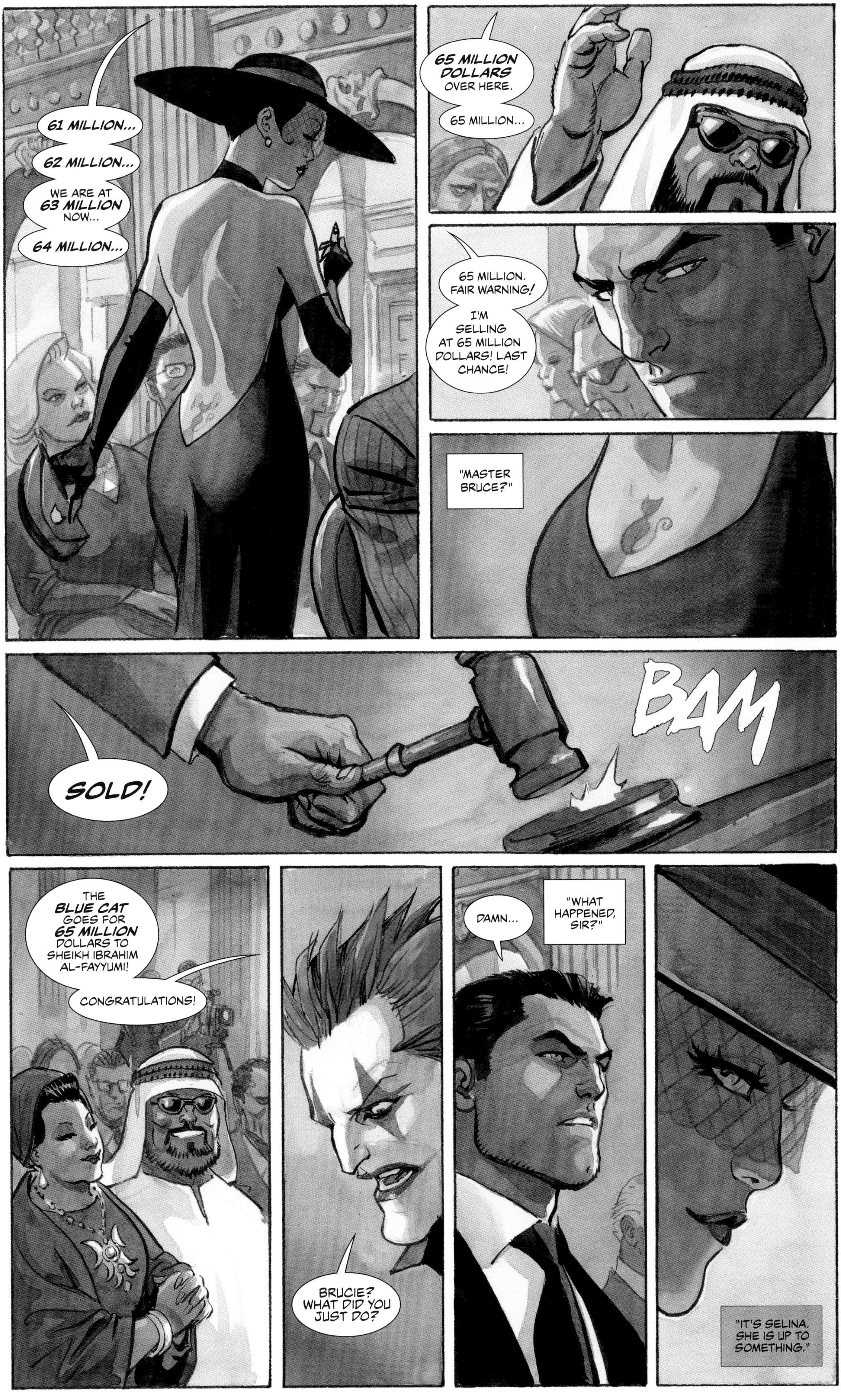
61 MILLION...
62 MILLION...
WE ARE AT 63 MILLION NOW...
64 MILLION...
65 MILLION DOLLARS OVER HERE.
65 MILLION...
65 MILLION. FAIR WARNING!
I'M SELLING AT 65 MILLION DOLLARS! LAST CHANCE!
"MASTER BRUCE?"
SOLD!
BAM
THE BLUE CAT GOES FOR 65 MILLION DOLLARS TO SHEIKH IBRAHIM AL-FAYYUMI!
CONGRATULATIONS!
BRUCIE? WHAT DID YOU JUST DO?
DAMN...
"WHAT HAPPENED, SIR?"
"IT'S SELINA. SHE IS UP TO SOMETHING."

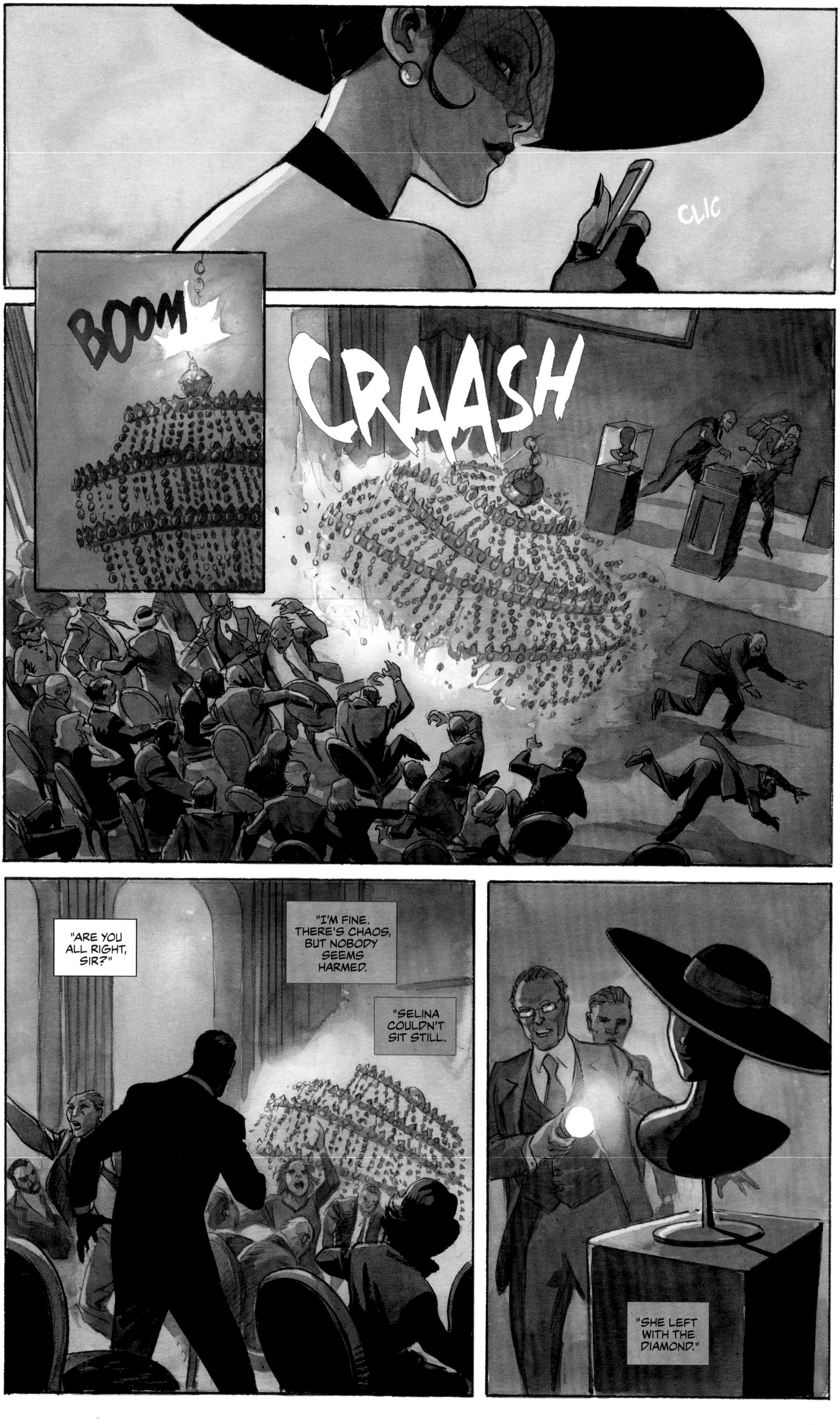
CLIC
BOOM
CRAASH
"ARE YOU ALL RIGHT, SIR?"
"I'M FINE. THERE'S CHAOS, BUT NOBODY SEEMS HARMED.
"SELINA COULDN'T SIT STILL.
"SHE LEFT WITH THE DIAMOND."

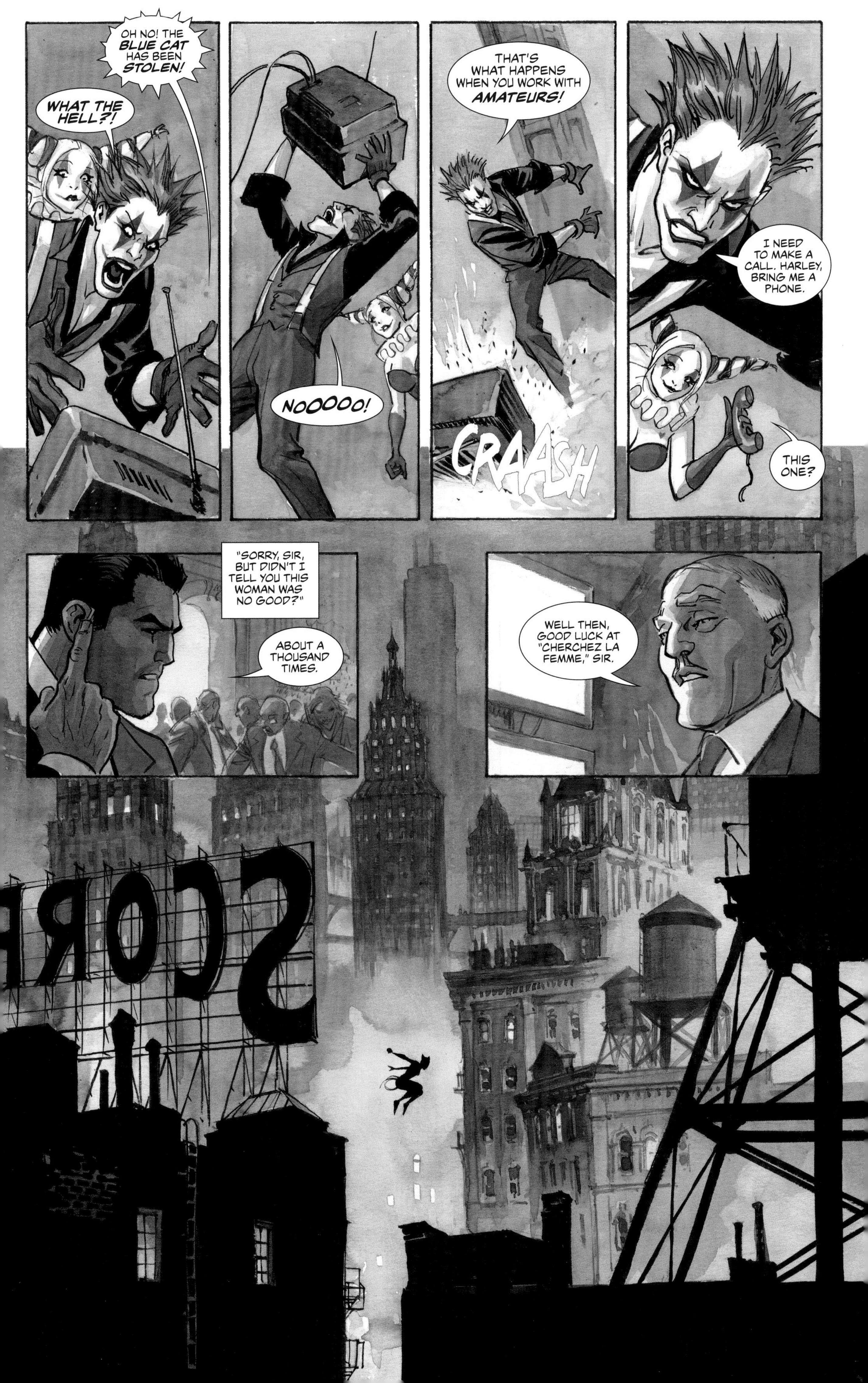

OH NO! THE BLUE CAT HAS BEEN STOLEN!
WHAT THE HELL?!
NOOOOO!
THAT'S WHAT HAPPENS WHEN YOU WORK WITH AMATEURS!
CRAASH
I NEED TO MAKE A CALL. HARLEY, BRING ME A PHONE.
THIS ONE?
"SORRY, SIR, BUT DIDN'T I TELL YOU THIS WOMAN WAS NO GOOD?"
ABOUT A THOUSAND TIMES.
WELL THEN, GOOD LUCK AT "CHERCHEZ LA FEMME," SIR.
SCOR

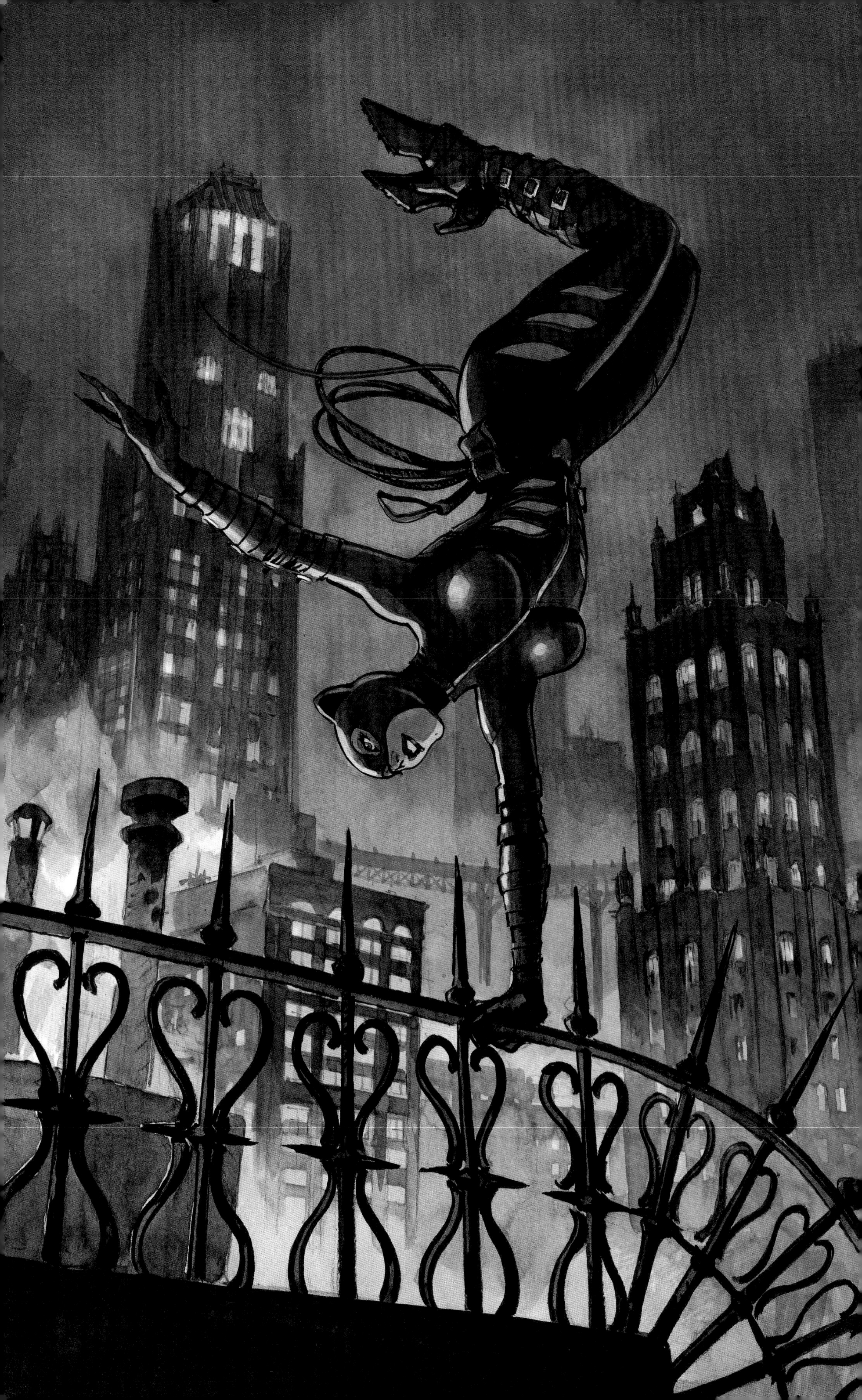

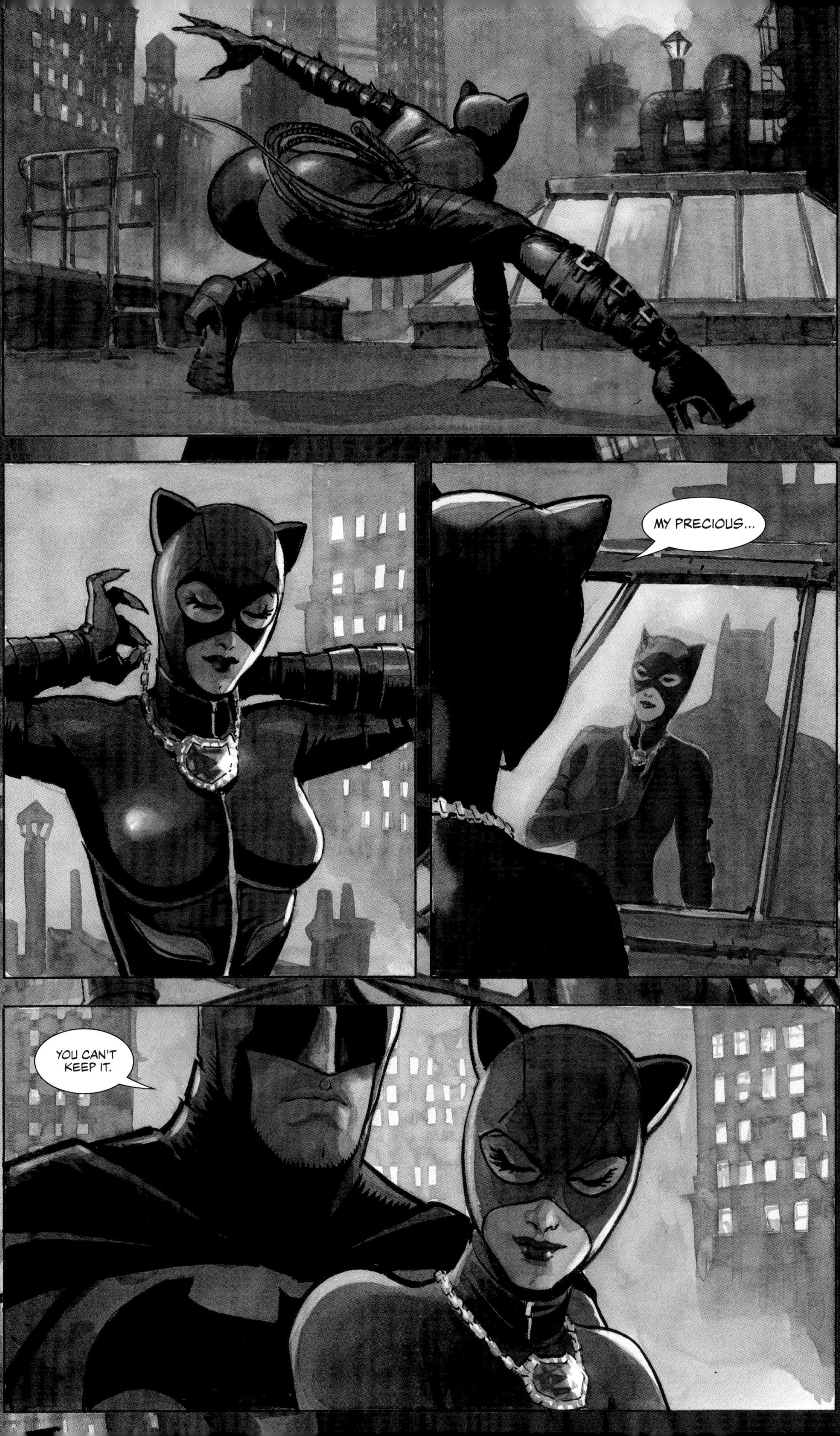
MY PRECIOUS...
YOU CAN'T KEEP IT.

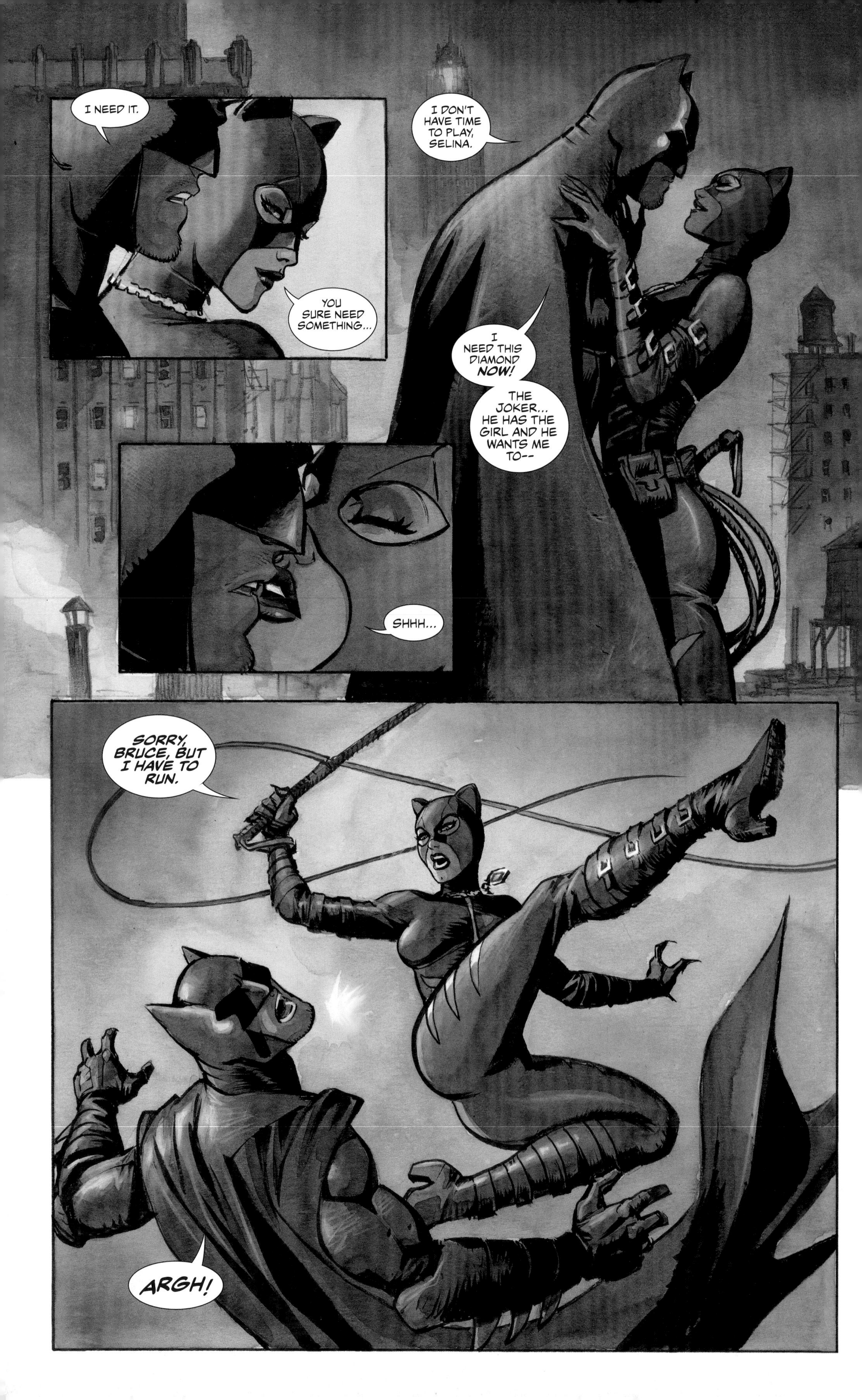
I NEED IT.
I DON'T HAVE TIME TO PLAY, SELINA.
YOU SURE NEED SOMETHING...
I NEED THIS DIAMOND *NOW!*
THE JOKER... HE HAS THE GIRL AND HE WANTS ME TO--
SHHH...
SORRY, BRUCE, BUT I HAVE TO RUN.
ARGH!

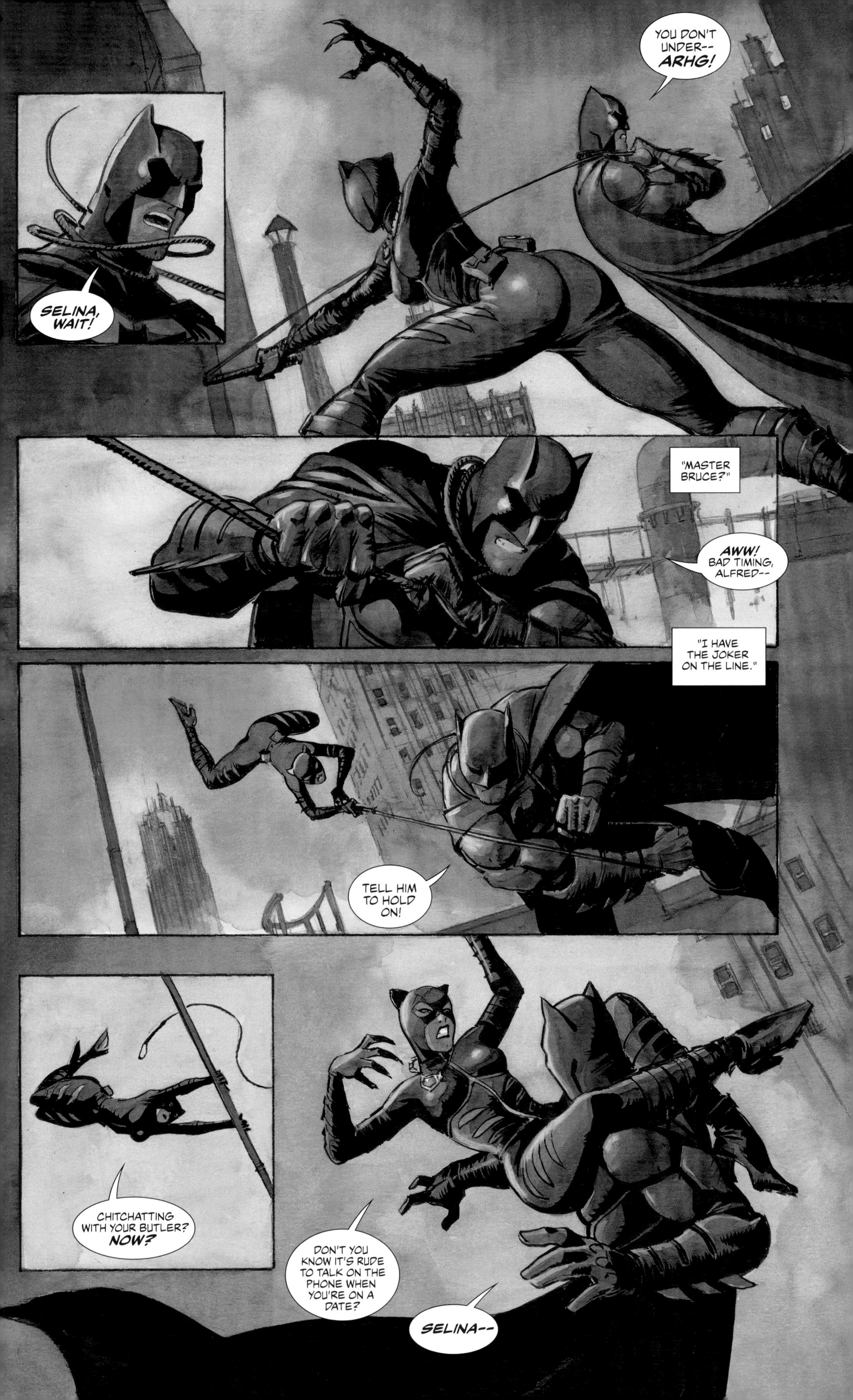

YOU DON'T UNDER-- ARHG!
SELINA, WAIT!
"MASTER BRUCE?"
AWW! BAD TIMING, ALFRED--
"I HAVE THE JOKER ON THE LINE."
TELL HIM TO HOLD ON!
CHITCHATTING WITH YOUR BUTLER? NOW?
DON'T YOU KNOW IT'S RUDE TO TALK ON THE PHONE WHEN YOU'RE ON A DATE?
SELINA--

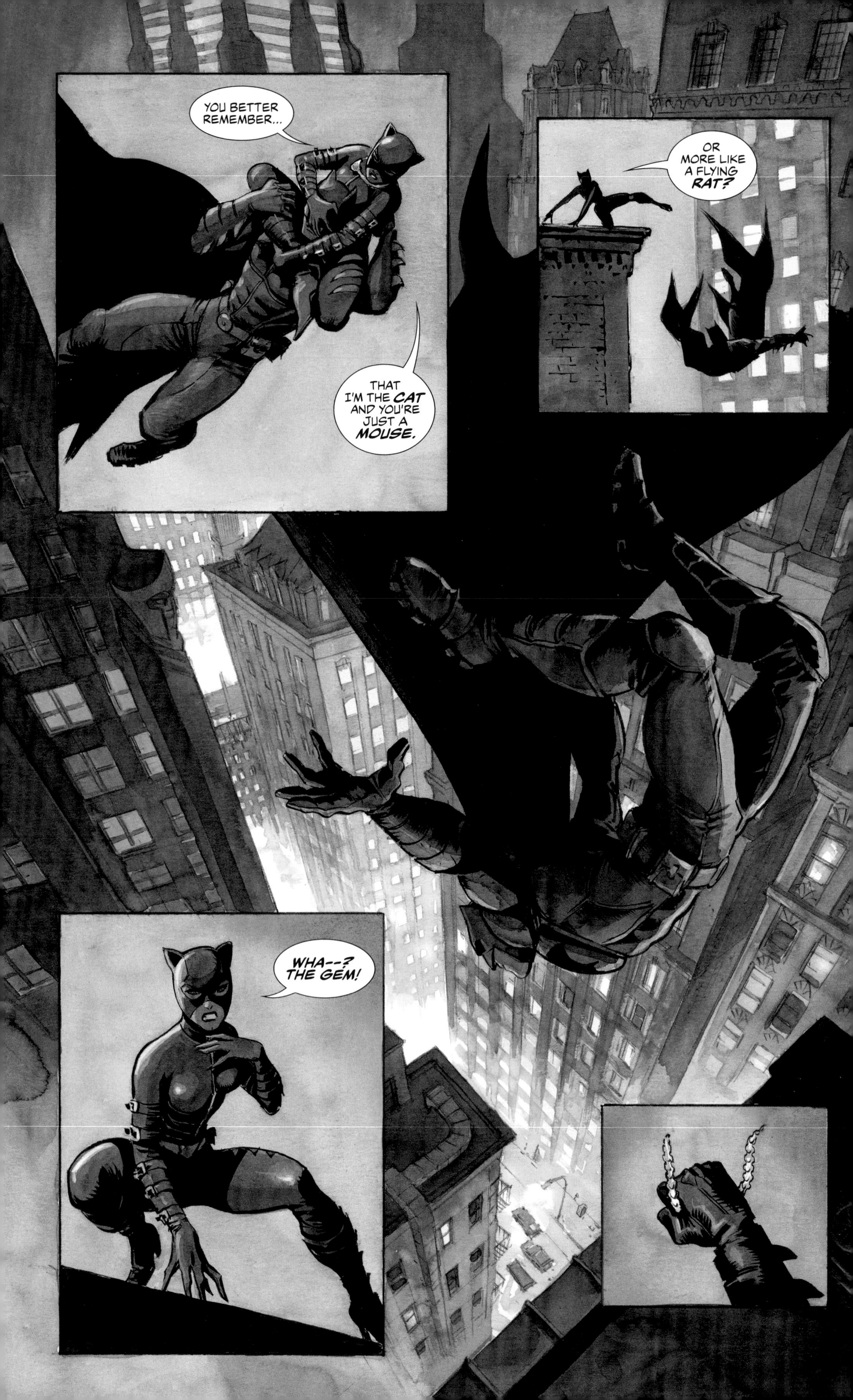
YOU BETTER REMEMBER...
THAT I'M THE CAT AND YOU'RE JUST A MOUSE.
OR MORE LIKE A FLYING RAT?
WHA--? THE GEM!

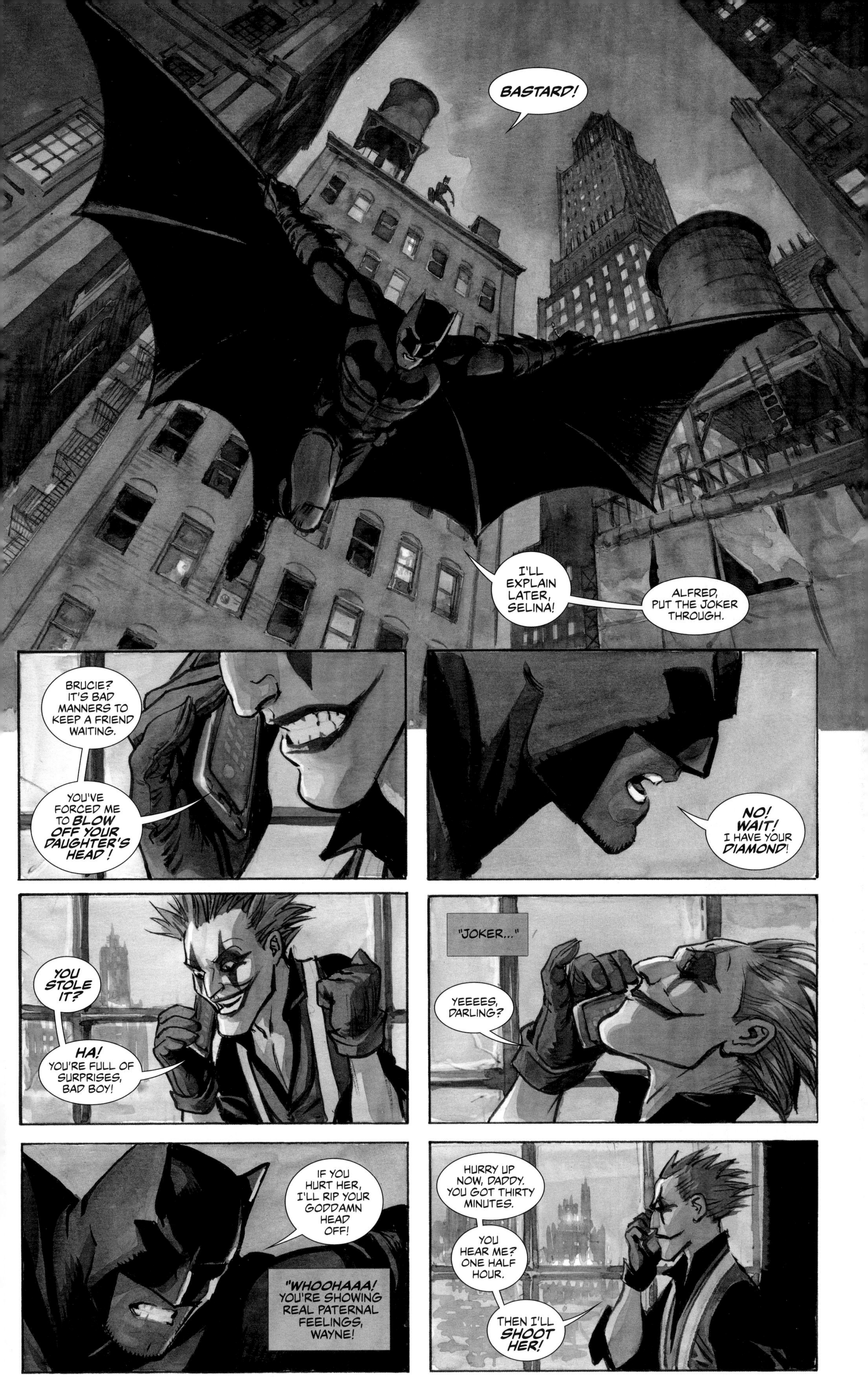
BASTARD!
I'LL EXPLAIN LATER, SELINA!
ALFRED, PUT THE JOKER THROUGH.
BRUCIE? IT'S BAD MANNERS TO KEEP A FRIEND WAITING.
YOU'VE FORCED ME TO BLOW OFF YOUR DAUGHTER'S HEAD!
NO! WAIT! I HAVE YOUR DIAMOND!
YOU STOLE IT?
HA! YOU'RE FULL OF SURPRISES, BAD BOY!
"JOKER..."
YEEEES, DARLING?
IF YOU HURT HER, I'LL RIP YOUR GODDAMN HEAD OFF!
"WHOOHAAA! YOU'RE SHOWING REAL PATERNAL FEELINGS, WAYNE!
HURRY UP NOW, DADDY. YOU GOT THIRTY MINUTES.
YOU HEAR ME? ONE HALF HOUR.
THEN I'LL SHOOT HER!

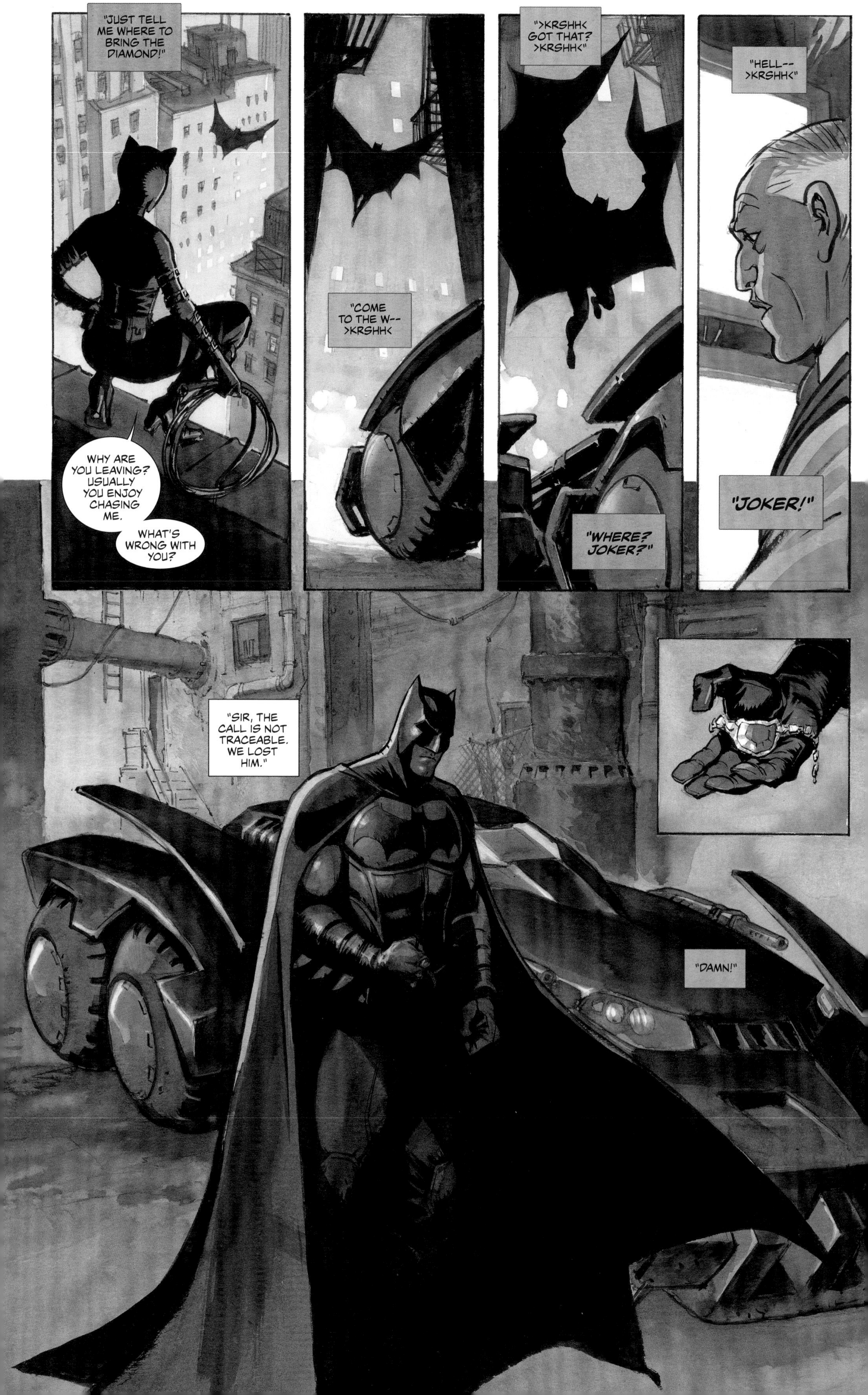
"JUST TELL ME WHERE TO BRING THE DIAMOND!"
WHY ARE YOU LEAVING? USUALLY YOU ENJOY CHASING ME.
WHAT'S WRONG WITH YOU?
"COME TO THE W-- >KRSHH<
">KRSHH< GOT THAT? >KRSHH<"
"WHERE? JOKER?"
"HELL-- >KRSHH<"
"JOKER!"
"SIR, THE CALL IS NOT TRACEABLE. WE LOST HIM."
"DAMN!"

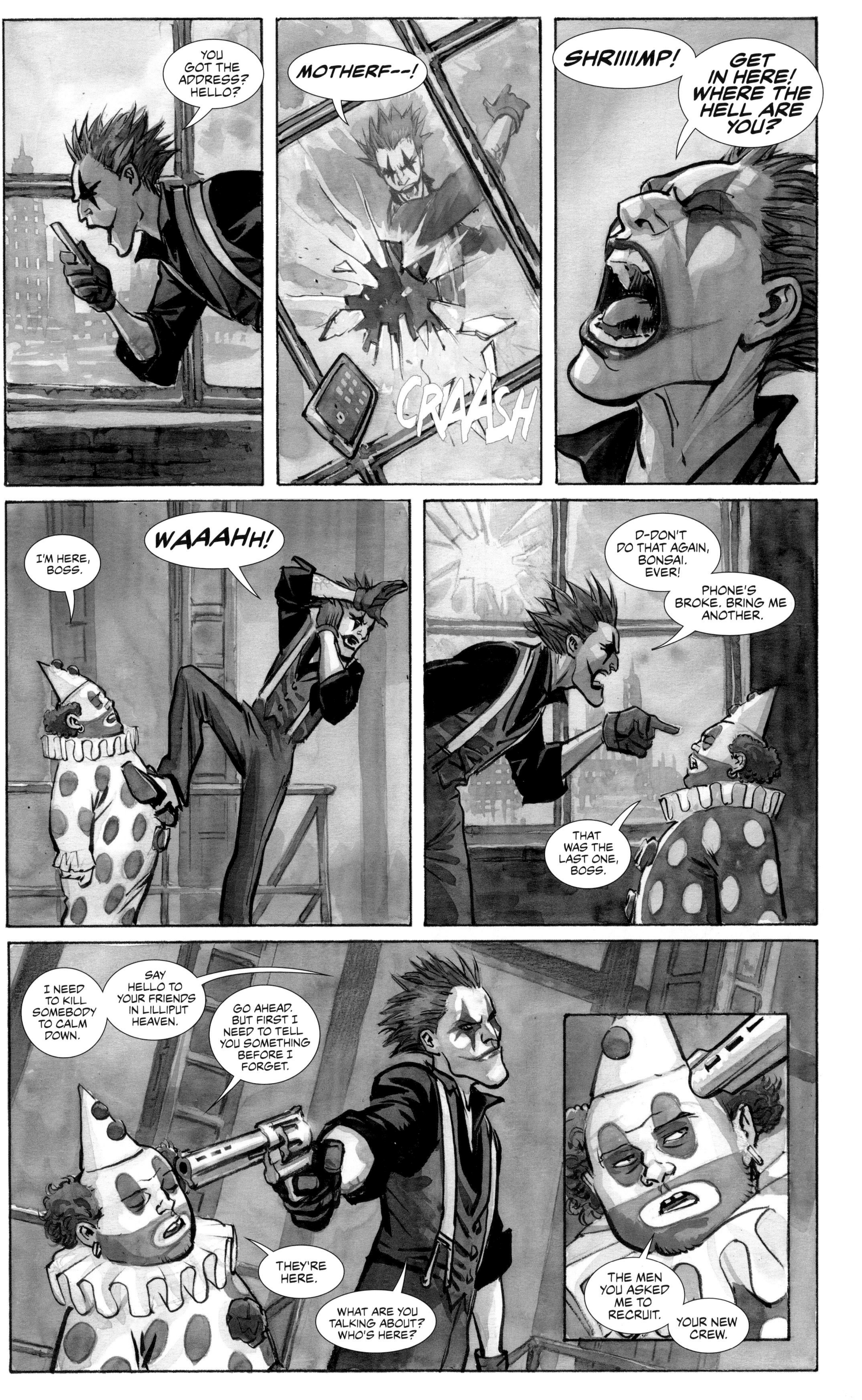
YOU GOT THE ADDRESS? HELLO?
MOTHERF--!
CRAAASH
SHRIIIIMP!
GET IN HERE! WHERE THE HELL ARE YOU?
I'M HERE, BOSS.
WAAAHH!
D-DON'T DO THAT AGAIN, BONSAI. EVER!
PHONE'S BROKE. BRING ME ANOTHER.
THAT WAS THE LAST ONE, BOSS.
I NEED TO KILL SOMEBODY TO CALM DOWN.
SAY HELLO TO YOUR FRIENDS IN LILLIPUT HEAVEN.
GO AHEAD. BUT FIRST I NEED TO TELL YOU SOMETHING BEFORE I FORGET.
THEY'RE HERE.
WHAT ARE YOU TALKING ABOUT? WHO'S HERE?
THE MEN YOU ASKED ME TO RECRUIT.
YOUR NEW CREW.

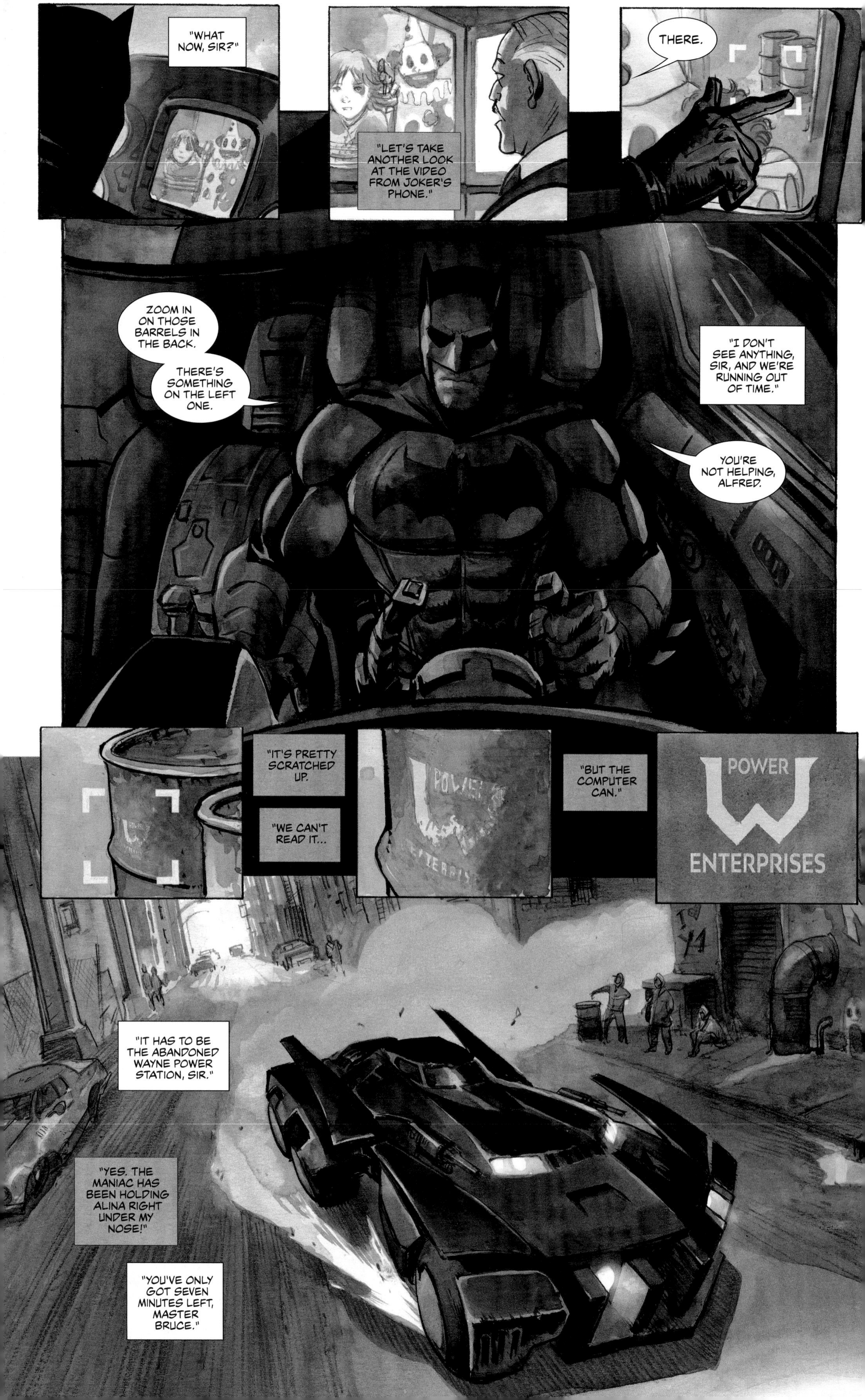
"WHAT NOW, SIR?"
"LET'S TAKE ANOTHER LOOK AT THE VIDEO FROM JOKER'S PHONE."
THERE.
ZOOM IN ON THOSE BARRELS IN THE BACK.
THERE'S SOMETHING ON THE LEFT ONE.
"I DON'T SEE ANYTHING, SIR, AND WE'RE RUNNING OUT OF TIME."
YOU'RE NOT HELPING, ALFRED.
"IT'S PRETTY SCRATCHED UP.
"WE CAN'T READ IT...
"BUT THE COMPUTER CAN."
POWER
W
ENTERPRISES
"IT HAS TO BE THE ABANDONED WAYNE POWER STATION, SIR."
"YES. THE MANIAC HAS BEEN HOLDING ALINA RIGHT UNDER MY NOSE!"
"YOU'VE ONLY GOT SEVEN MINUTES LEFT, MASTER BRUCE."

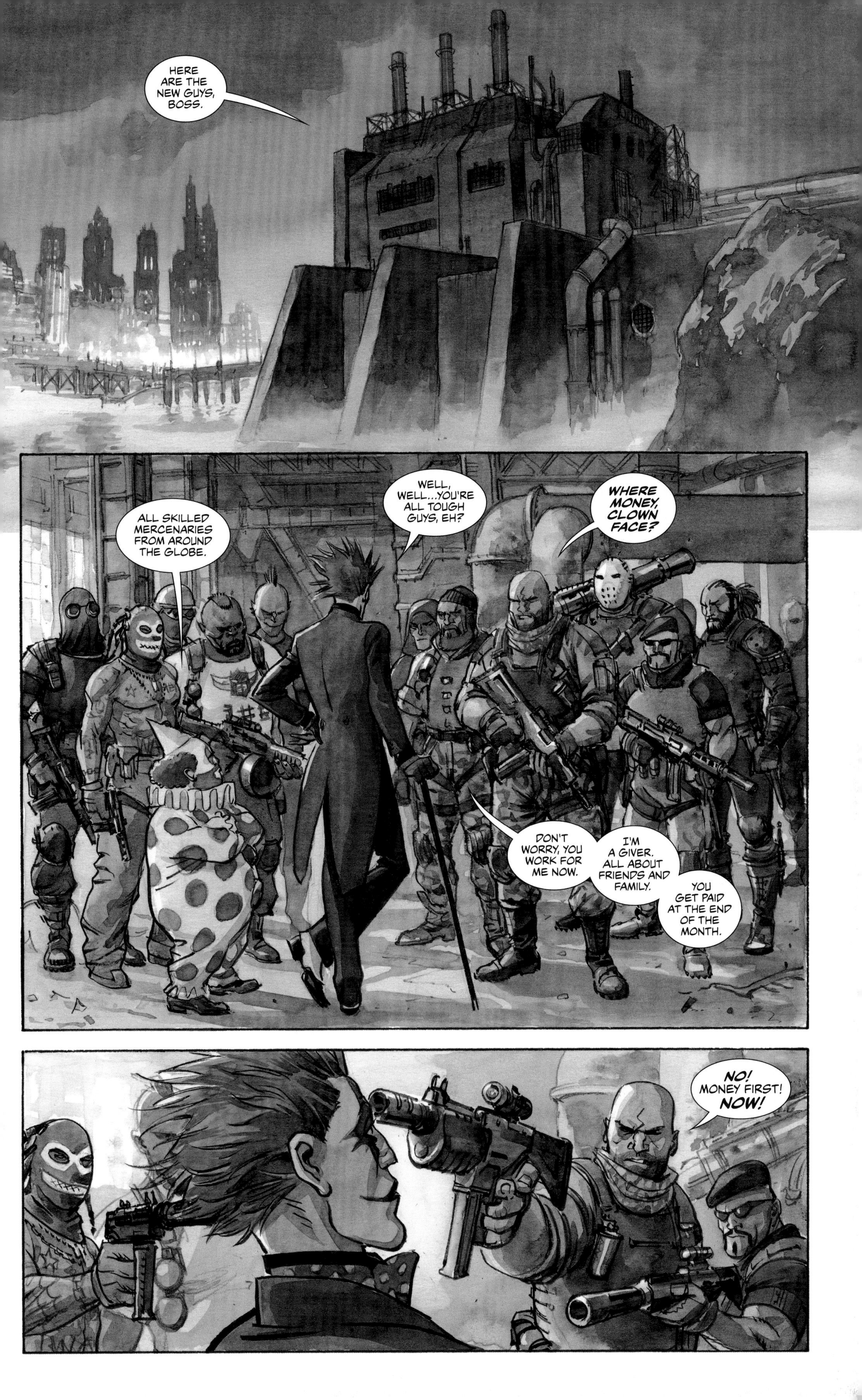
HERE ARE THE NEW GUYS, BOSS.
ALL SKILLED MERCENARIES FROM AROUND THE GLOBE.
WELL, WELL...YOU'RE ALL TOUGH GUYS, EH?
WHERE MONEY, CLOWN FACE?
DON'T WORRY, YOU WORK FOR ME NOW.
I'M A GIVER. ALL ABOUT FRIENDS AND FAMILY.
YOU GET PAID AT THE END OF THE MONTH.
NO! MONEY FIRST! NOW!

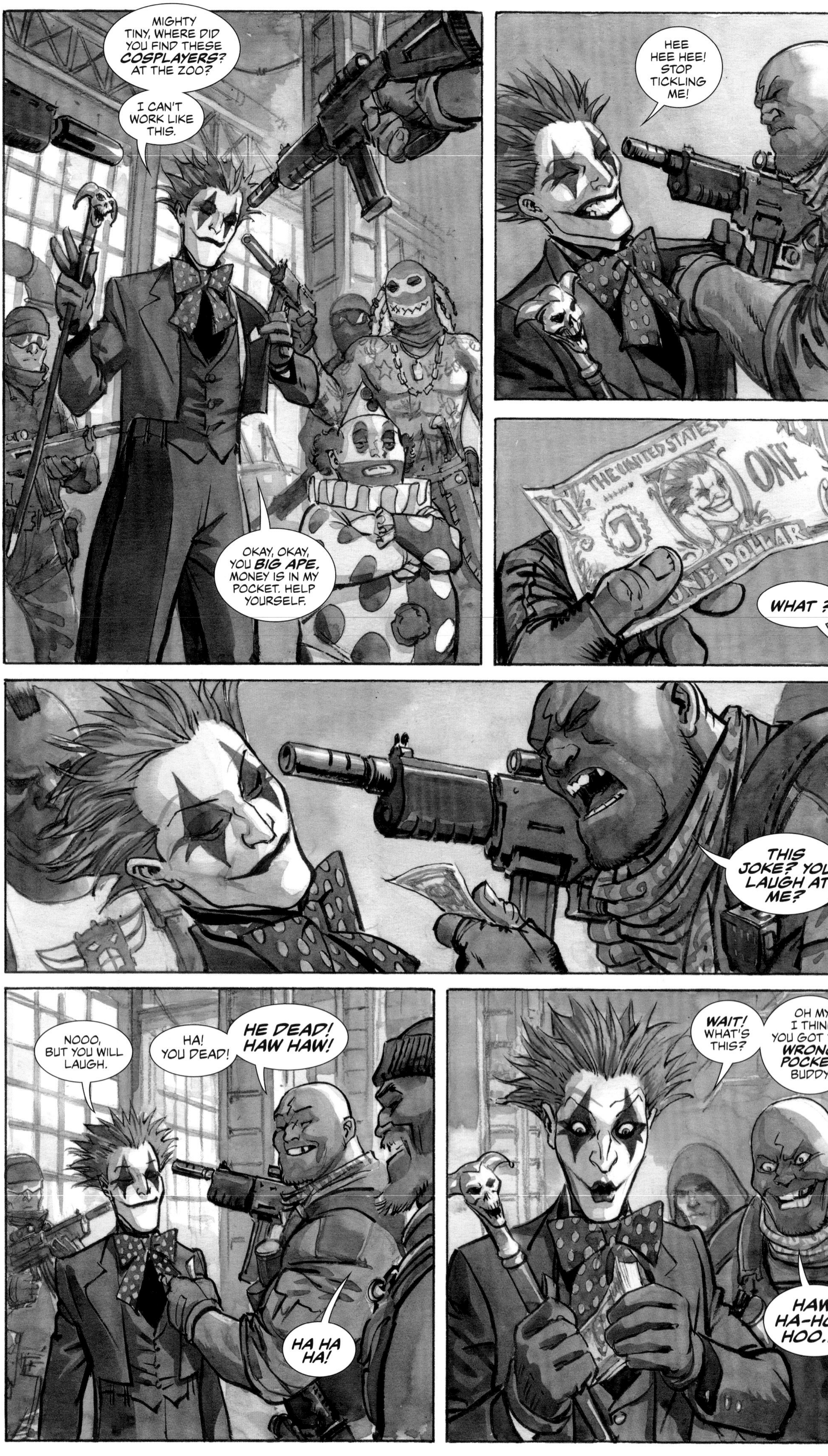

MIGHTY TINY, WHERE DID YOU FIND THESE COSPLAYERS? AT THE ZOO?
I CAN'T WORK LIKE THIS.
OKAY, OKAY, YOU BIG APE. MONEY IS IN MY POCKET. HELP YOURSELF.
HEE HEE HEE! STOP TICKLING ME!
THE UNITED STATES
ONE
ONE DOLLAR
WHAT ?
THIS JOKE? YOU LAUGH AT ME?
HA! YOU DEAD!
HE DEAD! HAW HAW!
NOOO, BUT YOU WILL LAUGH.
HA HA HA!
WAIT! WHAT'S THIS?
OH MY, I THINK YOU GOT THE WRONG POCKET, BUDDY.
HAW HA-HOO HOO...!

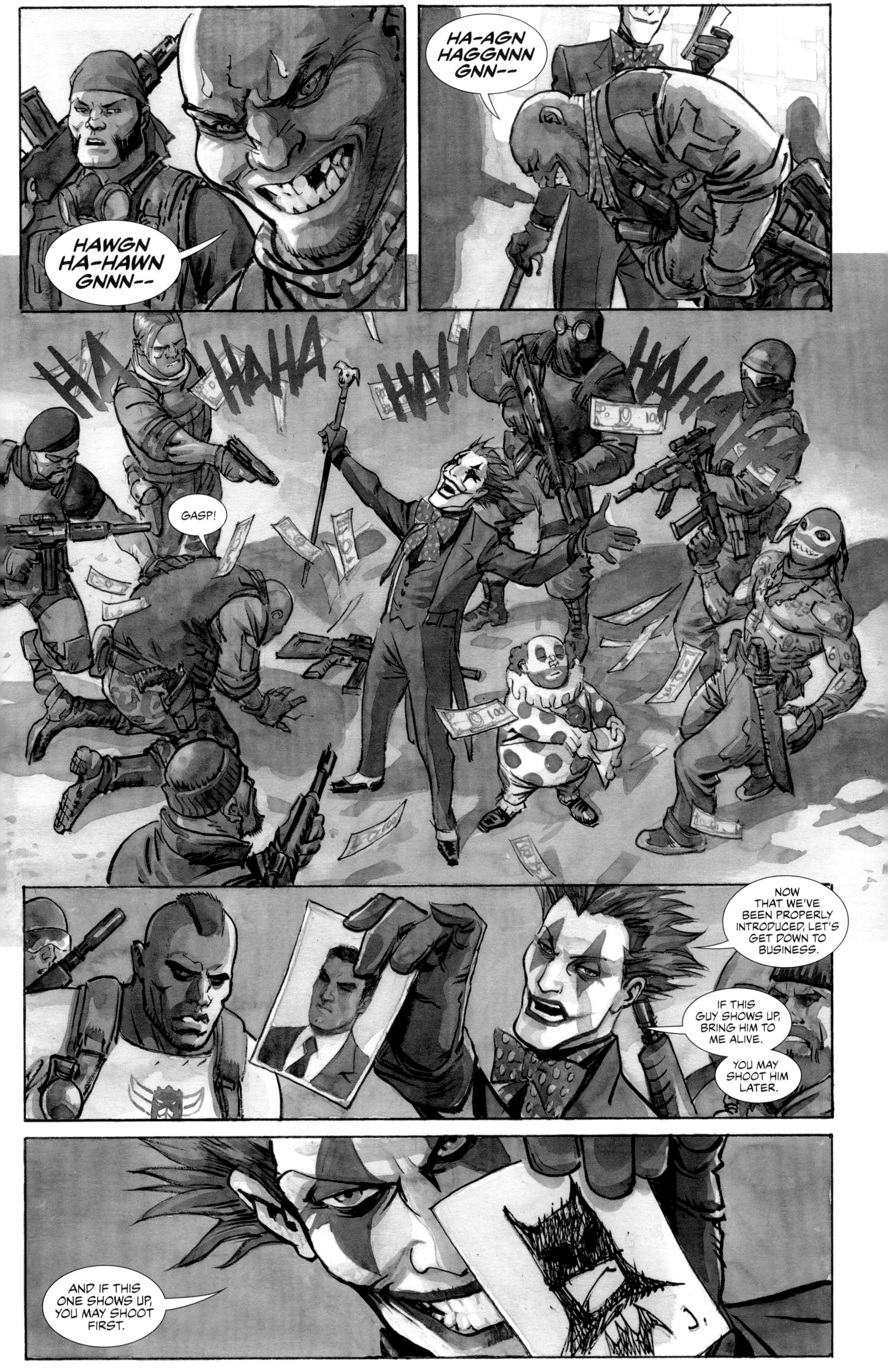
HAWGN HA-HAWN GNNN--
HA-AGN HAGGNNN GNN--
HA HAHA HAHA HAHA
GASP!
NOW THAT WE'VE BEEN PROPERLY INTRODUCED, LET'S GET DOWN TO BUSINESS.
IF THIS GUY SHOWS UP, BRING HIM TO ME ALIVE.
YOU MAY SHOOT HIM LATER.
AND IF THIS ONE SHOWS UP, YOU MAY SHOOT FIRST.

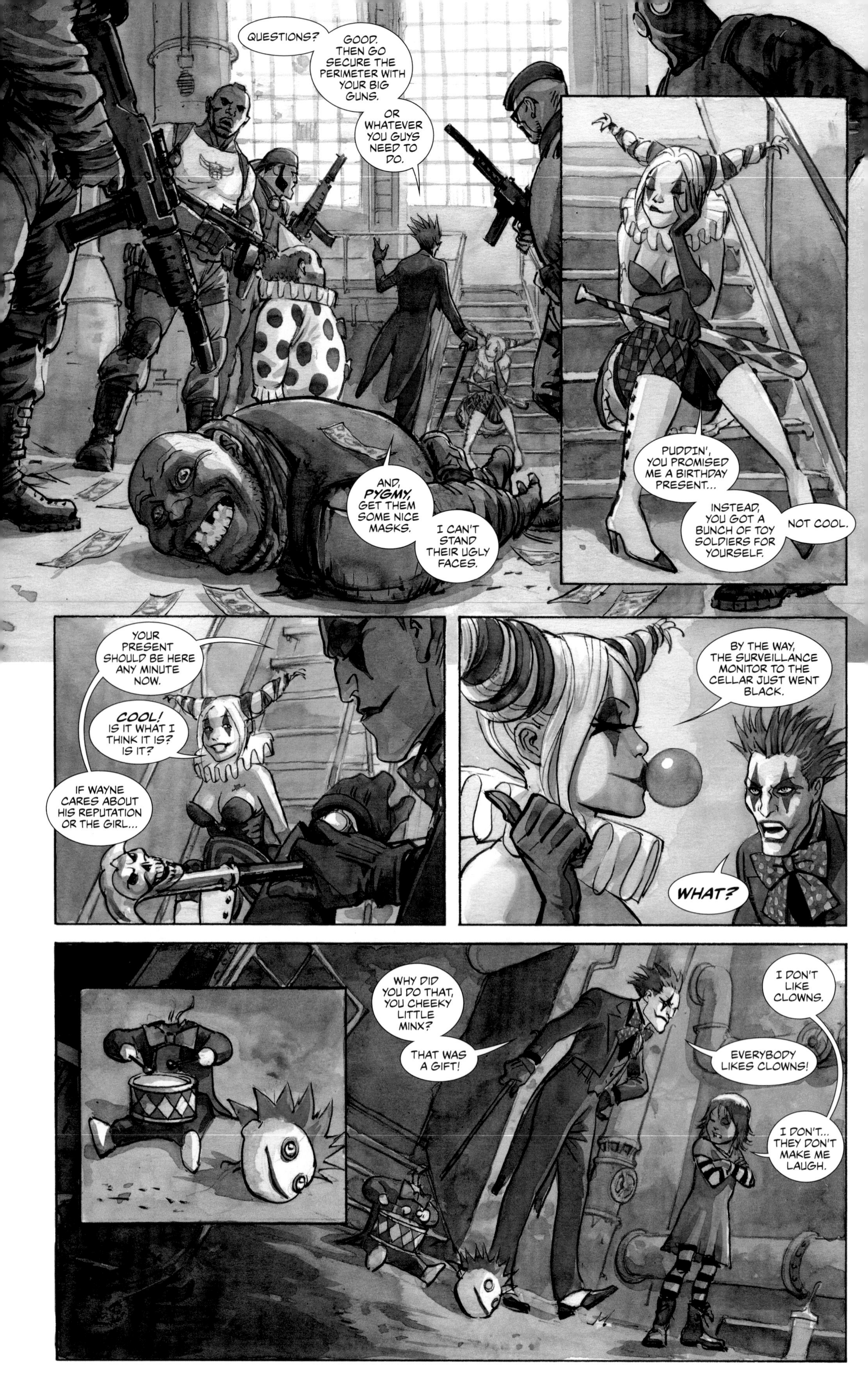
QUESTIONS?
GOOD. THEN GO SECURE THE PERIMETER WITH YOUR BIG GUNS.
OR WHATEVER YOU GUYS NEED TO DO.
AND, PYGMY, GET THEM SOME NICE MASKS.
I CAN'T STAND THEIR UGLY FACES.
PUDDIN', YOU PROMISED ME A BIRTHDAY PRESENT...
INSTEAD, YOU GOT A BUNCH OF TOY SOLDIERS FOR YOURSELF.
NOT COOL.
YOUR PRESENT SHOULD BE HERE ANY MINUTE NOW.
COOL! IS IT WHAT I THINK IT IS? IS IT?
IF WAYNE CARES ABOUT HIS REPUTATION OR THE GIRL...
BY THE WAY, THE SURVEILLANCE MONITOR TO THE CELLAR JUST WENT BLACK.
WHAT?
WHY DID YOU DO THAT, YOU CHEEKY LITTLE MINX?
THAT WAS A GIFT!
I DON'T LIKE CLOWNS.
EVERYBODY LIKES CLOWNS!
I DON'T... THEY DON'T MAKE ME LAUGH.

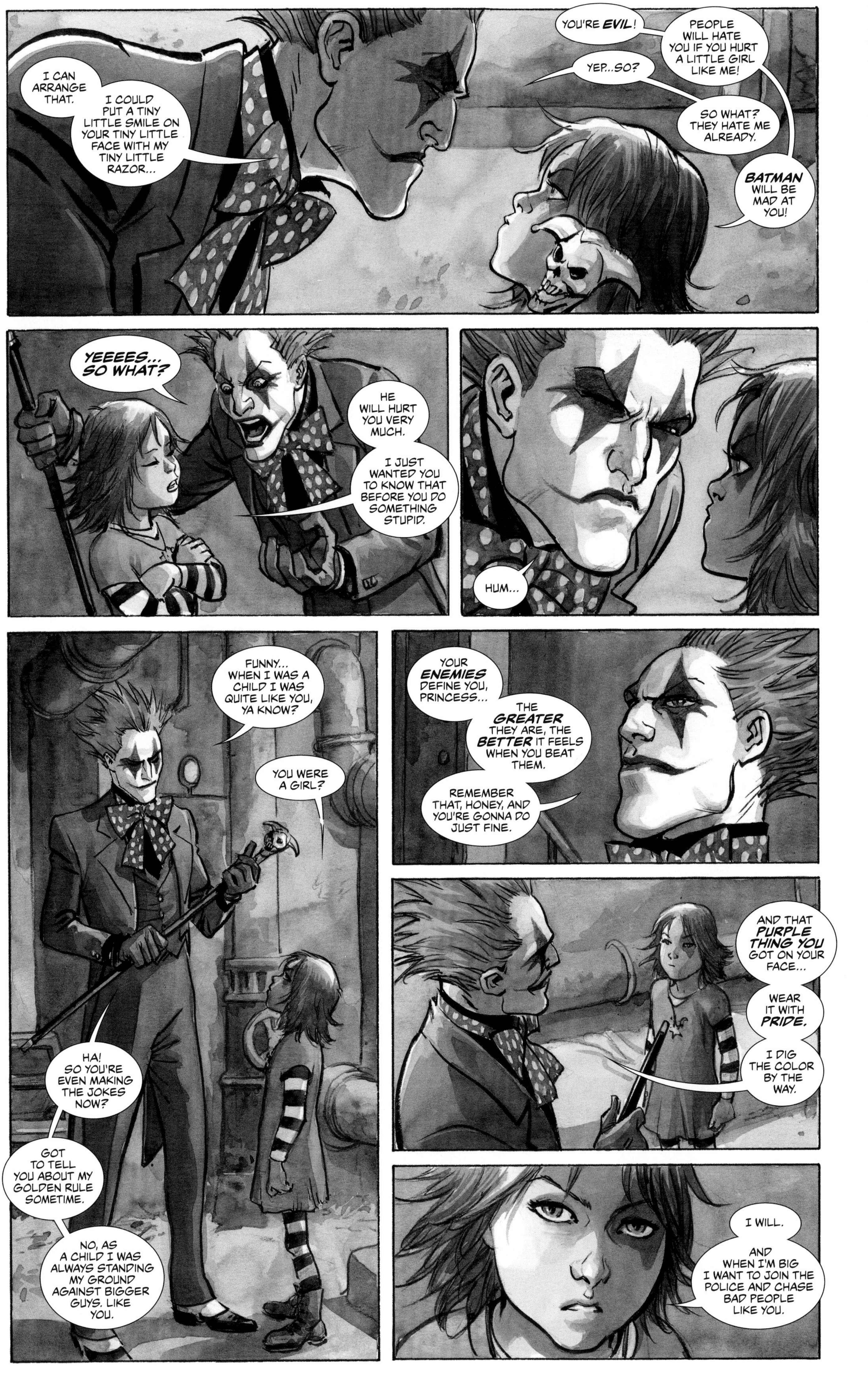
I CAN ARRANGE THAT.
I COULD PUT A TINY LITTLE SMILE ON YOUR TINY LITTLE FACE WITH MY TINY LITTLE RAZOR...
YOU'RE EVIL!
PEOPLE WILL HATE YOU IF YOU HURT A LITTLE GIRL LIKE ME!
YEP...SO?
SO WHAT? THEY HATE ME ALREADY.
BATMAN WILL BE MAD AT YOU!
YEEEES... SO WHAT?
HE WILL HURT YOU VERY MUCH.
I JUST WANTED YOU TO KNOW THAT BEFORE YOU DO SOMETHING STUPID.
HUM...
FUNNY... WHEN I WAS A CHILD I WAS QUITE LIKE YOU, YA KNOW?
YOU WERE A GIRL?
HA! SO YOU'RE EVEN MAKING THE JOKES NOW?
GOT TO TELL YOU ABOUT MY GOLDEN RULE SOMETIME.
NO, AS A CHILD I WAS ALWAYS STANDING MY GROUND AGAINST BIGGER GUYS. LIKE YOU.
YOUR ENEMIES DEFINE YOU, PRINCESS...
THE GREATER THEY ARE, THE BETTER IT FEELS WHEN YOU BEAT THEM.
REMEMBER THAT, HONEY, AND YOU'RE GONNA DO JUST FINE.
AND THAT PURPLE THING YOU GOT ON YOUR FACE...
WEAR IT WITH PRIDE.
I DIG THE COLOR BY THE WAY.
I WILL.
AND WHEN I'M BIG I WANT TO JOIN THE POLICE AND CHASE BAD PEOPLE LIKE YOU.

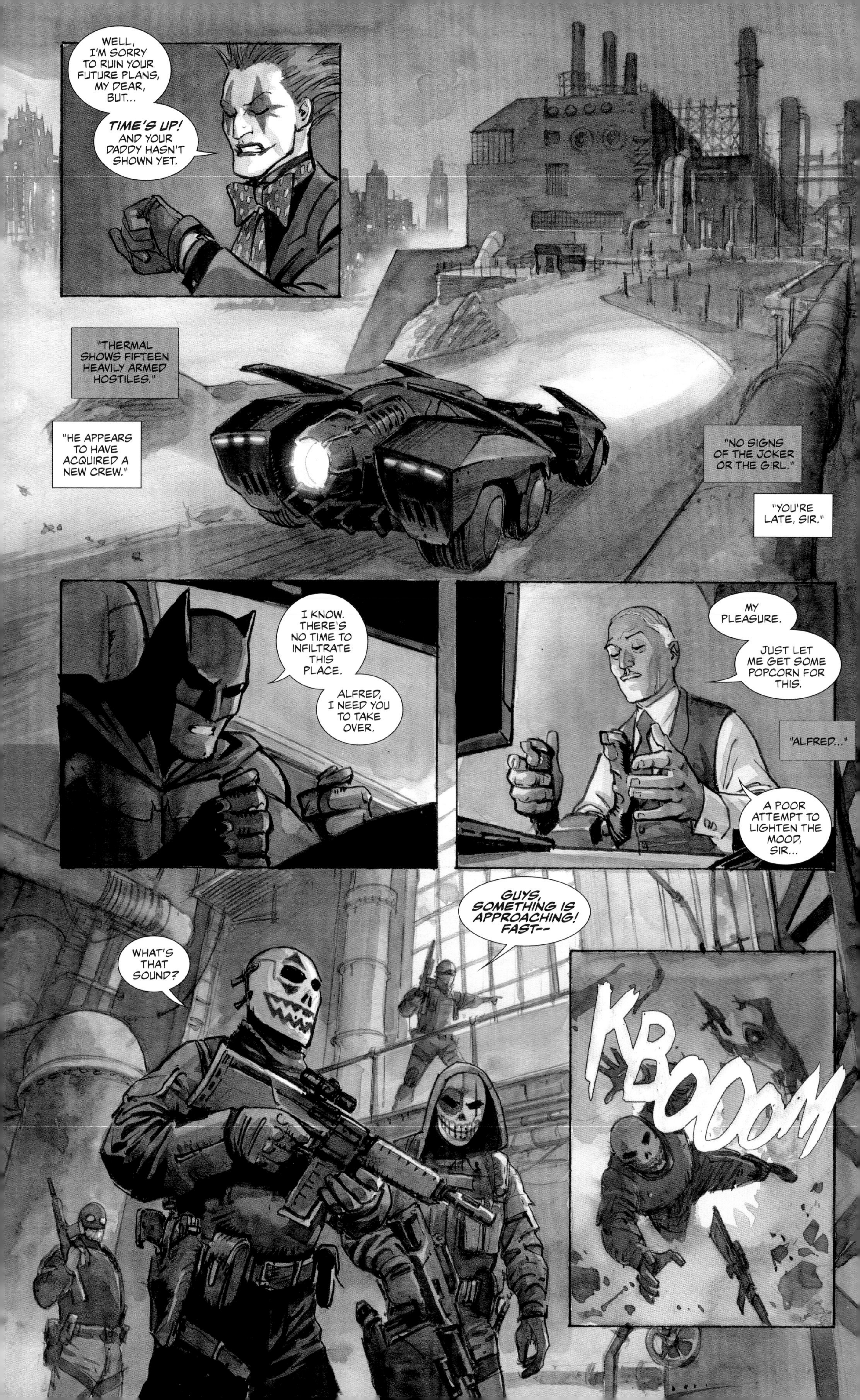
WELL, I'M SORRY TO RUIN YOUR FUTURE PLANS, MY DEAR, BUT...
TIME'S UP! AND YOUR DADDY HASN'T SHOWN YET.
"THERMAL SHOWS FIFTEEN HEAVILY ARMED HOSTILES."
"HE APPEARS TO HAVE ACQUIRED A NEW CREW."
"NO SIGNS OF THE JOKER OR THE GIRL."
"YOU'RE LATE, SIR."
I KNOW. THERE'S NO TIME TO INFILTRATE THIS PLACE.
ALFRED, I NEED YOU TO TAKE OVER.
MY PLEASURE.
JUST LET ME GET SOME POPCORN FOR THIS.
"ALFRED..."
A POOR ATTEMPT TO LIGHTEN THE MOOD, SIR...
WHAT'S THAT SOUND?
GUYS, SOMETHING IS APPROACHING! FAST--
KBOOOOM

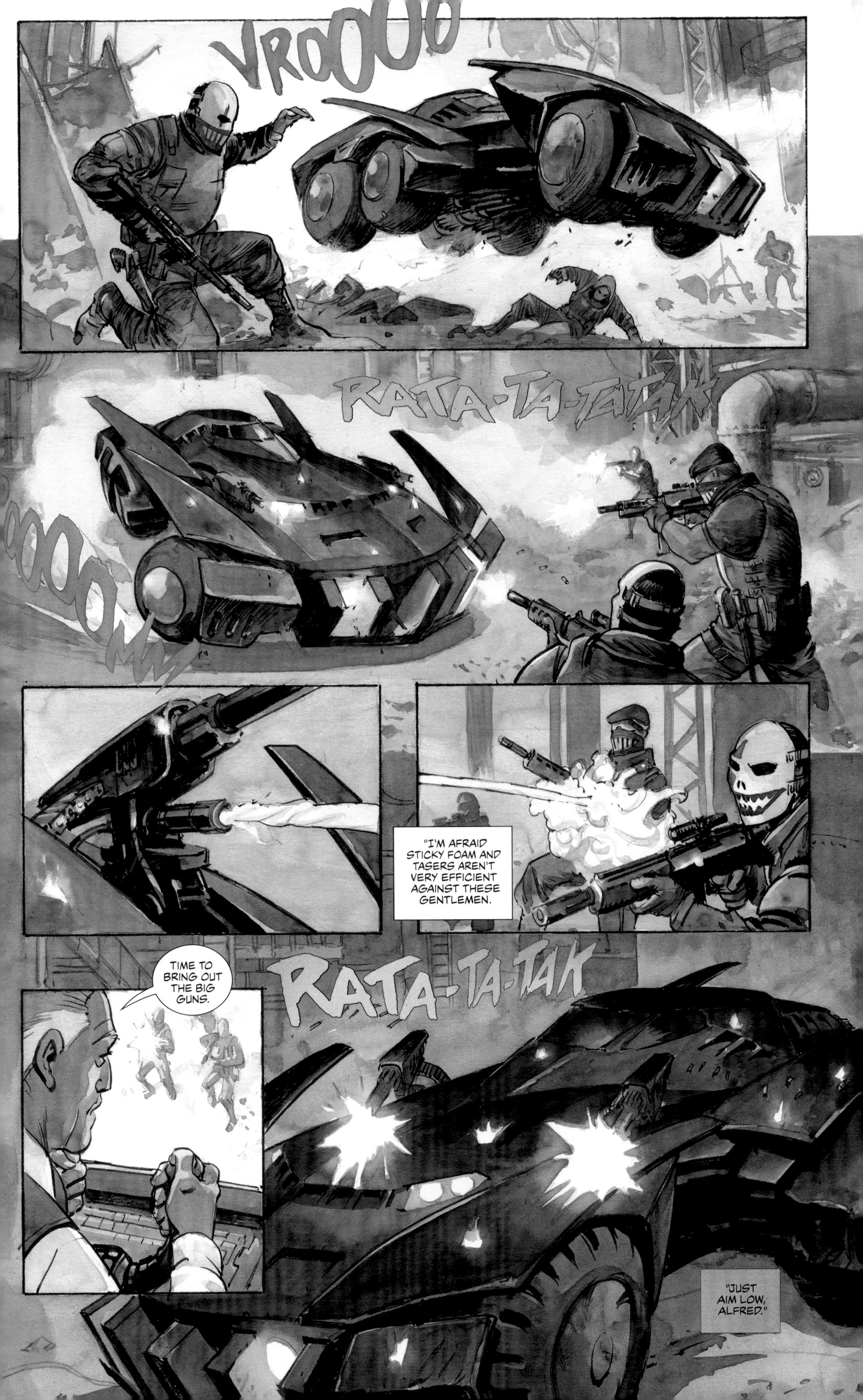
VROOOO
RATA-TA-TATAK
OOOOOM
"I'M AFRAID STICKY FOAM AND TASERS AREN'T VERY EFFICIENT AGAINST THESE GENTLEMEN.
TIME TO BRING OUT THE BIG GUNS.
RATA-TA-TAK
"JUST AIM LOW, ALFRED."

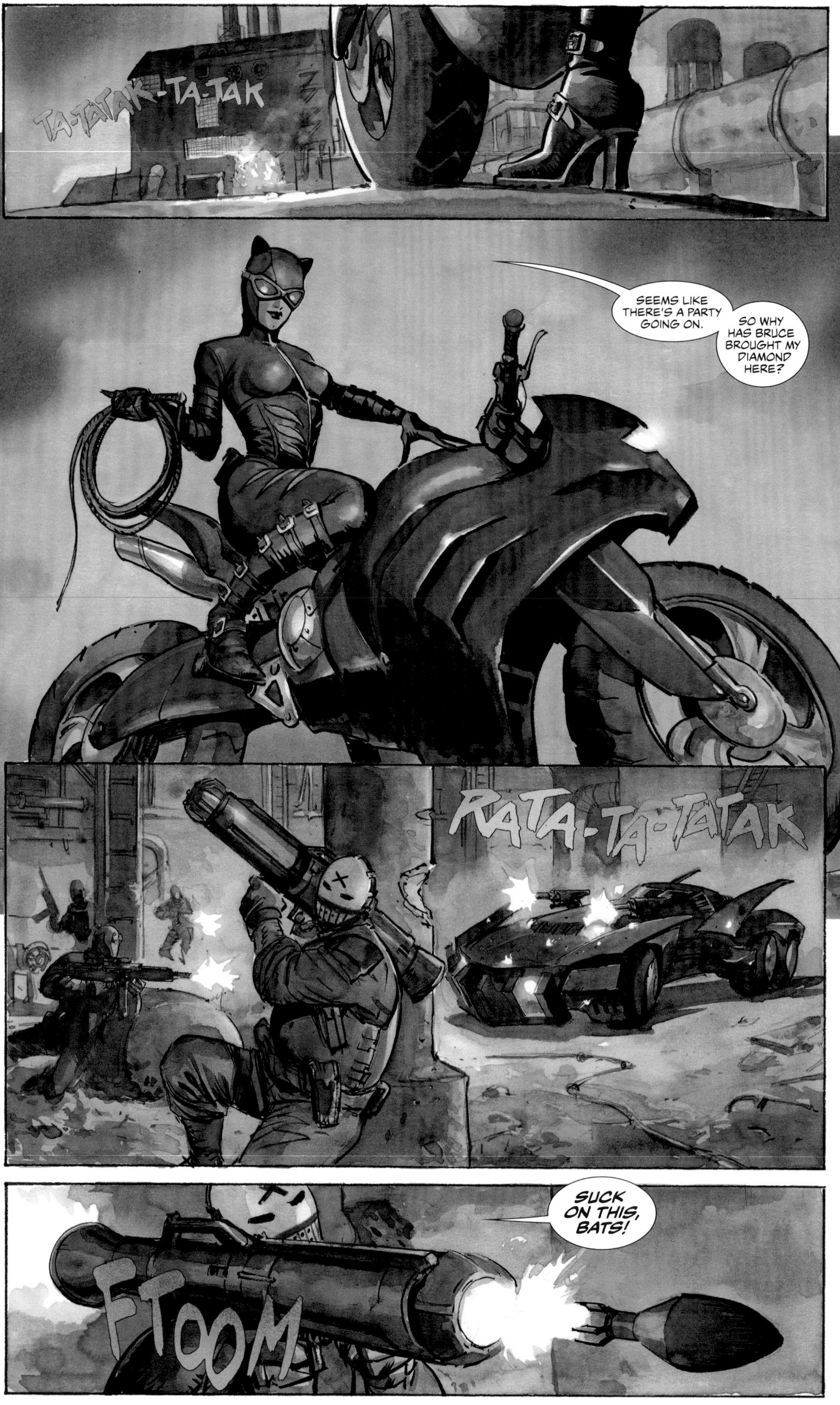
TA-TATAK-TA-TAK
SEEMS LIKE THERE'S A PARTY GOING ON.
SO WHY HAS BRUCE BROUGHT MY DIAMOND HERE?
RATA-TA-TATAK
SUCK ON THIS, BATS!
FTOOM

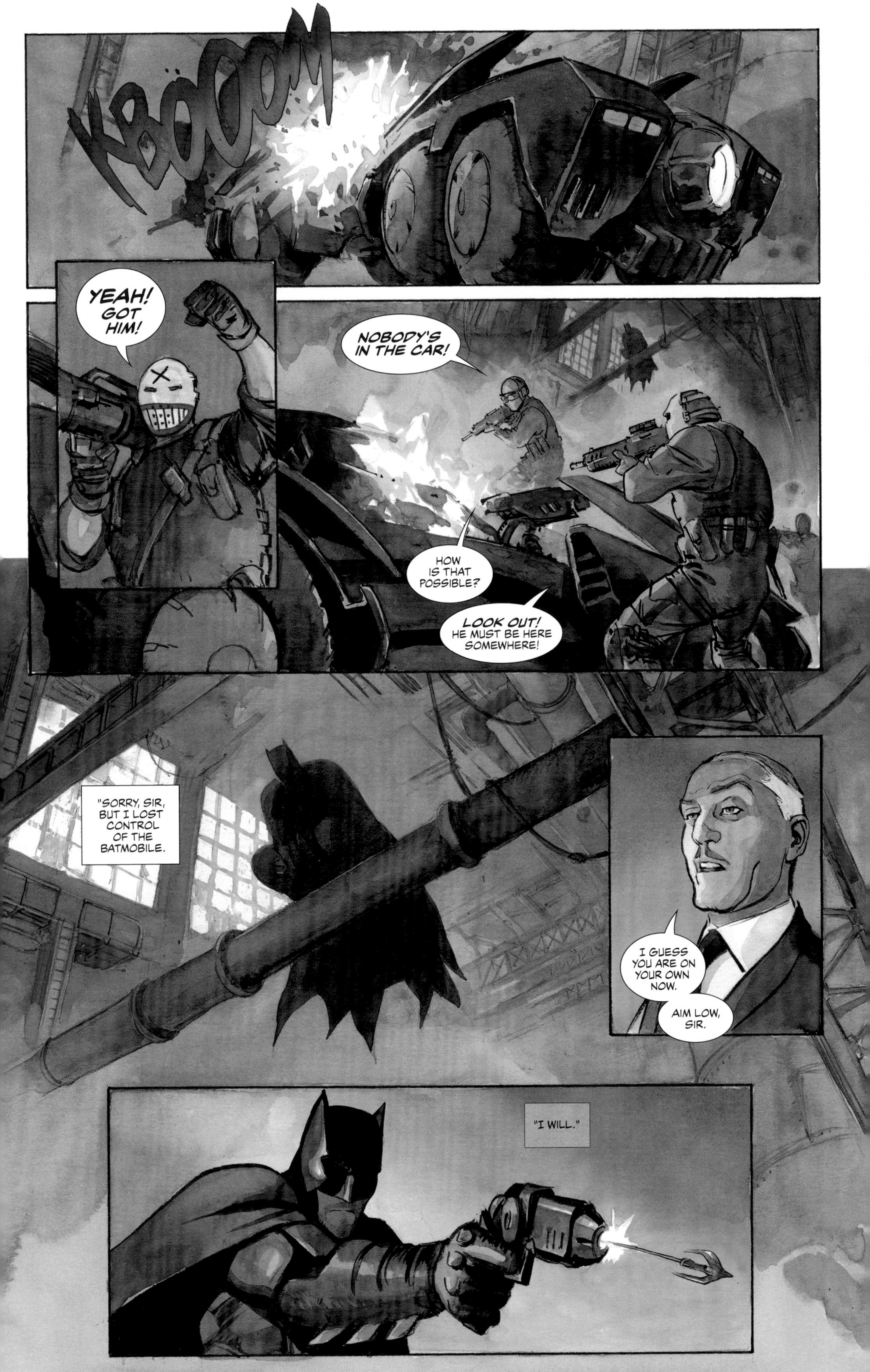
KBOOOM
YEAH! GOT HIM!
NOBODY'S IN THE CAR!
HOW IS THAT POSSIBLE?
LOOK OUT! HE MUST BE HERE SOMEWHERE!
"SORRY, SIR, BUT I LOST CONTROL OF THE BATMOBILE.
I GUESS YOU ARE ON YOUR OWN NOW.
AIM LOW, SIR.
"I WILL."

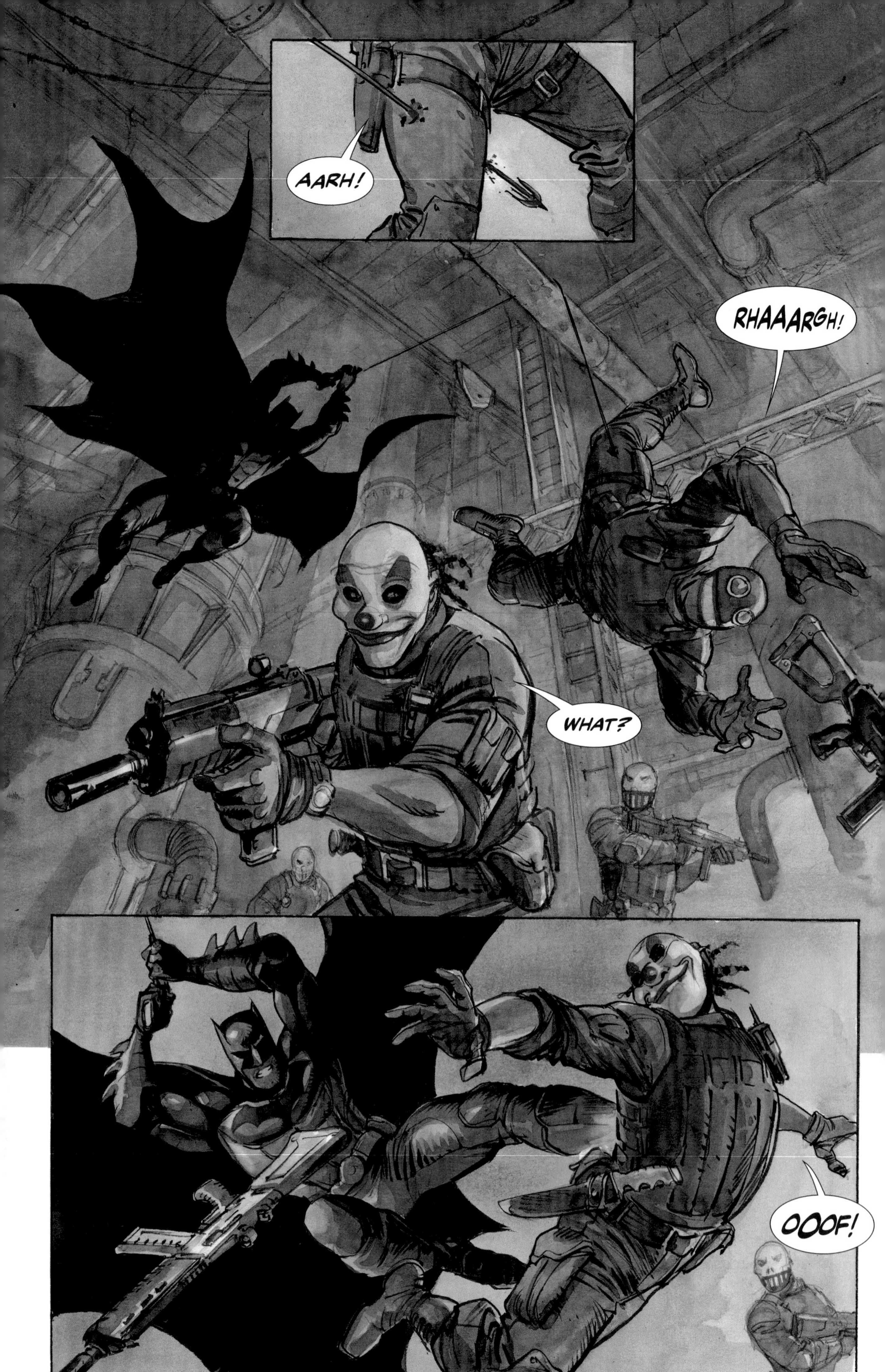
AARH!
RHAAARGH!
WHAT?
OOOF!

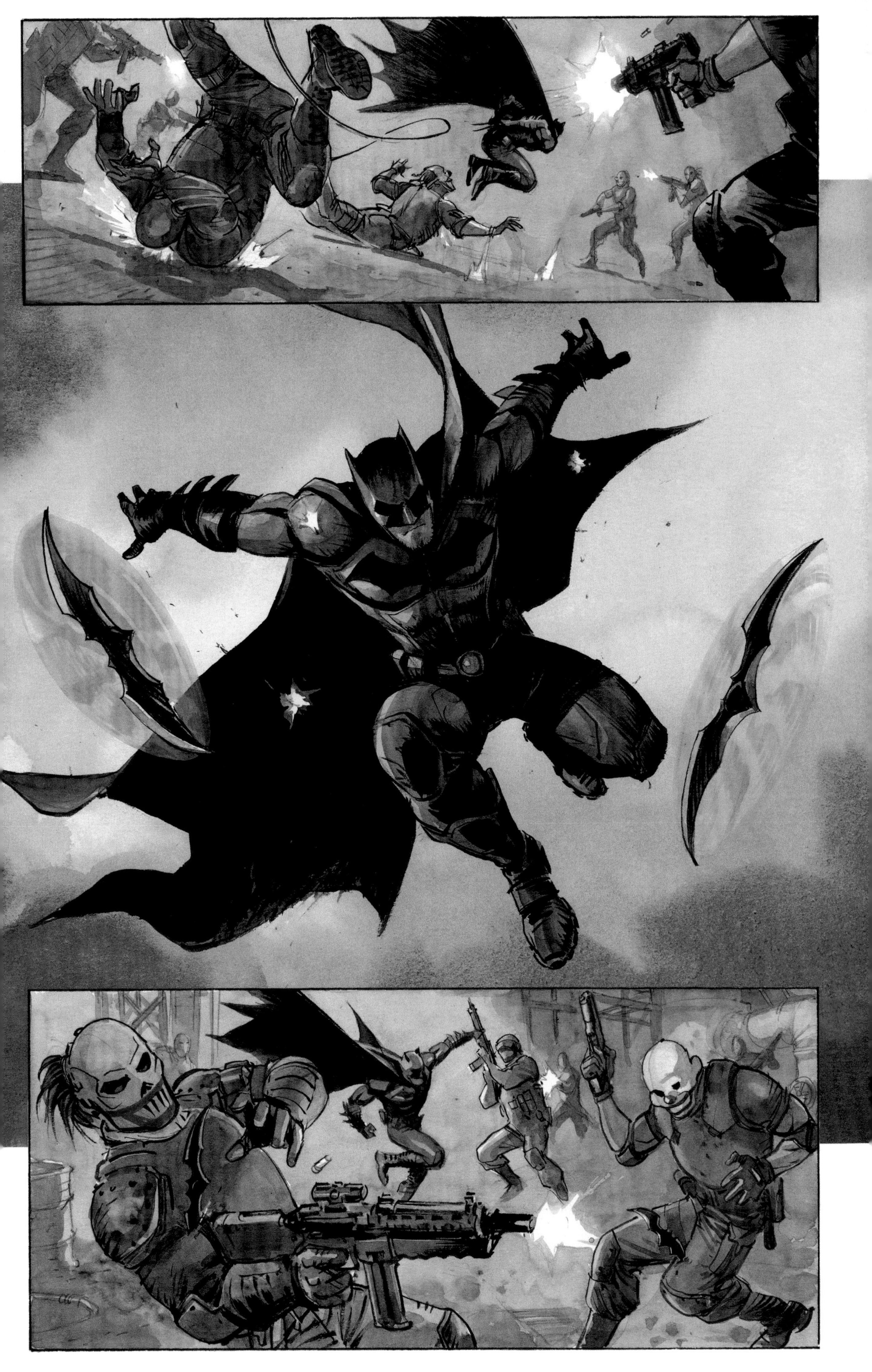

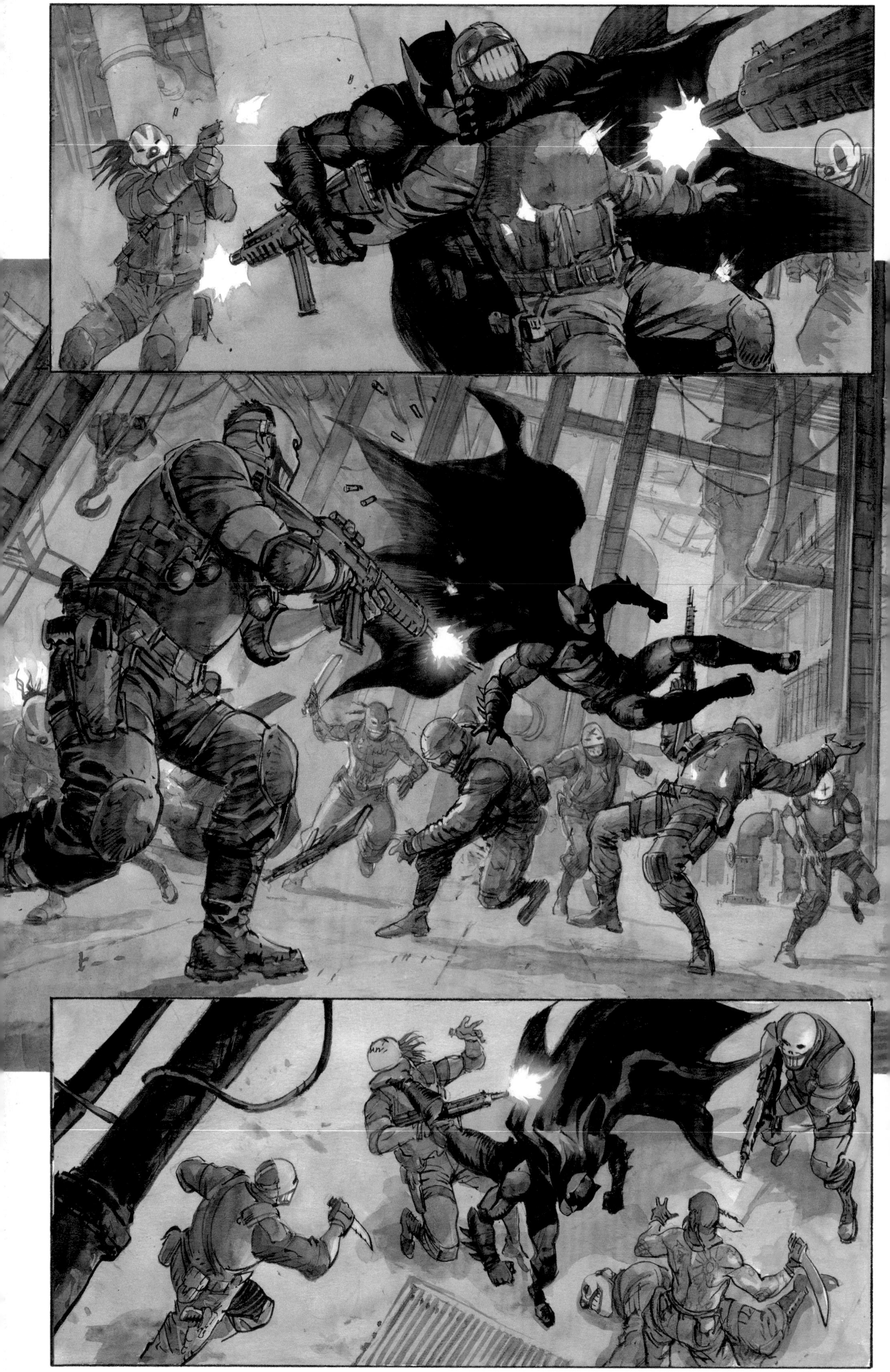

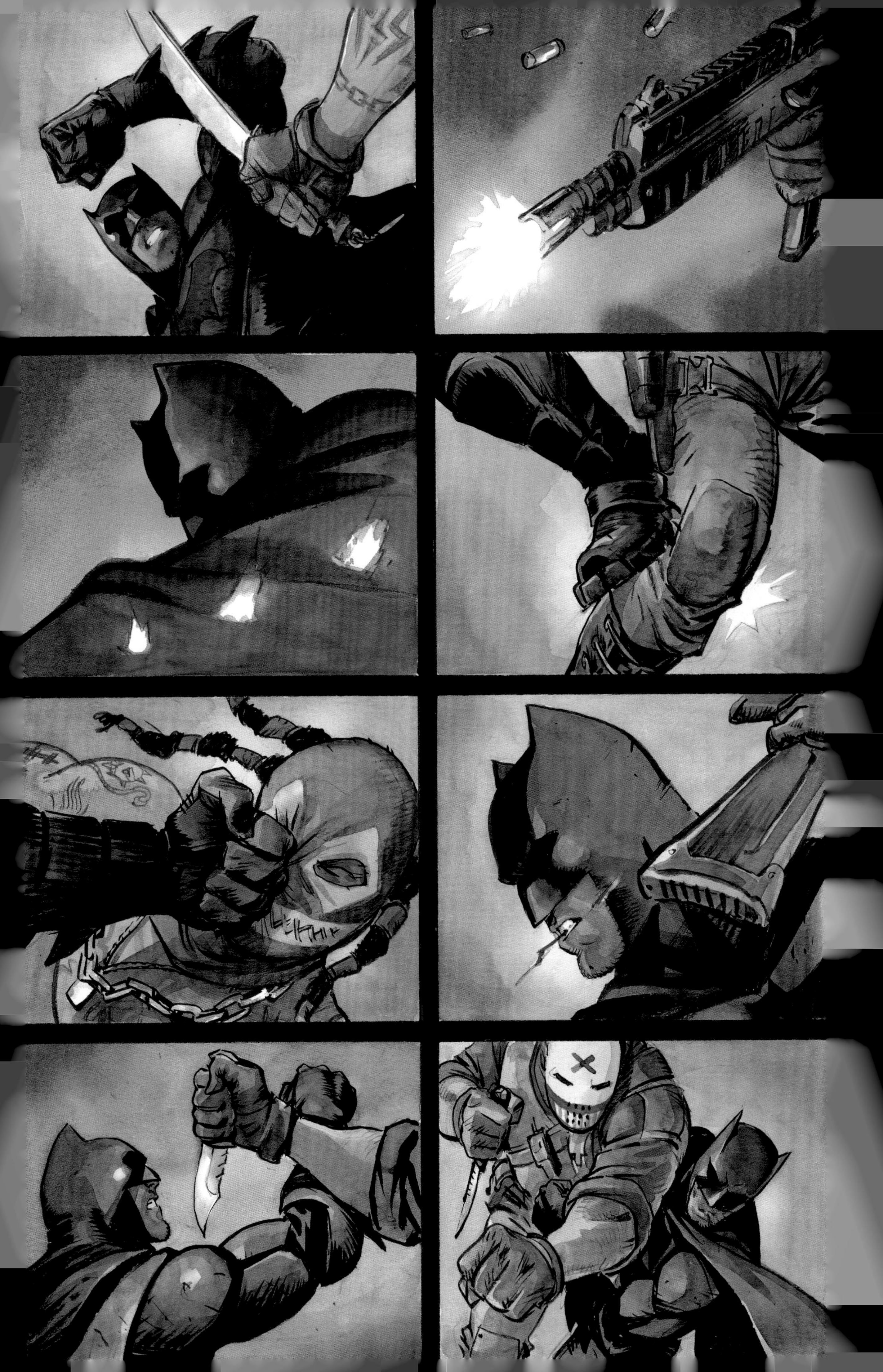

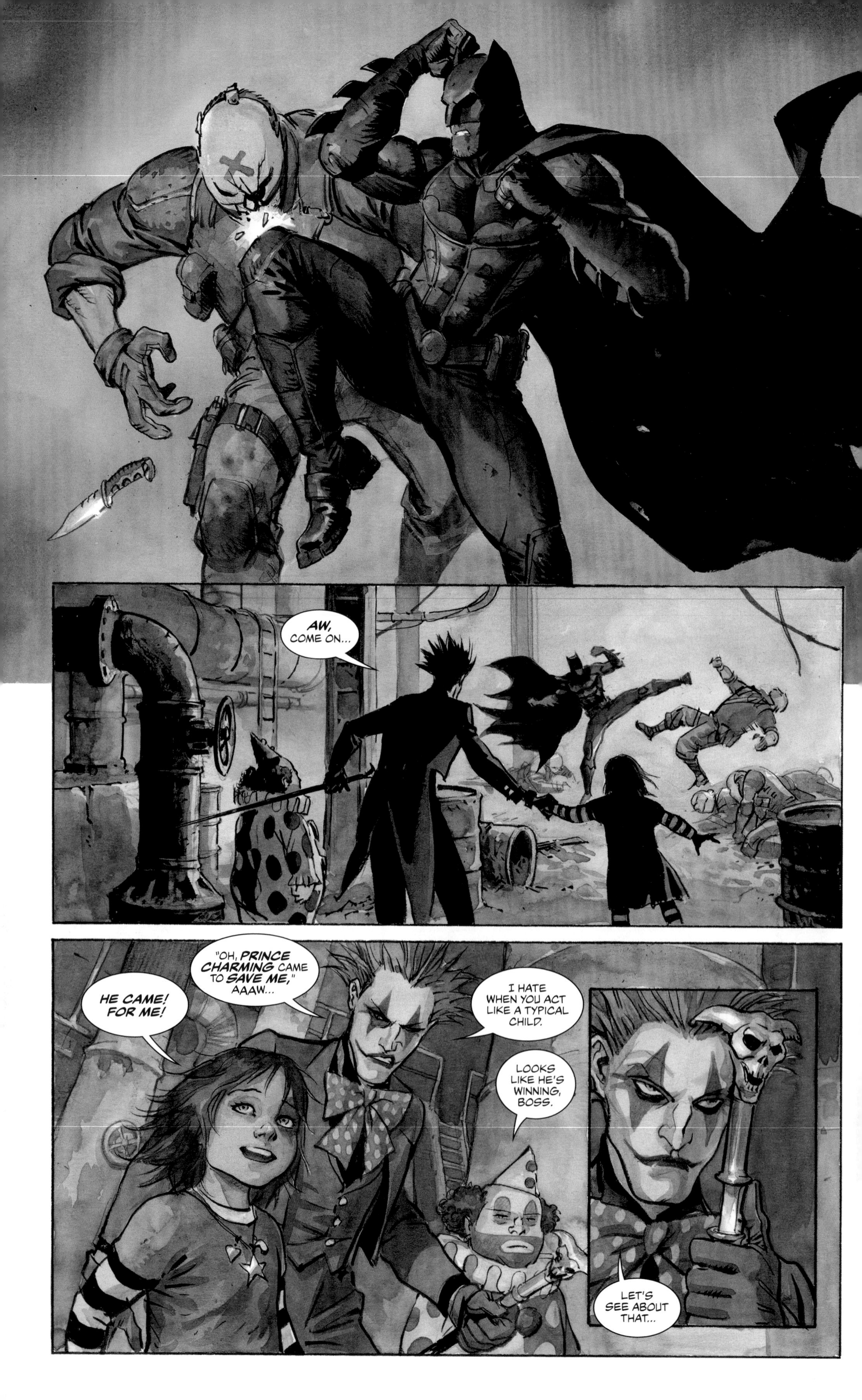

AW, COME ON...
HE CAME! FOR ME!
"OH, PRINCE CHARMING CAME TO SAVE ME," AAAW...
I HATE WHEN YOU ACT LIKE A TYPICAL CHILD.
LOOKS LIKE HE'S WINNING, BOSS.
LET'S SEE ABOUT THAT...

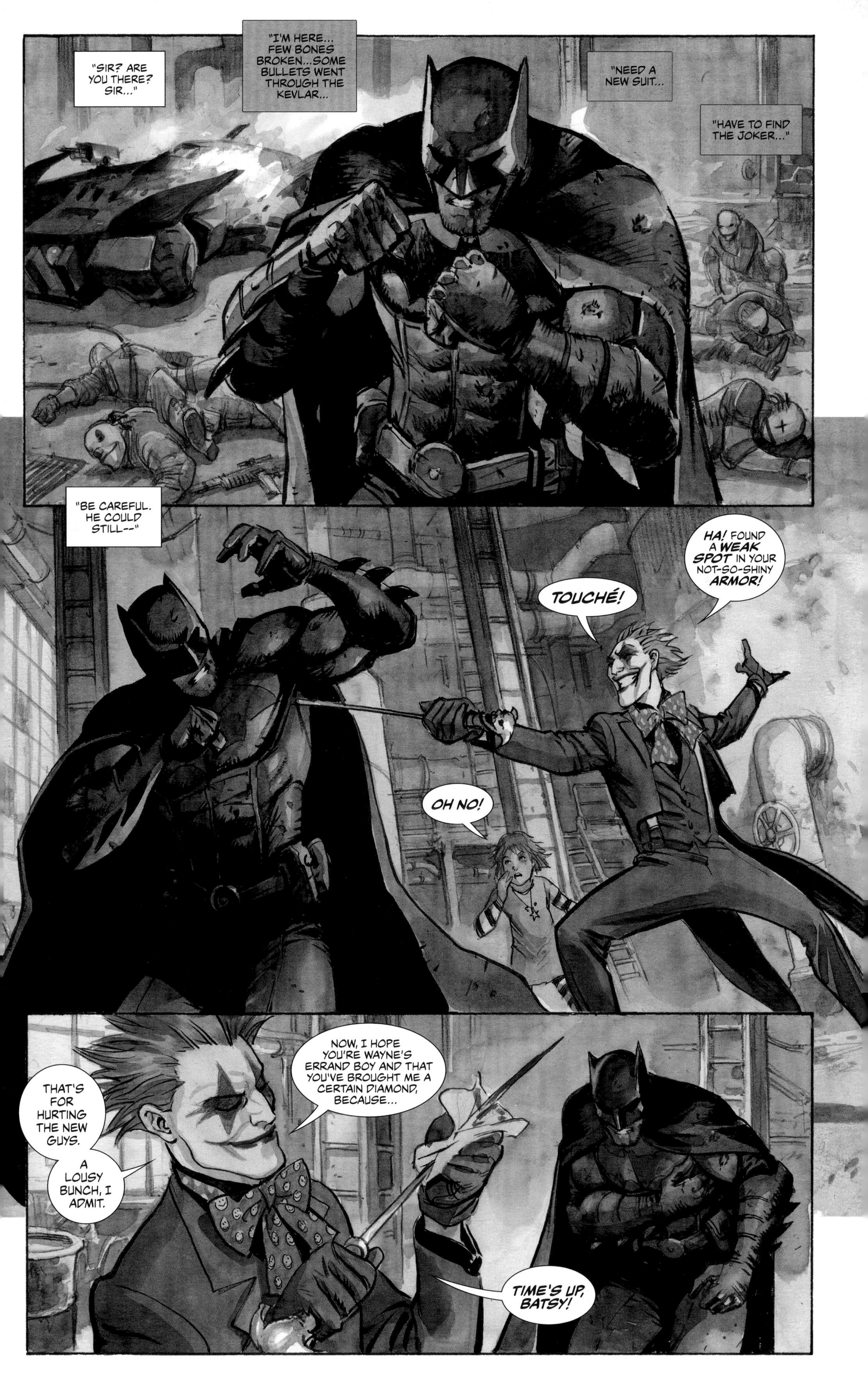
"SIR? ARE YOU THERE? SIR..."
"I'M HERE... FEW BONES BROKEN...SOME BULLETS WENT THROUGH THE KEVLAR...
"NEED A NEW SUIT...
"HAVE TO FIND THE JOKER..."
"BE CAREFUL. HE COULD STILL--"
HA! FOUND A WEAK SPOT IN YOUR NOT-SO-SHINY ARMOR!
TOUCHÉ!
OH NO!
THAT'S FOR HURTING THE NEW GUYS.
A LOUSY BUNCH, I ADMIT.
NOW, I HOPE YOU'RE WAYNE'S ERRAND BOY AND THAT YOU'VE BROUGHT ME A CERTAIN DIAMOND, BECAUSE...
TIME'S UP, BATSY!

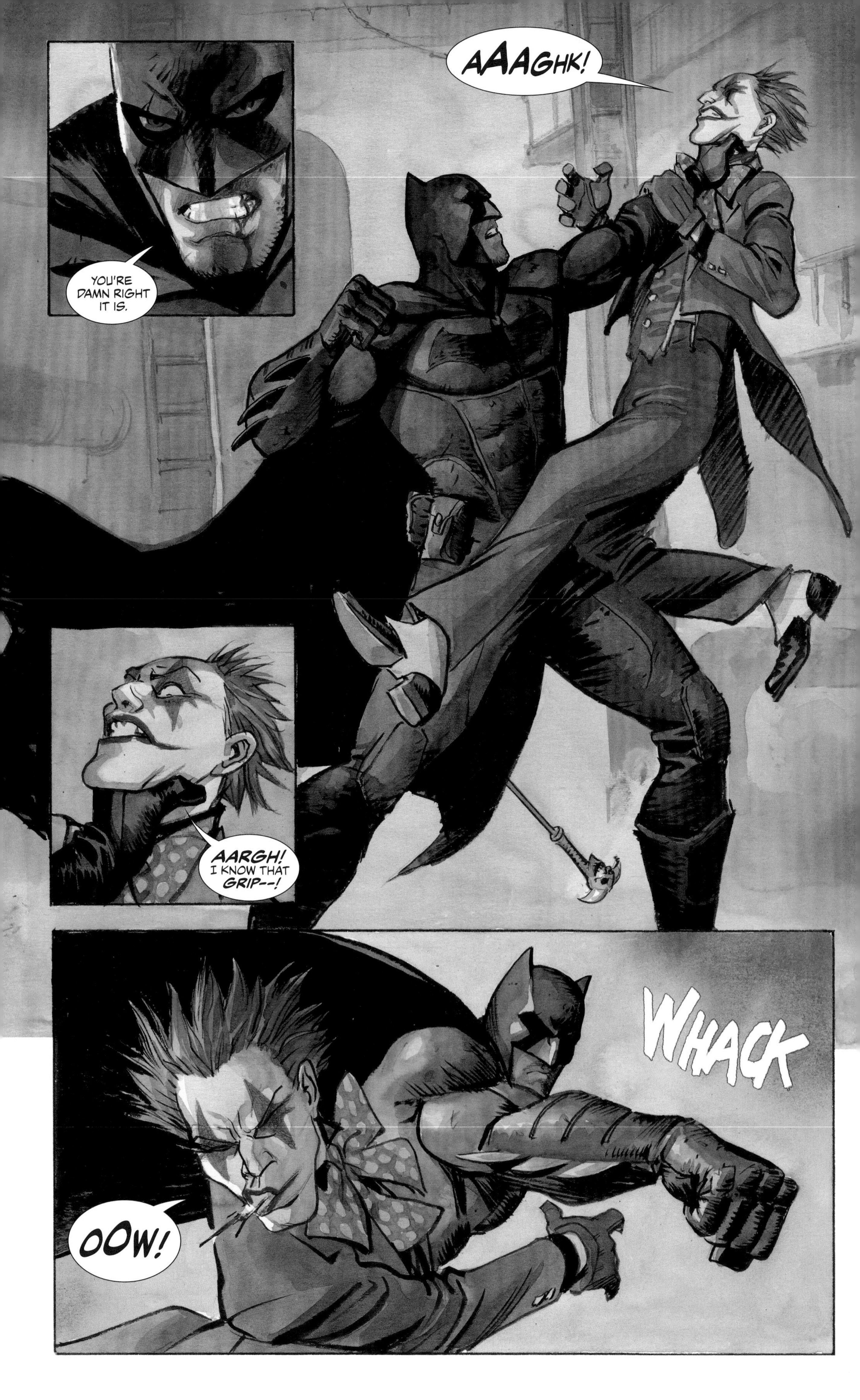
YOU'RE DAMN RIGHT IT IS.
AAAGHK!
AARGH! I KNOW THAT GRIP--!
WHACK
OOW!

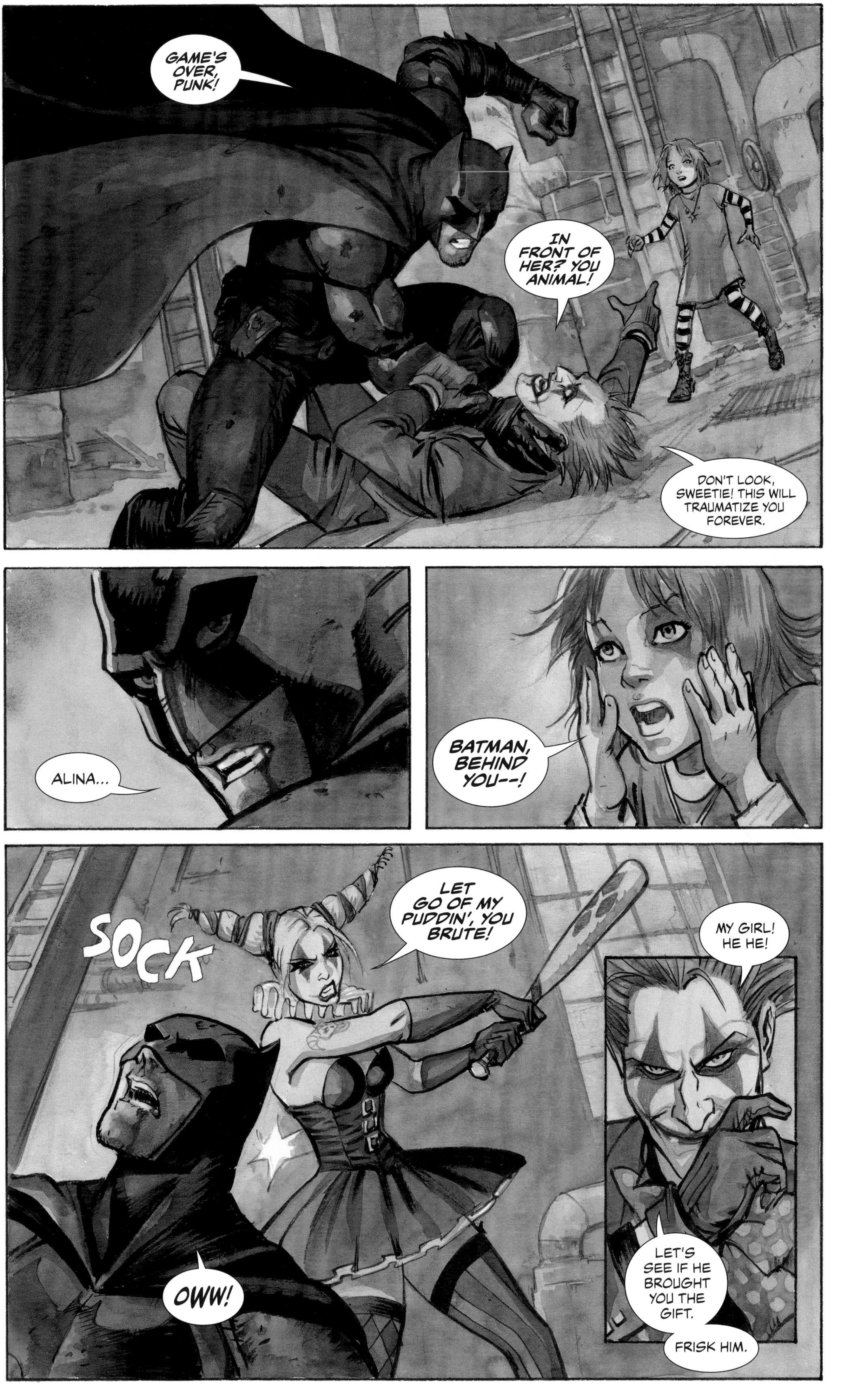
GAME'S OVER, PUNK!
IN FRONT OF HER? YOU ANIMAL!
DON'T LOOK, SWEETIE! THIS WILL TRAUMATIZE YOU FOREVER.
ALINA...
BATMAN, BEHIND YOU--!
SOCK
LET GO OF MY PUDDIN', YOU BRUTE!
OWW!
MY GIRL! HE HE!
LET'S SEE IF HE BROUGHT YOU THE GIFT.
FRISK HIM.

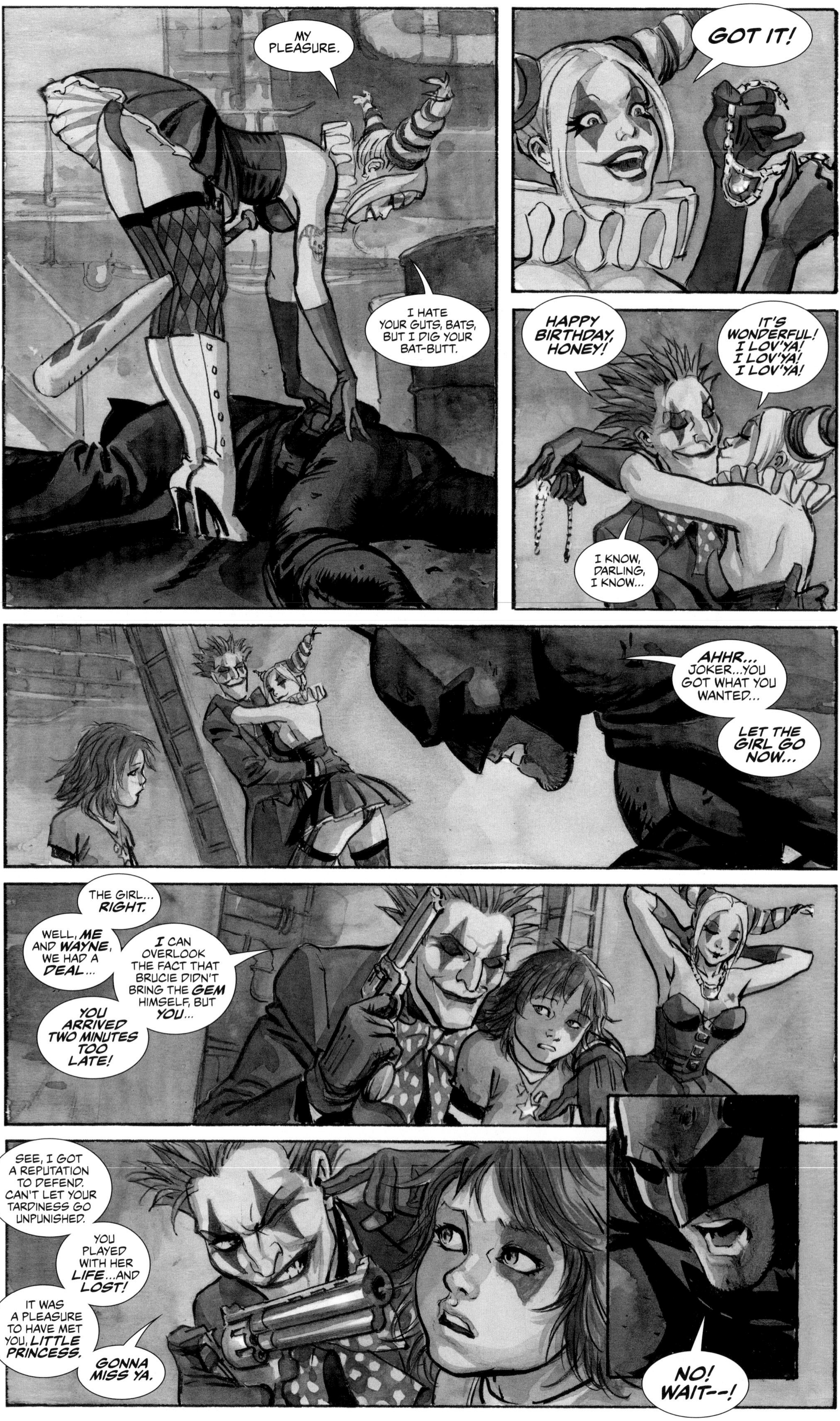
MY PLEASURE.
I HATE YOUR GUTS, BATS, BUT I DIG YOUR BAT-BUTT.
GOT IT!
HAPPY BIRTHDAY, HONEY!
IT'S WONDERFUL! I LOV'YA! I LOV'YA! I LOV'YA!
I KNOW, DARLING, I KNOW...
AHHR... JOKER...YOU GOT WHAT YOU WANTED...
LET THE GIRL GO NOW...
THE GIRL... RIGHT.
WELL, ME AND WAYNE, WE HAD A DEAL...
I CAN OVERLOOK THE FACT THAT BRUCIE DIDN'T BRING THE GEM HIMSELF, BUT YOU...
YOU ARRIVED TWO MINUTES TOO LATE!
SEE, I GOT A REPUTATION TO DEFEND. CAN'T LET YOUR TARDINESS GO UNPUNISHED.
YOU PLAYED WITH HER LIFE...AND LOST!
IT WAS A PLEASURE TO HAVE MET YOU, LITTLE PRINCESS.
GONNA MISS YA.
NO! WAIT--!

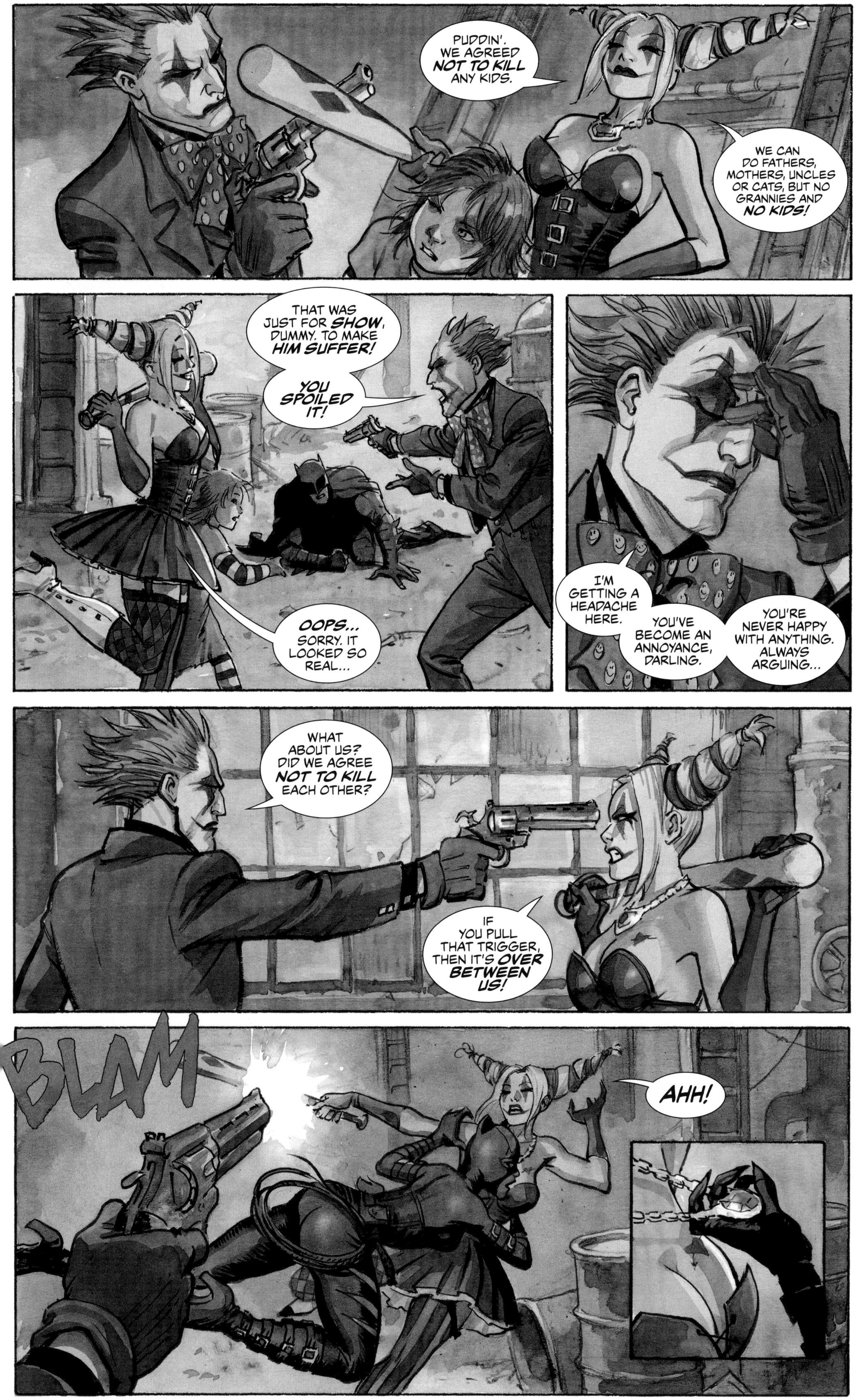
PUDDIN'. WE AGREED NOT TO KILL ANY KIDS.
WE CAN DO FATHERS, MOTHERS, UNCLES OR CATS, BUT NO GRANNIES AND NO KIDS!
THAT WAS JUST FOR SHOW, DUMMY. TO MAKE HIM SUFFER!
YOU SPOILED IT!
OOPS... SORRY. IT LOOKED SO REAL...
I'M GETTING A HEADACHE HERE.
YOU'VE BECOME AN ANNOYANCE, DARLING.
YOU'RE NEVER HAPPY WITH ANYTHING. ALWAYS ARGUING...
WHAT ABOUT US? DID WE AGREE NOT TO KILL EACH OTHER?
IF YOU PULL THAT TRIGGER, THEN IT'S OVER BETWEEN US!
BLAM
AHH!

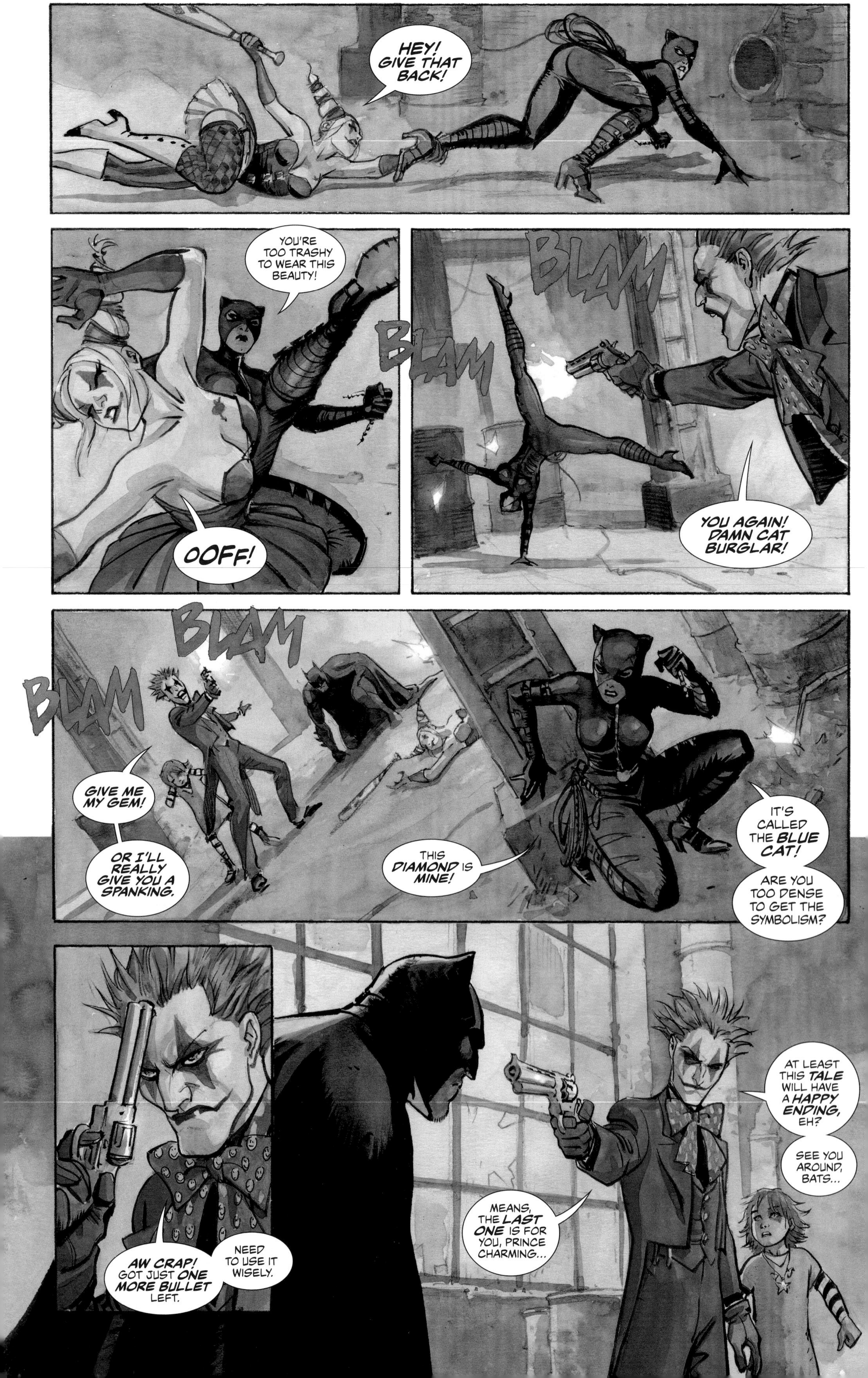
HEY! GIVE THAT BACK!
YOU'RE TOO TRASHY TO WEAR THIS BEAUTY!
OOFF!
BLAM
BLAM
YOU AGAIN! DAMN CAT BURGLAR!
BLAM
BLAM
GIVE ME MY GEM!
OR I'LL REALLY GIVE YOU A SPANKING.
THIS DIAMOND IS MINE!
IT'S CALLED THE BLUE CAT!
ARE YOU TOO DENSE TO GET THE SYMBOLISM?
AW CRAP! GOT JUST ONE MORE BULLET LEFT.
NEED TO USE IT WISELY.
MEANS, THE LAST ONE IS FOR YOU, PRINCE CHARMING...
AT LEAST THIS TALE WILL HAVE A HAPPY ENDING, EH?
SEE YOU AROUND, BATS...

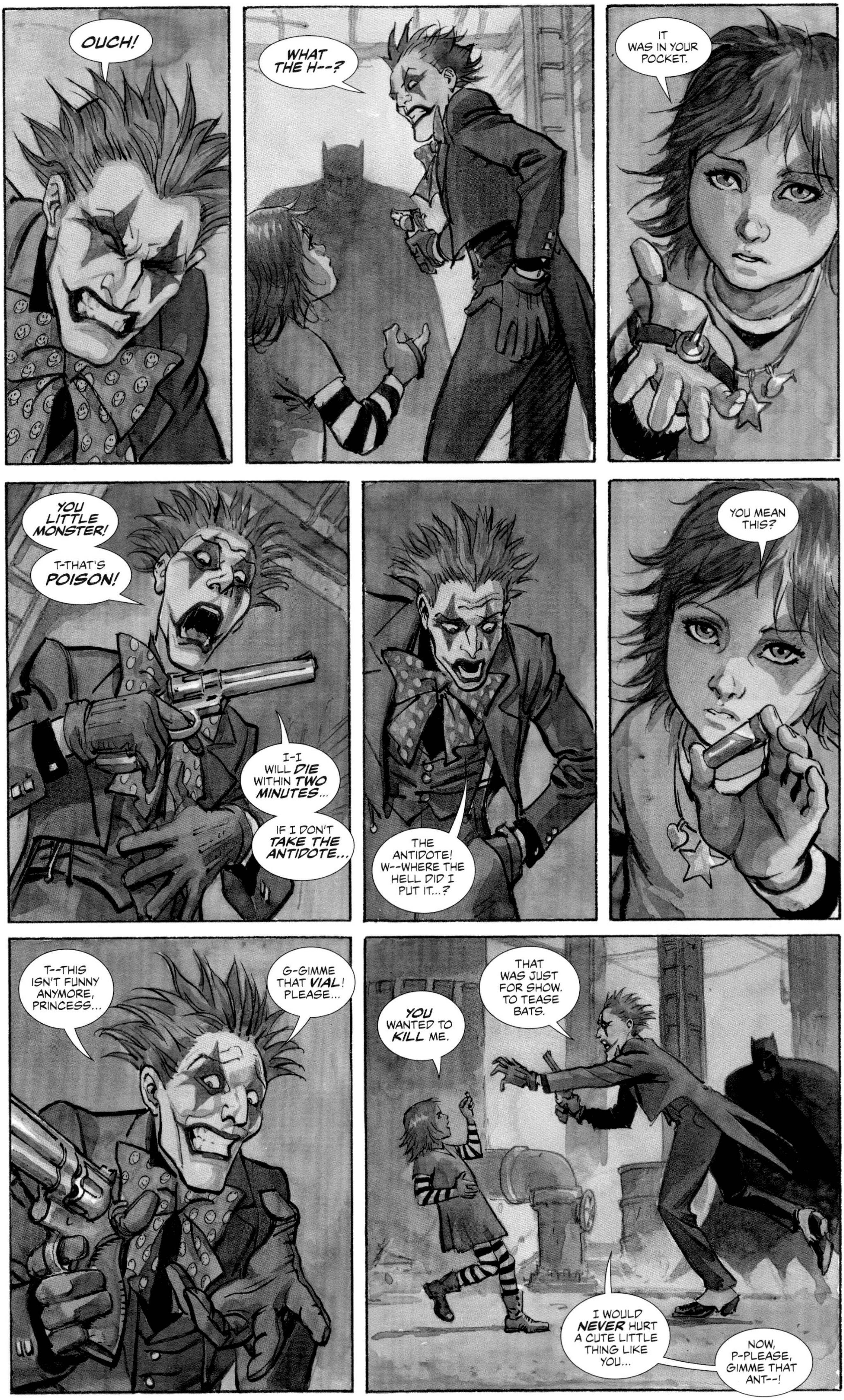
OUCH!
WHAT THE H--?
IT WAS IN YOUR POCKET.
YOU LITTLE MONSTER!
T-THAT'S POISON!
I-I WILL DIE WITHIN TWO MINUTES...
IF I DON'T TAKE THE ANTIDOTE...
THE ANTIDOTE! W--WHERE THE HELL DID I PUT IT...?
YOU MEAN THIS?
T--THIS ISN'T FUNNY ANYMORE, PRINCESS...
G-GIMME THAT VIAL! PLEASE...
YOU WANTED TO KILL ME.
THAT WAS JUST FOR SHOW. TO TEASE BATS.
I WOULD NEVER HURT A CUTE LITTLE THING LIKE YOU...
NOW, P-PLEASE, GIMME THAT ANT--!

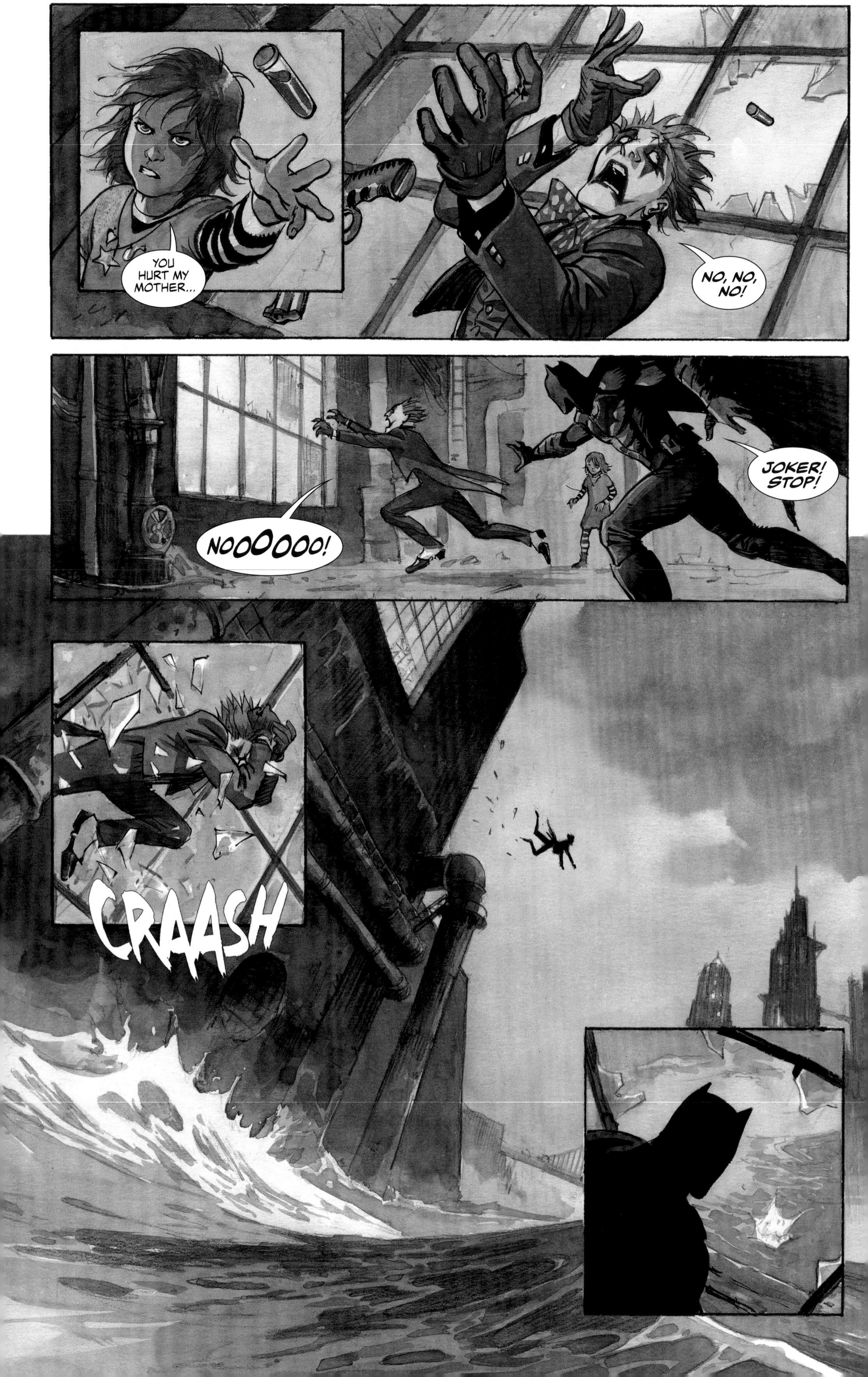
YOU HURT MY MOTHER...
NO, NO, NO!
NOOOOOO!
JOKER! STOP!
CRAASH

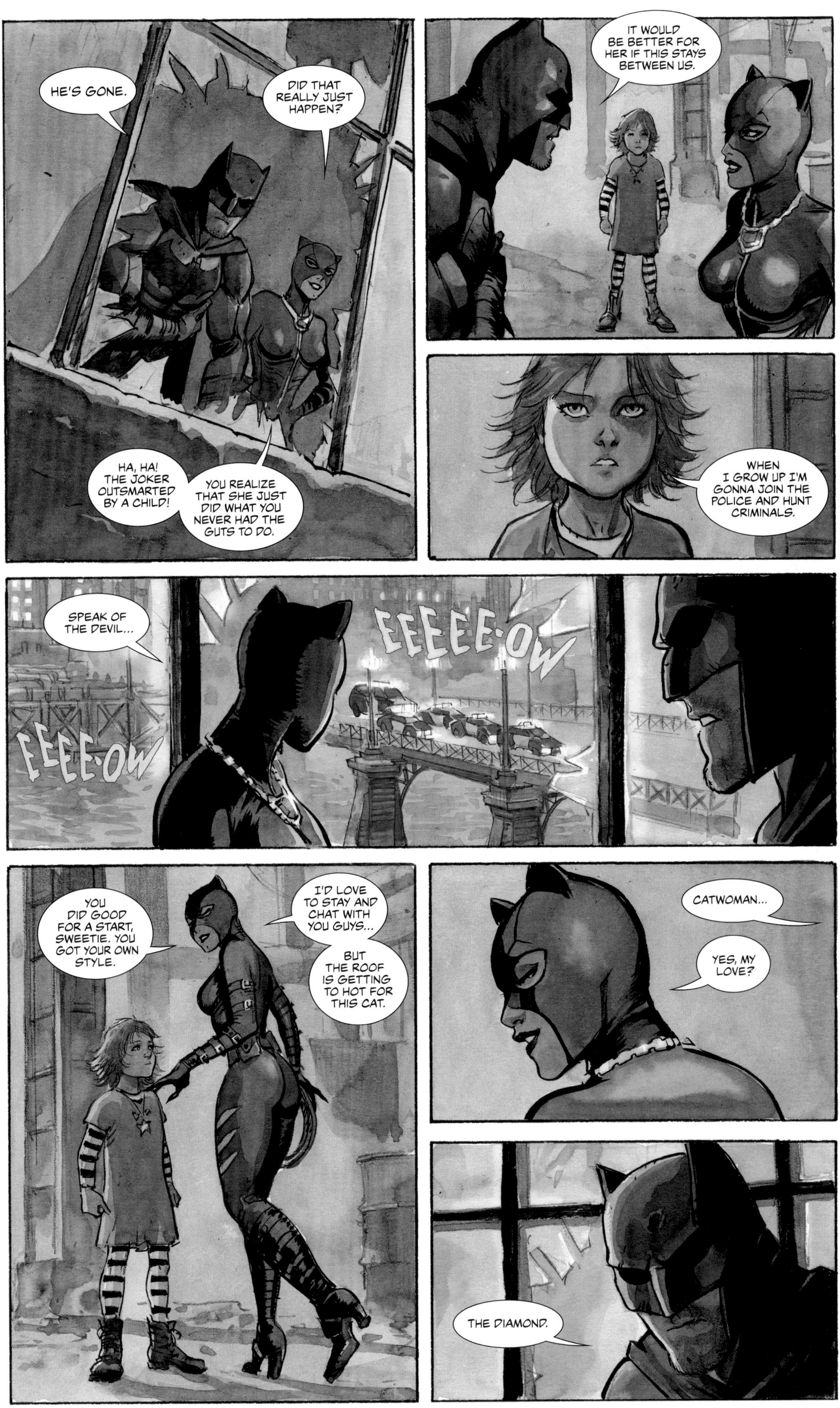
HE'S GONE.
DID THAT REALLY JUST HAPPEN?
HA, HA! THE JOKER OUTSMARTED BY A CHILD!
YOU REALIZE THAT SHE JUST DID WHAT YOU NEVER HAD THE GUTS TO DO.
IT WOULD BE BETTER FOR HER IF THIS STAYS BETWEEN US.
WHEN I GROW UP I'M GONNA JOIN THE POLICE AND HUNT CRIMINALS.
SPEAK OF THE DEVIL...
EEEEE-OW
EEEE-OW
YOU DID GOOD FOR A START, SWEETIE. YOU GOT YOUR OWN STYLE.
I'D LOVE TO STAY AND CHAT WITH YOU GUYS...
BUT THE ROOF IS GETTING TO HOT FOR THIS CAT.
CATWOMAN...
YES, MY LOVE?
THE DIAMOND.

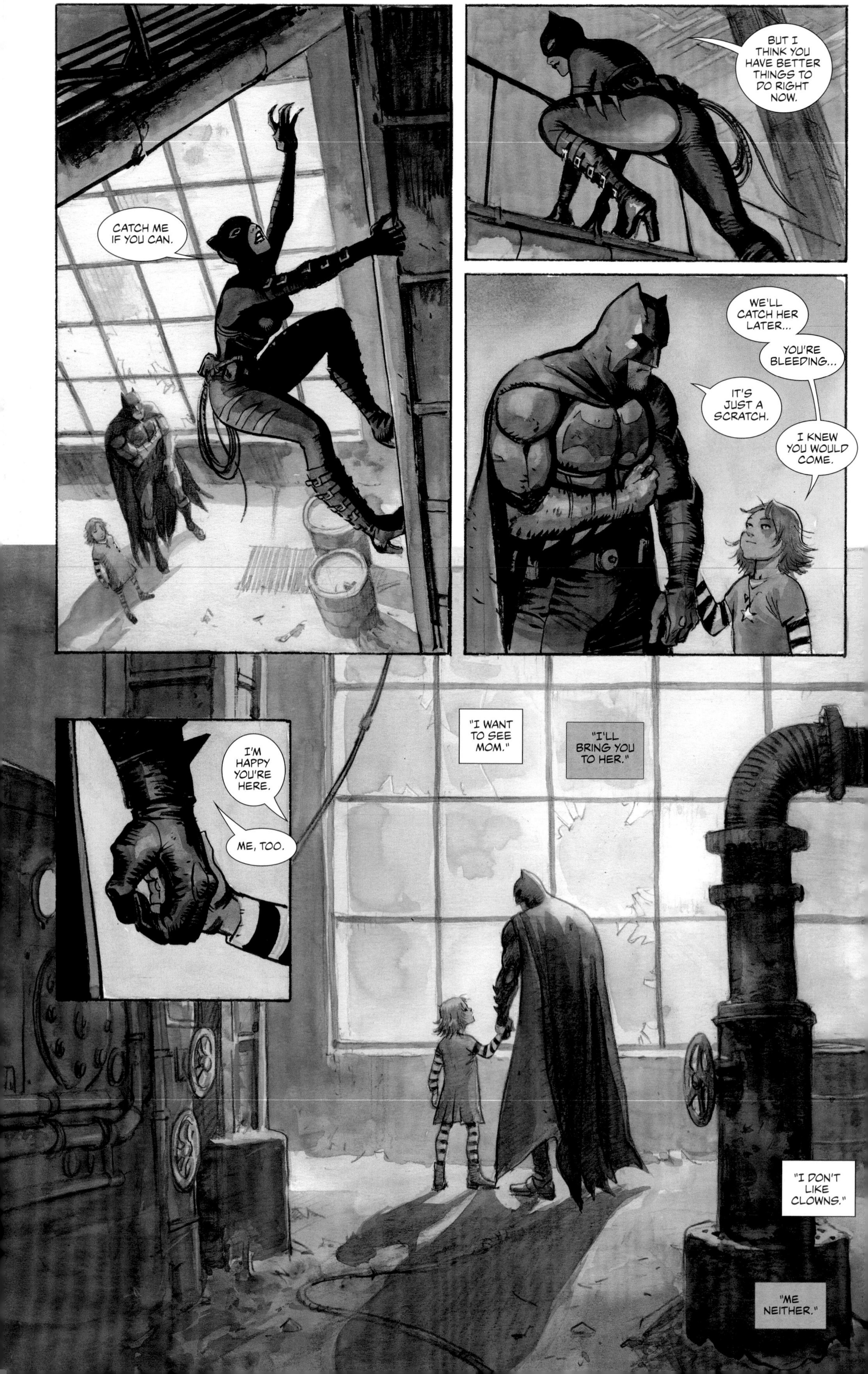
CATCH ME IF YOU CAN.
BUT I THINK YOU HAVE BETTER THINGS TO DO RIGHT NOW.
WE'LL CATCH HER LATER...
YOU'RE BLEEDING...
IT'S JUST A SCRATCH.
I KNEW YOU WOULD COME.
I'M HAPPY YOU'RE HERE.
ME, TOO.
"I WANT TO SEE MOM."
"I'LL BRING YOU TO HER."
"I DON'T LIKE CLOWNS."
"ME NEITHER."

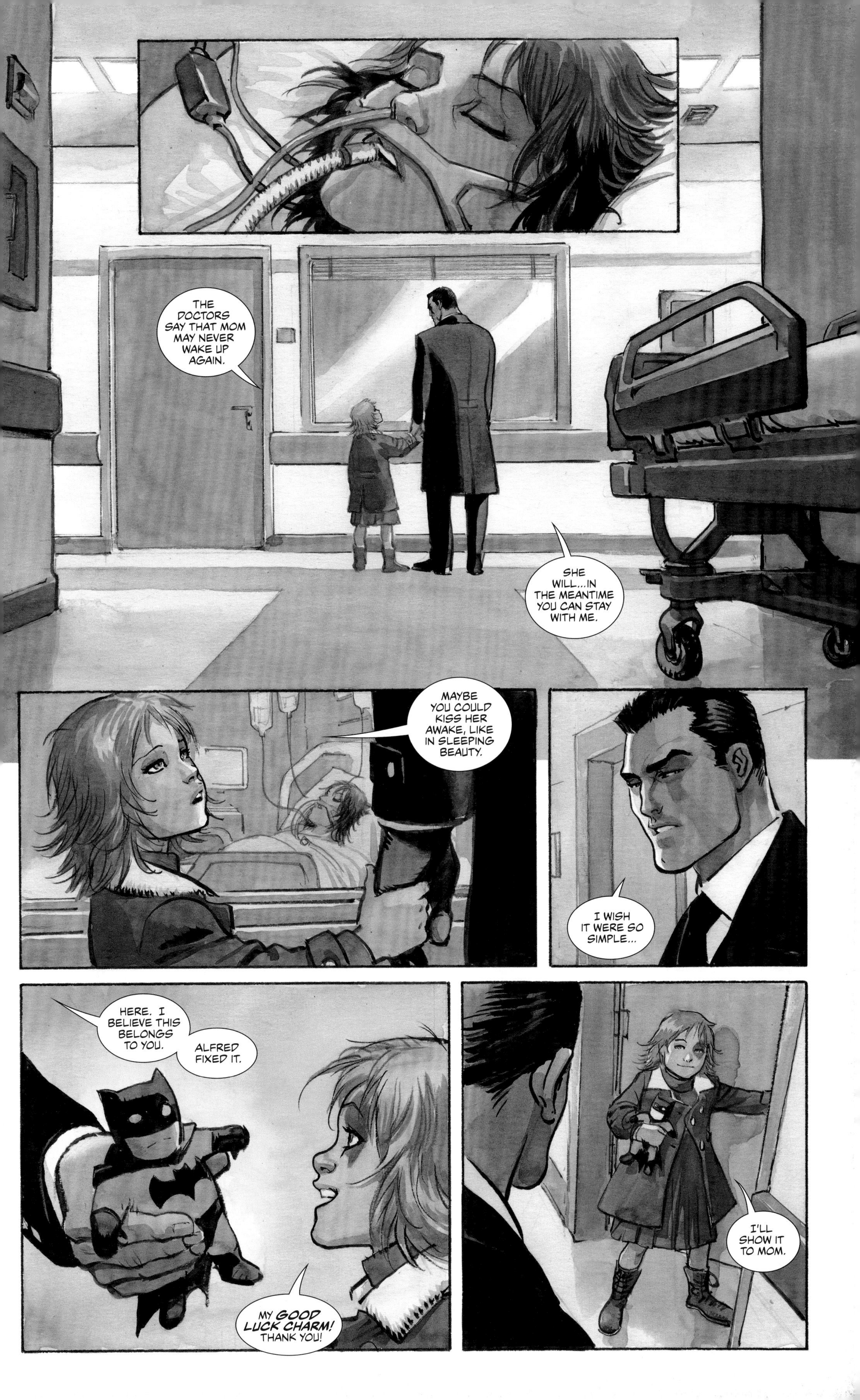
THE DOCTORS SAY THAT MOM MAY NEVER WAKE UP AGAIN.
SHE WILL...IN THE MEANTIME YOU CAN STAY WITH ME.
MAYBE YOU COULD KISS HER AWAKE, LIKE IN SLEEPING BEAUTY.
I WISH IT WERE SO SIMPLE...
HERE. I BELIEVE THIS BELONGS TO YOU.
ALFRED FIXED IT.
MY GOOD LUCK CHARM! THANK YOU!
I'LL SHOW IT TO MOM.

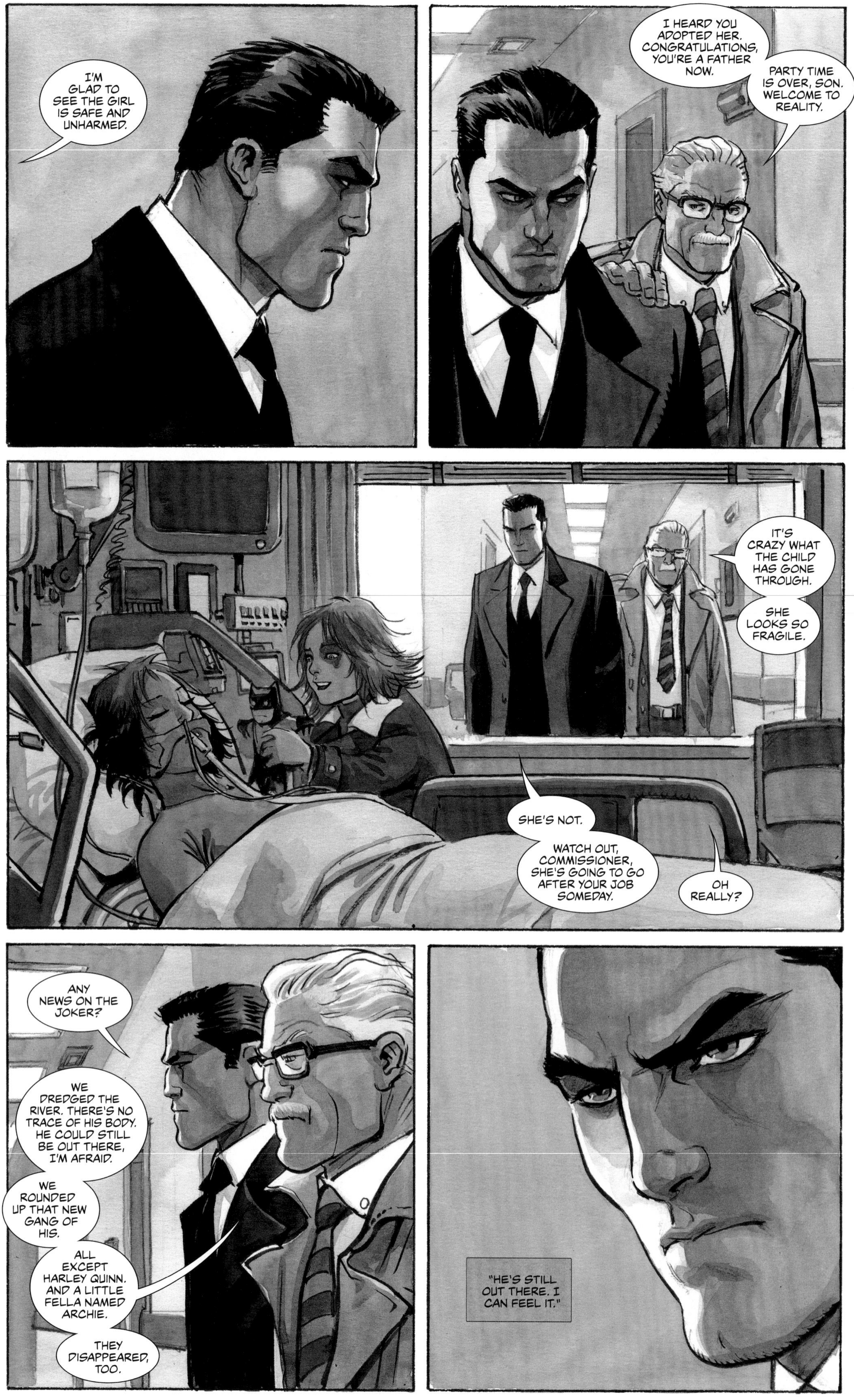
I'M GLAD TO SEE THE GIRL IS SAFE AND UNHARMED.
I HEARD YOU ADOPTED HER. CONGRATULATIONS, YOU'RE A FATHER NOW.
PARTY TIME IS OVER, SON. WELCOME TO REALITY.
IT'S CRAZY WHAT THE CHILD HAS GONE THROUGH.
SHE LOOKS SO FRAGILE.
SHE'S NOT.
WATCH OUT, COMMISSIONER, SHE'S GOING TO GO AFTER YOUR JOB SOMEDAY.
OH REALLY?
ANY NEWS ON THE JOKER?
WE DREDGED THE RIVER. THERE'S NO TRACE OF HIS BODY. HE COULD STILL BE OUT THERE, I'M AFRAID.
WE ROUNDED UP THAT NEW GANG OF HIS.
ALL EXCEPT HARLEY QUINN. AND A LITTLE FELLA NAMED ARCHIE.
THEY DISAPPEARED, TOO.
"HE'S STILL OUT THERE. I CAN FEEL IT."

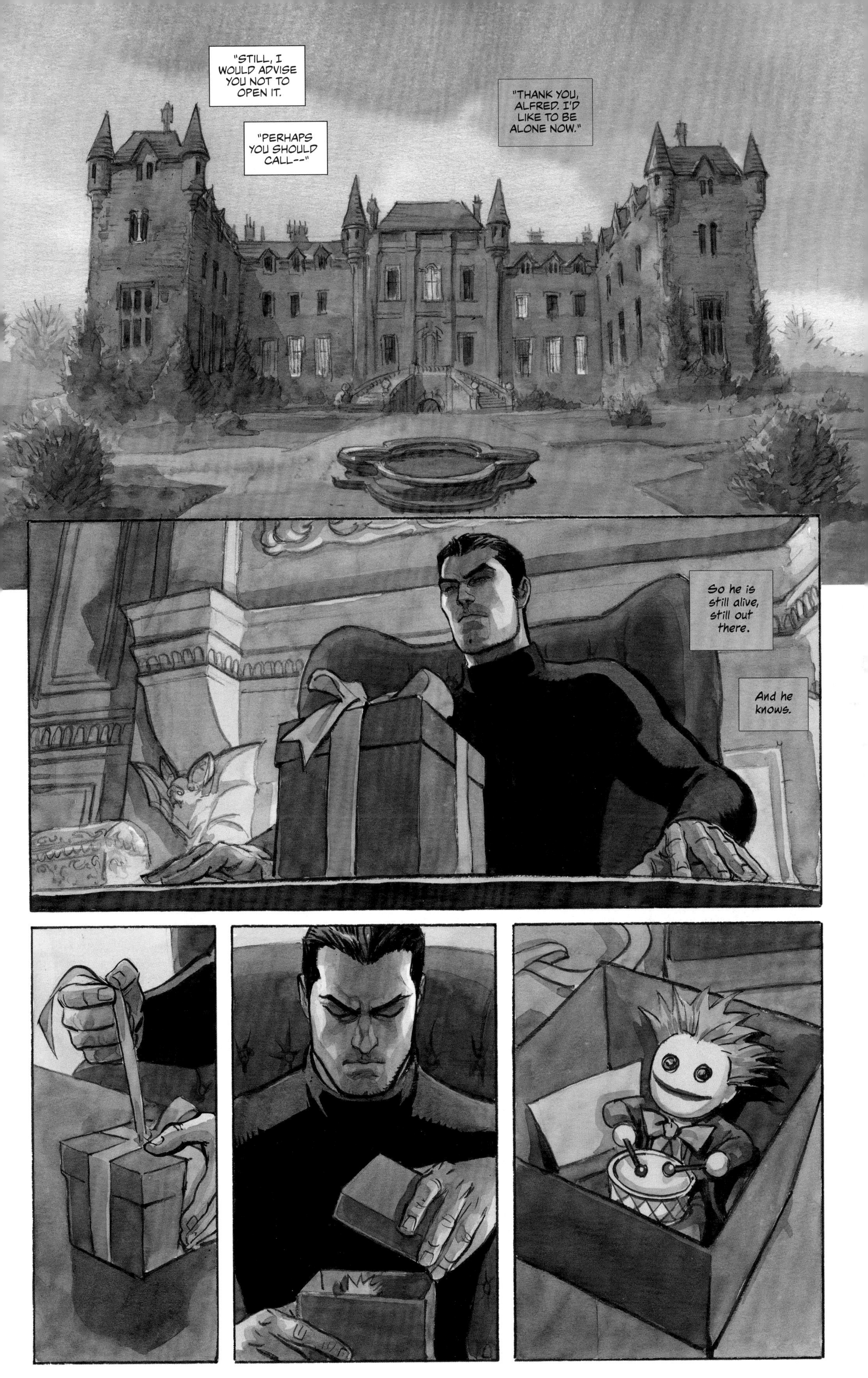
"STILL, I WOULD ADVISE YOU NOT TO OPEN IT.
"PERHAPS YOU SHOULD CALL--"
"THANK YOU, ALFRED. I'D LIKE TO BE ALONE NOW."
So he is still alive, still out there.
And he knows.

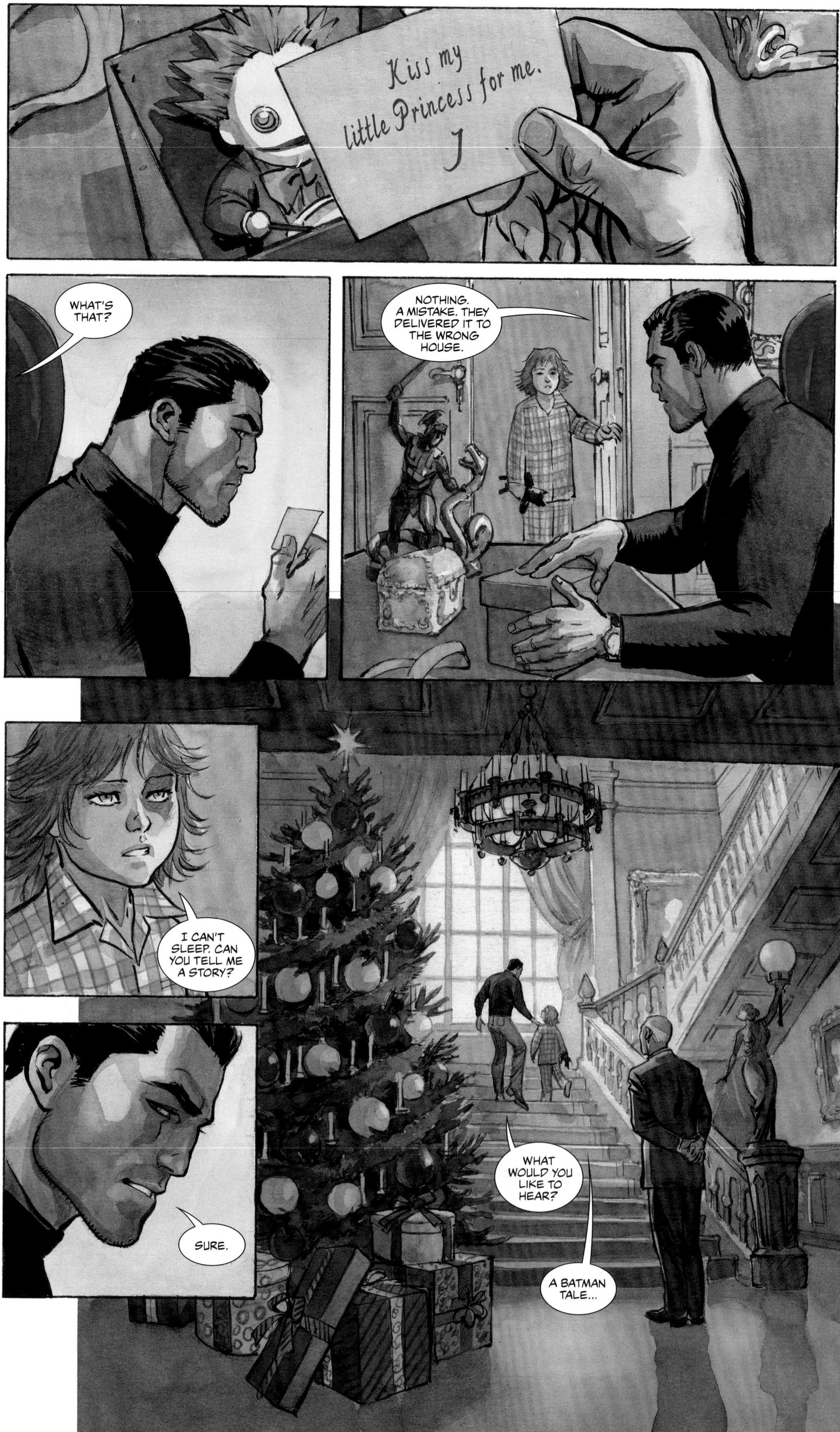
Kiss my
little Princess for me.
J
WHAT'S THAT?
NOTHING. A MISTAKE. THEY DELIVERED IT TO THE WRONG HOUSE.
I CAN'T SLEEP. CAN YOU TELL ME A STORY?
SURE.
WHAT WOULD YOU LIKE TO HEAR?
A BATMAN TALE...

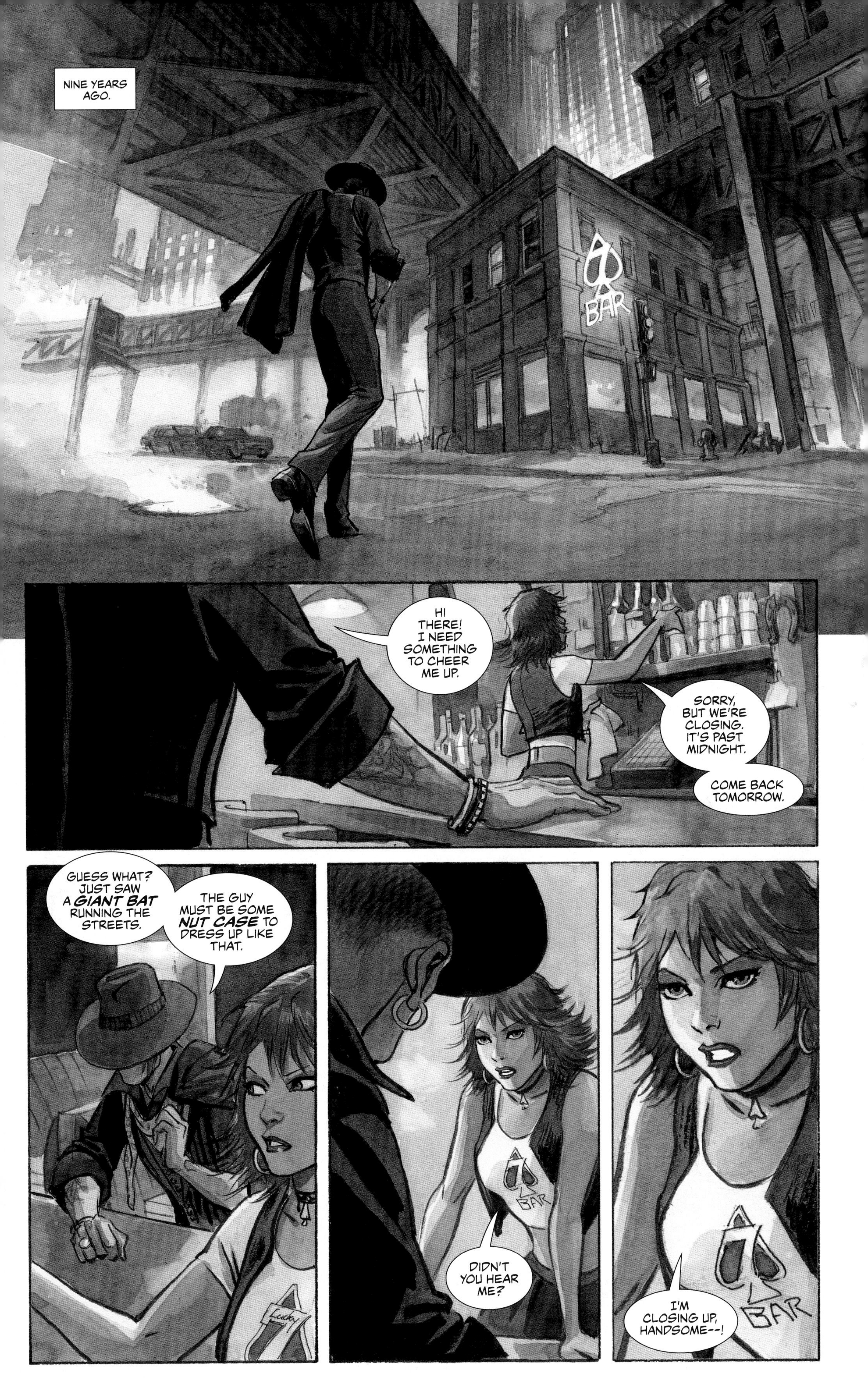
NINE YEARS AGO.
BAR
HI THERE! I NEED SOMETHING TO CHEER ME UP.
SORRY, BUT WE'RE CLOSING. IT'S PAST MIDNIGHT.
COME BACK TOMORROW.
GUESS WHAT? JUST SAW A GIANT BAT RUNNING THE STREETS.
THE GUY MUST BE SOME NUT CASE TO DRESS UP LIKE THAT.
DIDN'T YOU HEAR ME?
I'M CLOSING UP, HANDSOME--!

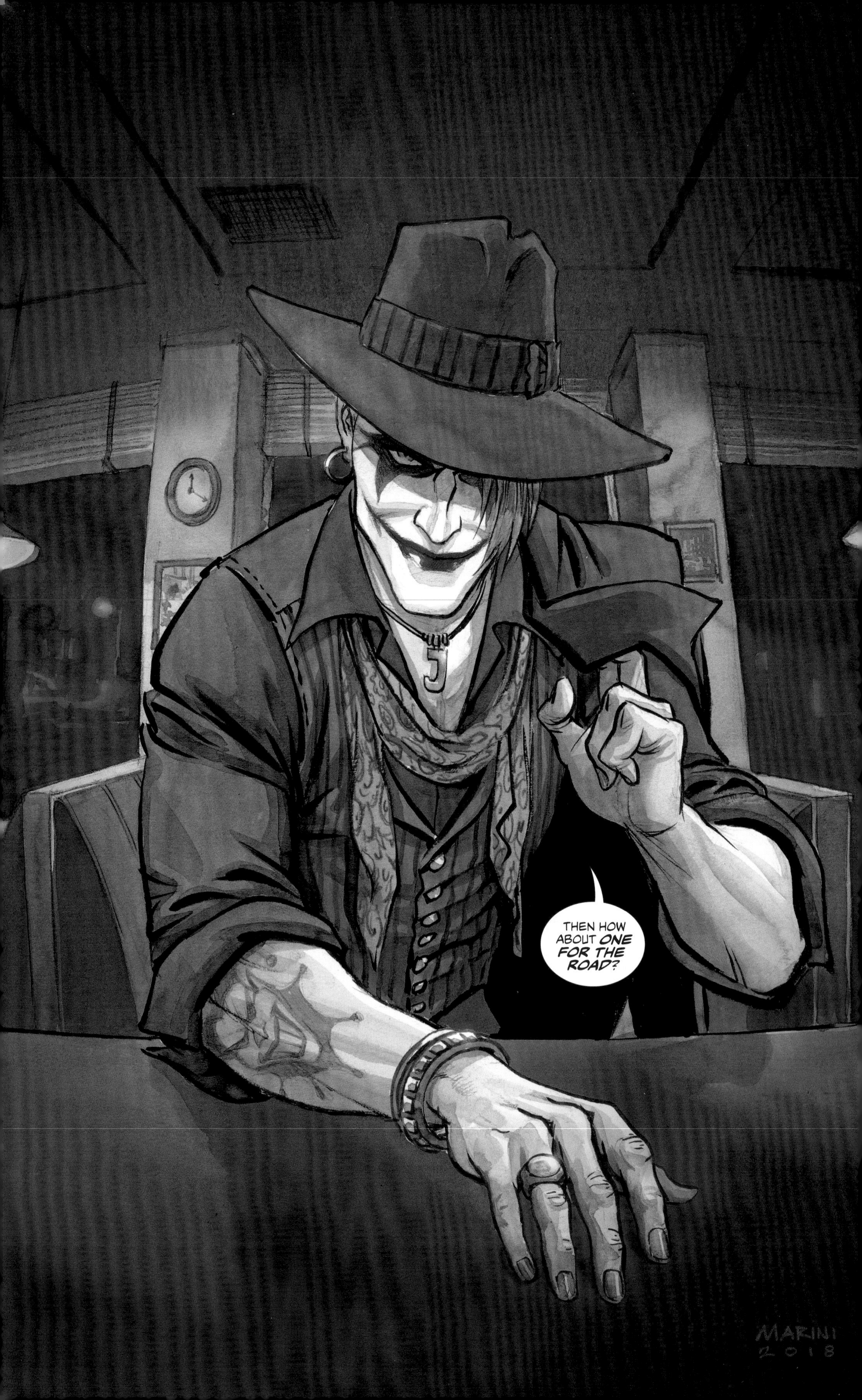
THEN HOW ABOUT ONE FOR THE ROAD?
MARINI 2018

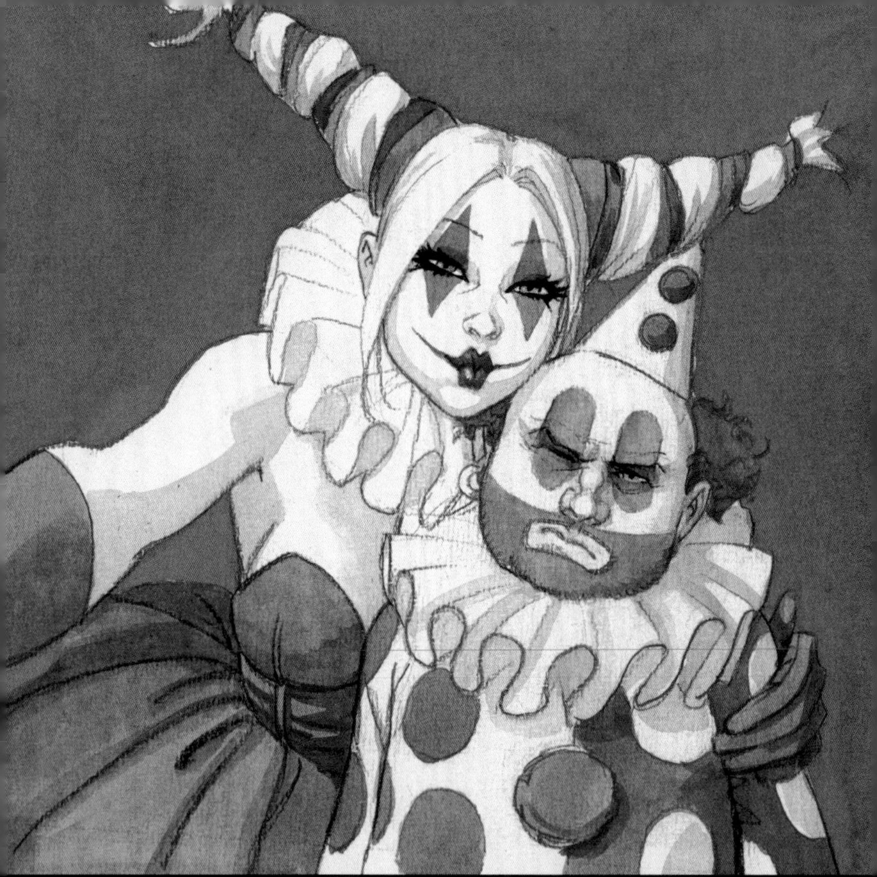

Yeah, so Harley and me, we got away. Kind of.

Now she says she wants to team up with me. Says I got what it takes to be Gotham's next crime boss. Really? She's all over me about it, won't leave me alone. What a pain. Trying to coach me and stuff. Says she wants to make an even more ridiculous costume for me.

But what bothers me the most is her crying all the time and wanting to hold my hand when she does. Says she misses her Mister J a lot.

Who needs this crap? I hope Joker survived and comes back to her. Too much more of this and I'm gonna throw myself off of Wayne Tower

SKETCHBOOK

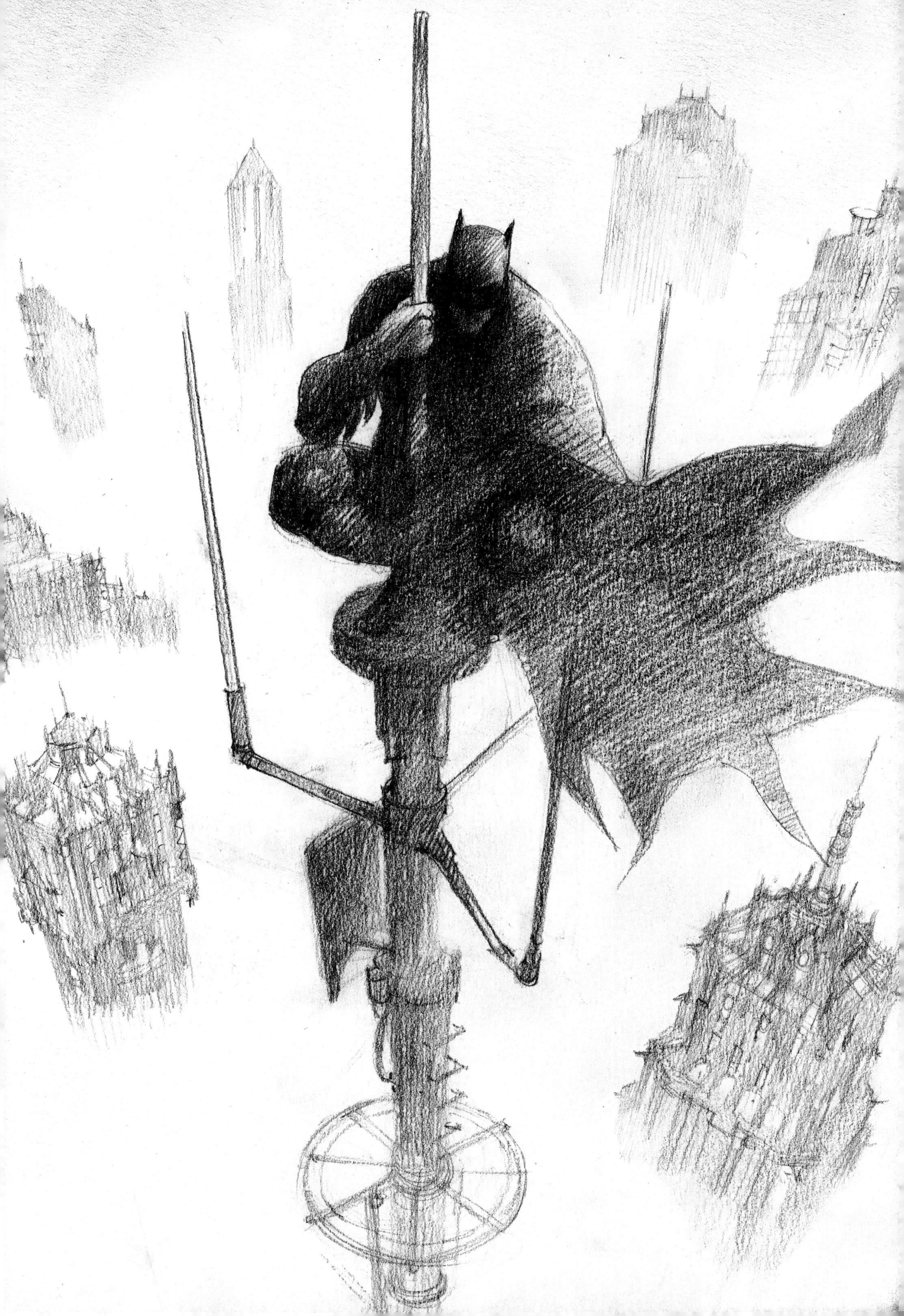

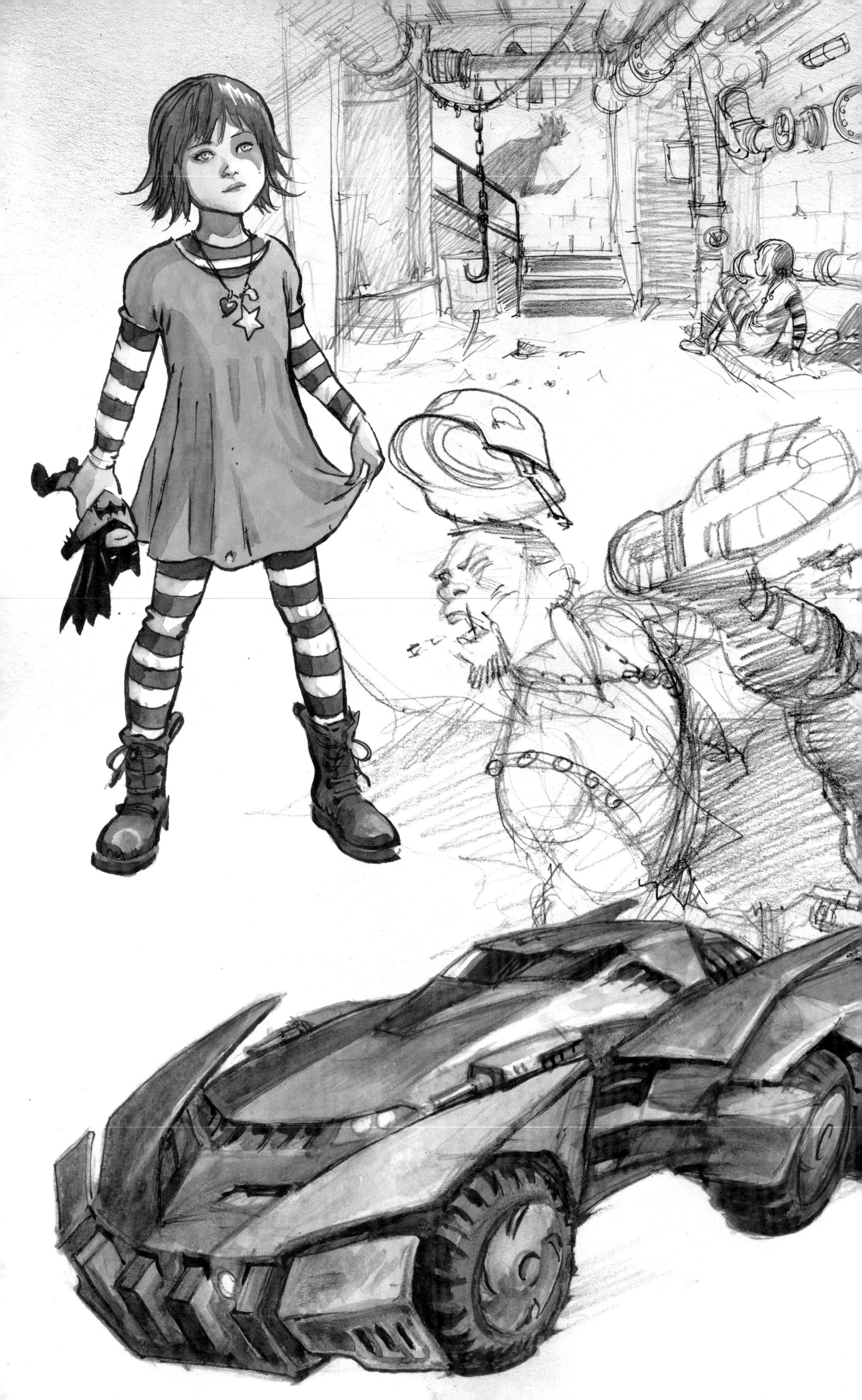

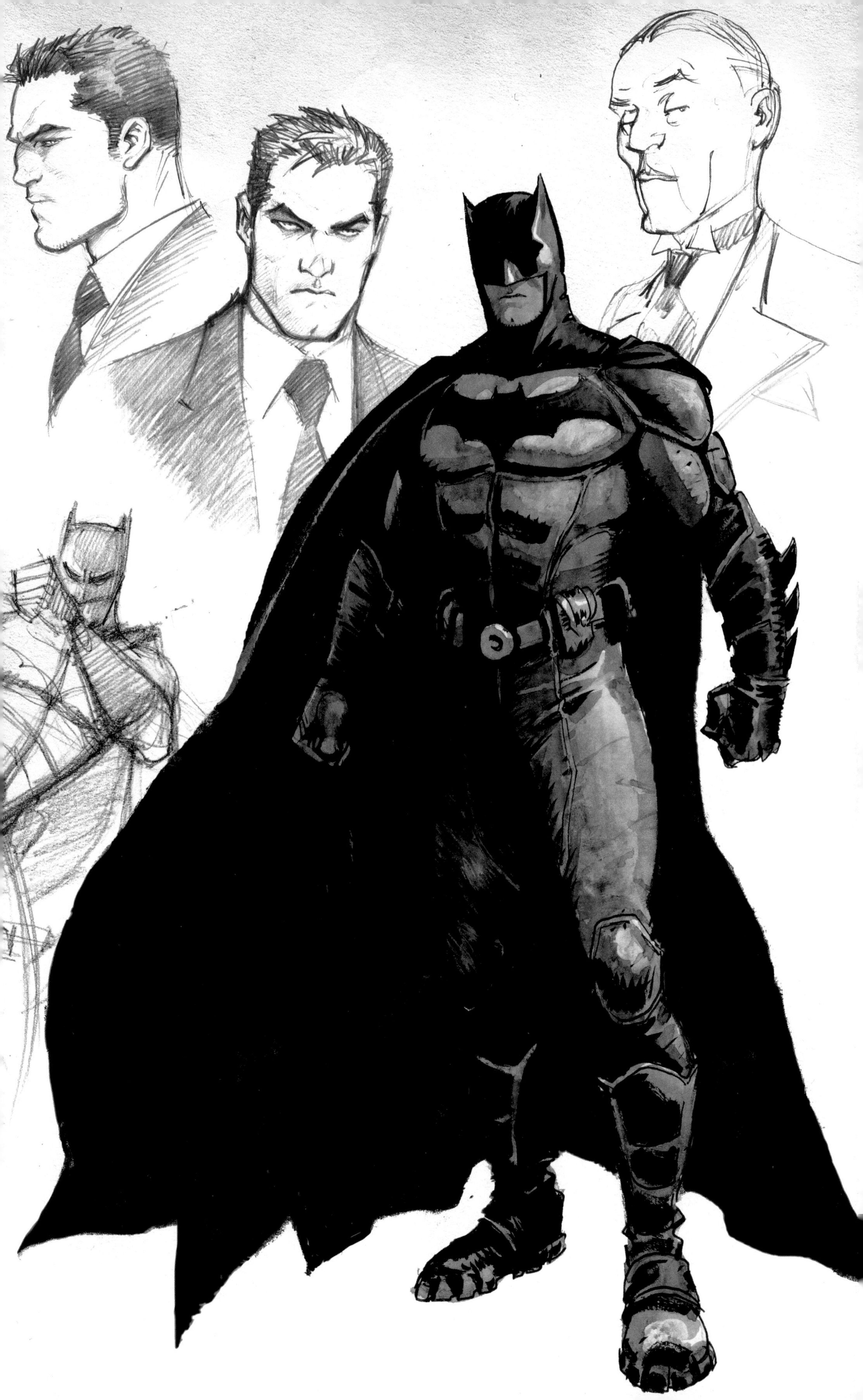

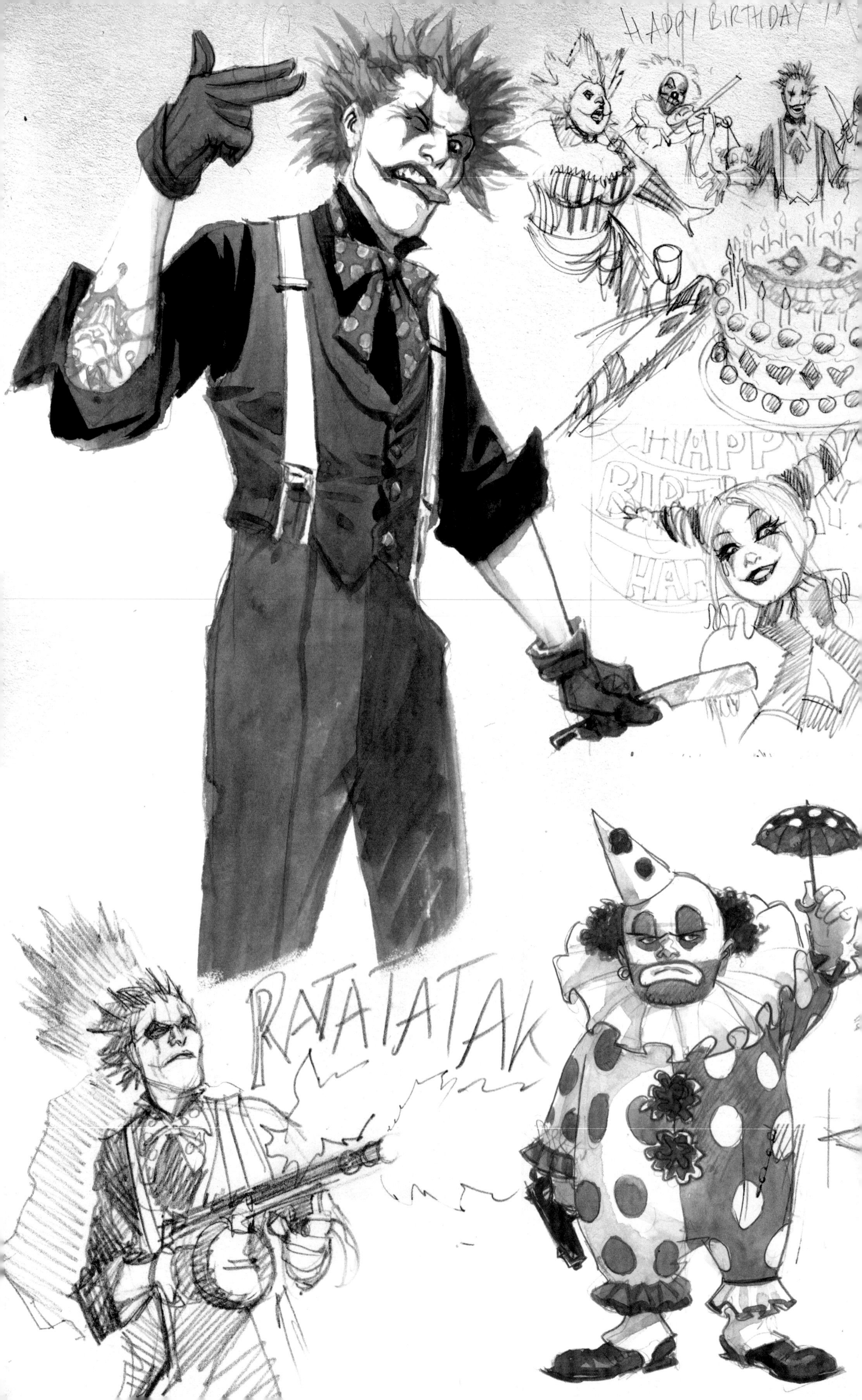
HAPPY BIRTHDAY !!
RATATATAK

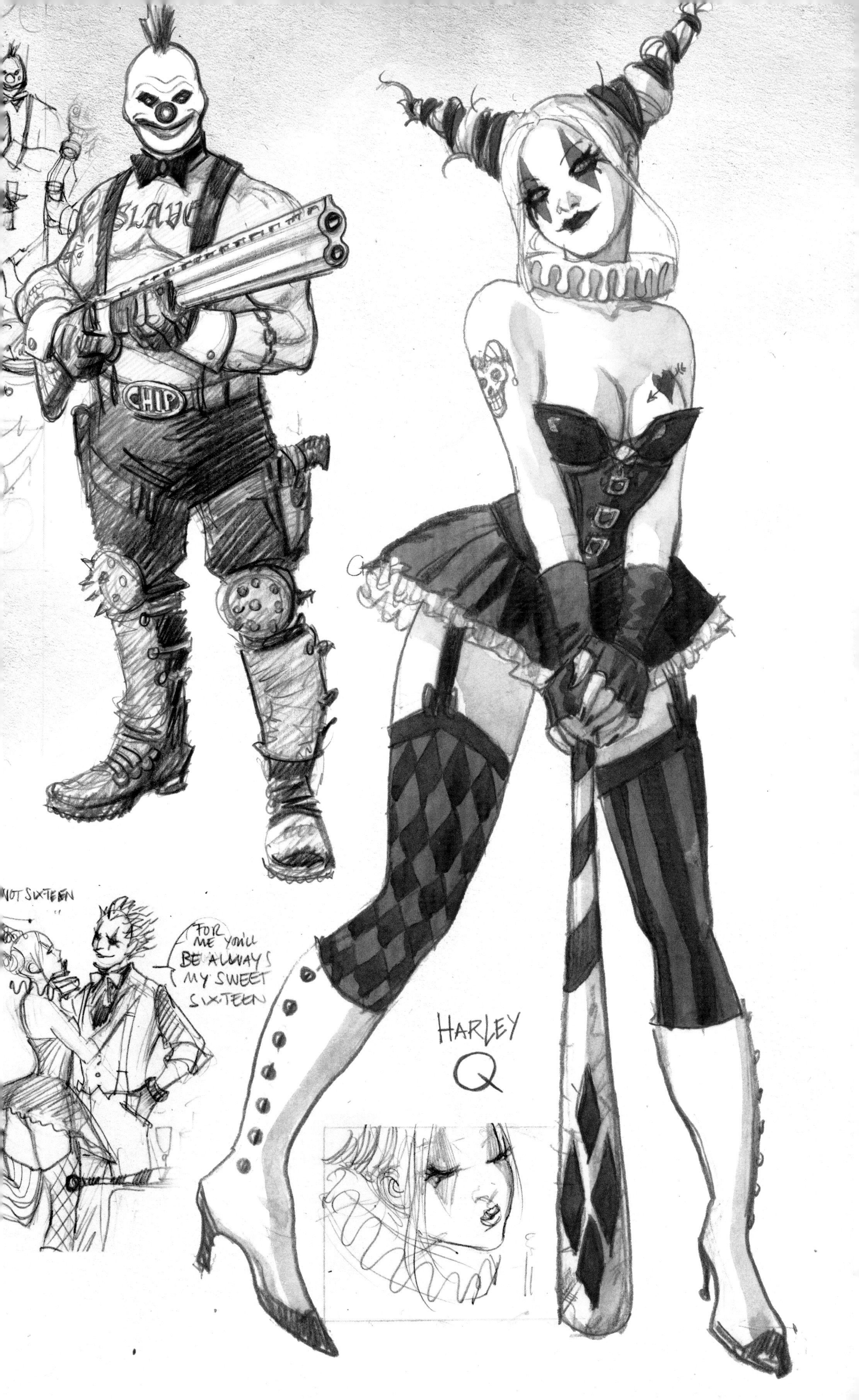
CHIP
NOT SIX-TEEN
FOR ME you'll BE ALLWAYS MY SWEET SIX-TEEN
HARLEY Q

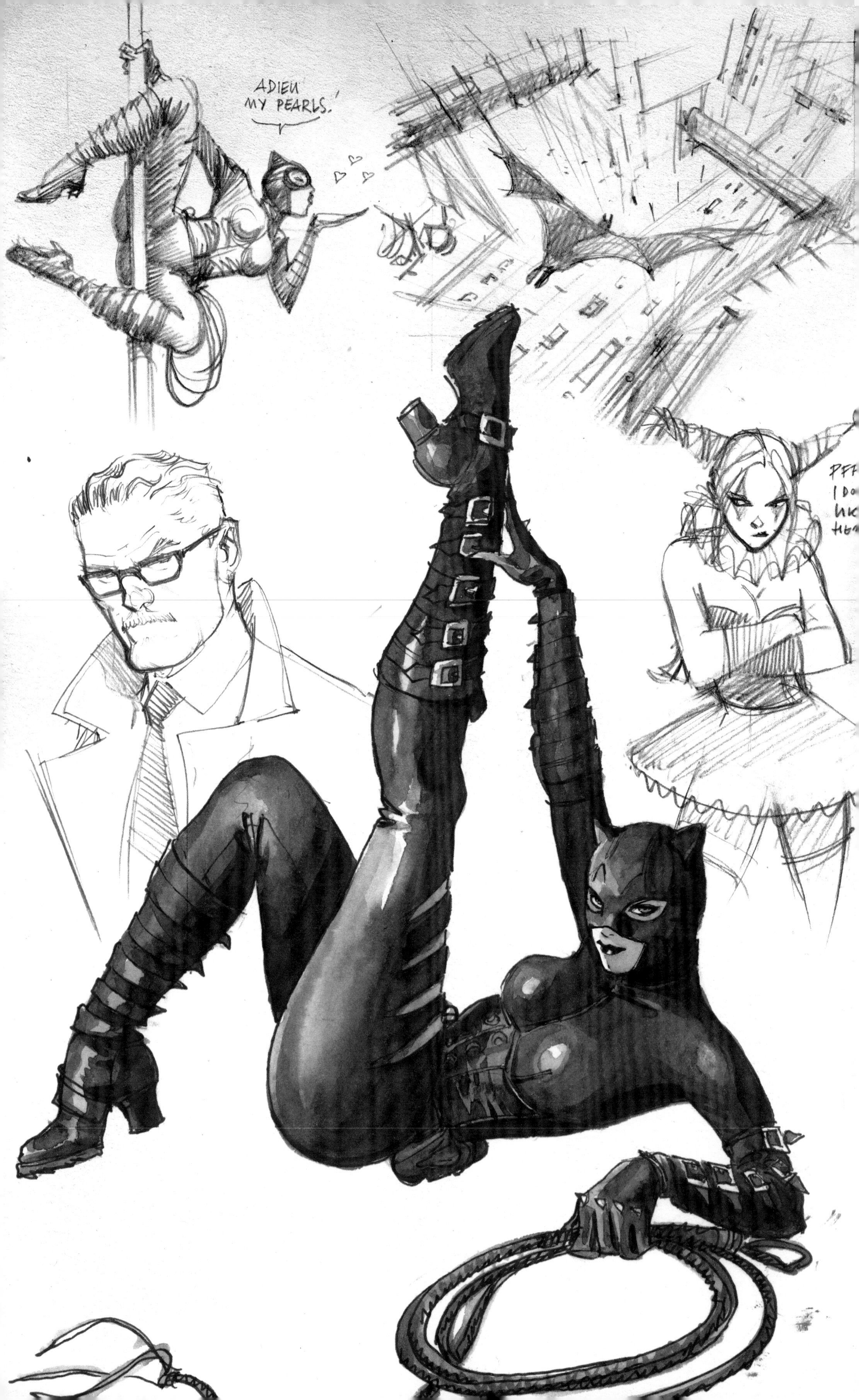
ADIEU MY PEARLS.